Windows 7 for Seniors

Studio Visual Steps

Windows 7
for Seniors

For everyone who wants to learn to use the computer at a later age

www.visualsteps.com

This book has been written using the Visual Steps™ method.
Cover design by Studio Willemien Haagsma bNO

© 2009 Visual Steps
Edited by Jolanda Ligthart, Mara Kok and Rilana Groot
Translated by Chris Hollingsworth, *1ˢᵗ Resources* and Irene Venditti, *i-write* translation services.
Editor in chief: Ria Beentjes

First printing: October 2009
ISBN 978 90 5905 126 3

Do you have questions or suggestions?
E-mail: info@visualsteps.com

Would you like more information?
www.visualsteps.com

Website for this book:
www.visualsteps.com/windows7
Here you can register your book.

Register your book
We will keep you aware of any important changes that are necessary to you as a user of the book. You can also take advantage of our periodic newsletter informing you of our product releases, company news, tips & tricks, special offers, free guides, etc.

Table of Contents

Appendices

Bonus Online Chapters

At the website accompanied to this book, you will find more bonus chapters. In *Chapter 9 Bonus Online Chapters and Extra Information* you can read how to open these chapters.

10. Text Layout
10.1 Text Layout
10.2 Text Layout in *WordPad*
10.3 Selecting Text
10.4 Underlining Words
10.5 Boldface
10.6 Italics
10.7 Colored Letters
10.8 Other Types of Layout Effects
10.9 Undoing Effects
10.10 The Font
10.11 The Font Size
10.12 Determining Layout in Advance
10.13 Inserting a Picture
10.13 Exercises
10.14 Background Information
10.15 Tips

11. How to Make Working with Your Computer More Pleasant
11.1 The *Control Panel*
11.2 Customizing the Mouse
11.3 The Pointer Speed
11.4 The Mouse Pointer Visibility
11.5 The Size of the Mouse Pointer

12. Photo Editing with Paint

Extra Appendix

Setting Up a Webmail Account in Windows Live Mail

Foreword

We wrote this book in order to introduce seniors to the computer. We will show you the basics of the operating system *Windows 7*, step-by-step. Use this book right next to your computer as you work through each chapter at your own pace. You will be amazed how easy it is to learn this way. When you have finished this book, you will know how to start programs, how to write a letter, how to surf the Internet and how to send an e-mail. This book makes use of the Visual Steps™ method specifically developed for adult learners by Addo Stuur. You do not need any prior computer experience to use this book.

We hope you will enjoy reading this book!

The Studio Visual Steps authors

P.S.
When you have completed this book, you will know how to send an e-mail. Your comments and suggestions are most welcome.
Our e-mail address is: mail@visualsteps.com

Visual Steps Newsletter

All Visual Steps books follow the same methodology: clear and concise step-by-step instructions with screenshots to demonstrate each task.
A complete list of all our books can be found on our website **www.visualsteps.com**
You can also sign up to receive our **free Visual Steps Newsletter**.

In this Newsletter you will receive periodic information by e-mail regarding:
- the latest titles and previously released books;
- special offers, supplemental chapters, tips and free informative booklets.

Also our Newsletter subscribers may download any of the documents listed on the web pages **www.visualsteps.com/info_downloads** and
www.visualsteps.com/tips

If you subscribe to our newsletter, be assured that we will never use your e-mail address for any purpose other than sending you the information as previously described. We will not share this address with any third-party. Each newsletter also contains a one-click link to unsubscribe.

Introduction to Visual Steps™

The Visual Steps handbooks and manuals are the best instructional materials available for learning how to work with computers. Nowhere else can you find better support for getting to know the computer, the Internet, *Windows* and related software programs.

Properties of the Visual Steps books:
- **Comprehensible contents**
  Addresses the needs of the beginner or intermediate computer user for a manual written in simple, straight-forward language.
- **Clear structure**
  Precise, easy to follow instructions. The material is broken down into small enough segments to allow for easy absorption.
- **Screenshots of every step**
  Quickly compare what you see on your screen with the screenshots in the book. Pointers and tips guide you when new windows are opened so you always know what to do next.
- **Get started right away**
  All you have to do is turn on your computer, place the book next to your keyboard, and begin at once.

In short, I believe these manuals will be excellent guides for you.

dr. H. van der Meij
Faculty of Applied Education, Department of Instruction Technology, University of Twente, the Netherlands

What You'll Need

In order to work through this book, you will need a number of things on your computer.

The primary requirement for working with this book is having one of the US versions of *Windows 7* installed on your computer:
- *Windows 7 Starter*
- *Windows 7 Home Premium*
- *Windows 7 Professional*
- *Windows 7 Ultimate/Enterprise*

You can check this yourself by turning on your computer and looking at the start-up screen.

If you have *Windows 7* on your computer, you will then also already have the following things on your computer.

Accessories WordPad Paint Calculator Games Solitaire	In *Windows 7*, the group *Accessories* will have been installed with the following programs: • *WordPad* • *Paint* • *Calculator* You should also see the group *Games*, in which you will find the program: • *Solitaire*
Network and Internet	A functioning Internet connection is needed for the two chapters about the Internet and downloading the Bonus Online Chapters (Chapters 7, 8 and 9). For the settings for your Internet connection, please see the software and information supplied by your Internet Service Provider.
Internet Explorer Windows Live Mail	In order to work with the Internet, you must have the following two programs installed on your computer: • *Windows Internet Explorer 8* • *Windows Live Mail* *Windows Live Mail* might not be installed to your computer yet. If so, follow the instructions in *Appendix D Downloading and Installing Windows Live Mail* to install this program.

You also need:

	A computer mouse. If you are working on a laptop with touchpad, you may want to purchase an external mouse in order to more easily follow the steps in this book.

The following things are useful. But it is not a problem if you do not have them. Simply skip over the relevant pages.

	An empty USB memory stick for saving files. (*Chapter 6 Libraries, Folders and Files*)

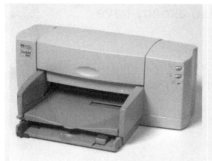

A printer is recommended for some of the exercises. If you do not have a printer, do not worry. Simply skip these exercises. (*Chapter 4 Writing a Letter*)

A music CD. (*Bonus Online Chapter 11 How to Make Working with Your Computer More Pleasant*)

How This Book Is Organized

This book is set up in such a way that you do not necessarily have to work through it from the beginning to the end.

The Basics
- Be sure to read and work carefully through *Chapters 1 and 2* first. These discuss the basics in *Windows 7*.
- Then you can continue with *Chapters 3, 4 and 5*. These chapters introduce the keyboard and the mouse, as well as basic word processing. These are skills that every computer user must master. The objective of these chapters is being able to write a letter.

Once you have mastered the basics, you can choose from the following topics:

Optional Subjects
- **Folders and files**
  You can choose to work with folders and files in *Chapter 6*. This chapter can be worked through separately.
- **Text layout**
  Or you can choose to layout text in *Bonus Online Chapter 10*.
- **Internet**
  If you want to learn how to use the Internet, read *Chapters 7 and 8*. For this you will need a functioning Internet connection.

- **Customizing computer settings**
  In *Bonus Online Chapter 11*, you can learn how to customize your computer settings to suit your individual needs or desires.
- **Photo Editing**
  In *Bonus Online Chapter 12*, you can learn how to open and edit your digital photos.

Please note: You can find the Bonus Online Chapters at the website that goes with this book: www.visualsteps.com/windows7
In *Chapter 9 Bonus Online Chapters and Extra Information* you can read how to open these chapters.

Website

At the website that accompanies this book, **www.visualsteps.com/windows7**, you will find some Bonus Online Chapters and more information about the book. This website will also keep you informed of changes you need to know of as a user of the book.
Please, also take a look at our website **www.visualsteps.com** from time to time to read about new books and gather other useful information.

Register Your Book

You can register your book. We will keep you aware of any important changes that are necessary to you as a user of the book. You can also take advantage of:
Our periodic newsletter informing you of our product releases, company news, tips & tricks, special offers, etcetera.
You can find information on how to register your book in *Chapter 7 Surfing the Internet*.

How To Use This Book

This book has been written using the Visual Steps™ method. You can work through this book independently at your own pace.

In this Visual Steps™ book, you will see various icons. This is what they mean:

Techniques
These icons indicate an action to be carried out:

 The mouse icon means you should do something with the mouse.

 The keyboard icon means you should type something on the keyboard.

 The hand icon means you should do something else, for example insert a CD-ROM in the computer. It is also used to remind you of something you learned before.

In addition to these actions, in some spots in the book *extra assistance* is provided so that you can successfully work through each chapter.

Help
These icons indicate that extra help is available:

The arrow icon warns you about something.

The bandage icon will help you if something has gone wrong.

Have you forgotten how to do something? The number next to the footsteps tells you where to look it up at the end of the book in the appendix *How Do I Do That Again?*

In separate boxes you find tips or additional, background information.

Extra information
Information boxes are denoted by these icons:

 The book icon gives you extra background information that you can read at your convenience. This extra information is not necessary for working through the book.

 The light bulb icon indicates an extra tip for using the program.

Test Your Knowledge

Have you finished reading this book? Test your knowledge then with the test *Windows 7*. Visit the website: **www.ccforseniors.com**

This multiple-choice test will show you how good your knowledge of *Windows 7* is. If you pass the test, you will receive your *free Computer Certificate* by e-mail.

For Teachers

This book is designed as a self-study guide. It is also well suited for use in a group or a classroom setting. For this purpose, we offer a free teacher's manual containing information about how to prepare for the course (including didactic teaching methods) and testing materials. You can download this teacher's manual (PDF file) from the website which accompanies this book: **www.visualsteps.com/windows7**

The Screen Shots

The screen shots in this book were made on a computer running *Windows 7 Ultimate*. The screen shots used in this book indicate which button, folder, file or hyperlink you need to click on your computer screen. In the instruction text (in **bold** letters) you will see a small image of the item you need to click. The black line will point you to the right place on your screen.
The small screen shots that are printed in this book are not meant to be completely legible all the time. This is not necessary, as you will see these images on your own computer screen in real size and fully legible.

Here you see an example of an instruction text and a screen shot. The black line indicates where to find this item on your own computer screen:

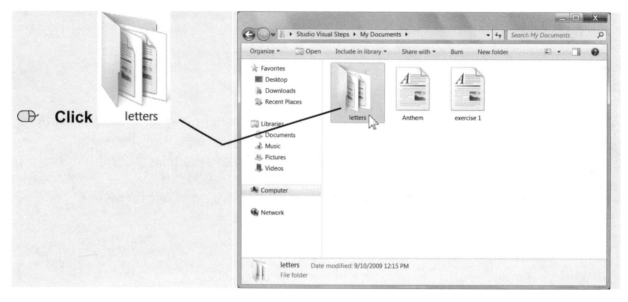

Sometimes the screen shot shows only a portion of a window. Here is an example:

It really will **not be necessary** for you to read all the information in the screen shots in this book. Always use the screen shots in combination with the image you see on your own computer screen.

1. Starting Windows 7

The computer you are sitting in front of is also called a *PC*. This is an abbreviation for *Personal Computer*. In the past twenty-five years, the PC has conquered the world, marching from the office to the home.

Nowadays nearly everyone has heard of *Windows*. But it was not all that long ago 1993 in fact - that *Windows* was used on PCs for the first time. Since then, *Windows* has evolved in step with the PC.

But what exactly is *Windows?* It is a program used to manage your computer's software and hardware resources. Before *Windows*, computers were operated by typing various complicated commands. With *Windows* you use your mouse to operate your computer. You can perform many different tasks by pointing and clicking the objects on your screen with your mouse.

As you work through this chapter, you will understand why this operating system is called *Windows.* You will see that nearly everything that happens is displayed in 'window panes' on your screen.

In this chapter, you will learn how to:

- turn on your computer and start *Windows 7*;
- point and click with the mouse;
- enter commands;
- open and close programs;
- minimize and maximize a window;
- use the taskbar;
- turn off your computer.

Please note:

This book assumes that you are working with a computer mouse. If you are working on a laptop with touchpad, you may want to purchase an external mouse in order to more easily follow the steps in this book.

1.1 Desktop Computer or Laptop

Computers come in different sizes and shapes. Desktop computers are designed for use at a desk or table. Desktop computers consist of separate components.

This is a desktop computer:

Monitor:

Computer case or housing:

Keyboard:

Mouse:

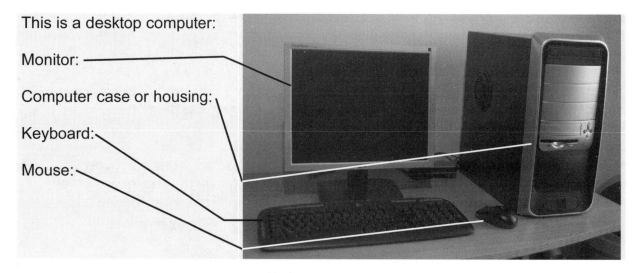

Laptop computers are lightweight portable PCs. They are often called *notebook computers* because of their small size. Laptops can operate on batteries, so you can take them anywhere. The screen folds down onto the keyboard when not in use. Laptops combine all computer components in a single case.

This is a laptop computer:

Screen:

Keyboard:

Touch pad:

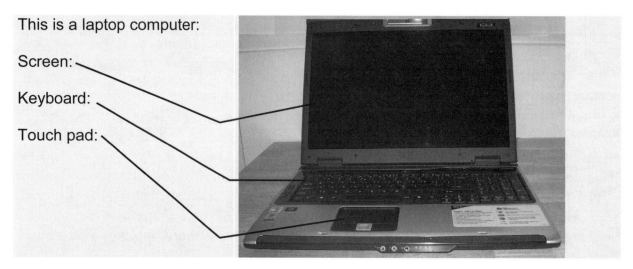

Operating *Windows 7* on either type of computer is the same. It does not matter whether you use a desktop or a laptop.

In order to use your computer, you first need to turn it on. You will learn how to do this in the next section.

1.2 Turning On Your Desktop Computer or Laptop

First, make sure your computer is plugged into an electrical outlet. You turn on your computer by pressing the power button found on the case. Turn on your monitor by pressing its power button. You will see this symbol: on or near this button. If you are using a computer for the first time it may take a little while to locate these power buttons.

Here you see how to turn on your computer.

If you are using a desktop computer, the power button is often located on the front of the case:

☞ **Press the power button**

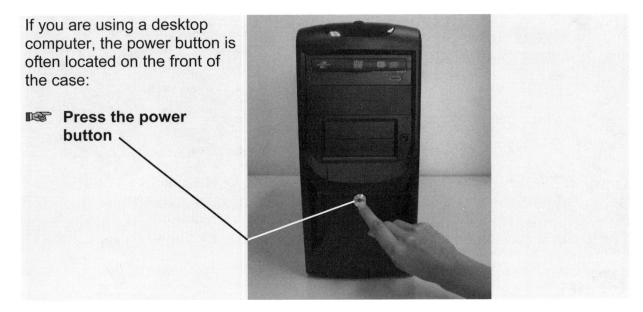

With many computers, the monitor will also be automatically started. With other computers, you must do this yourself.
If you do not see anything happening on your monitor after a short wait then your monitor most likely has not yet been turned on.

☞ **Press the power button**

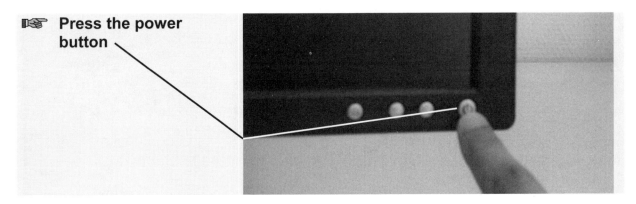

Your computer is now turned on.

✖️ HELP! I can not find the power button.

If you are unable to locate the power button, consult your computer's instruction manual or ask the person who sold it to you where the power button is located.

On a laptop, the power button is most likely found on the keyboard. You can easily identify this button by this symbol: ⏻.

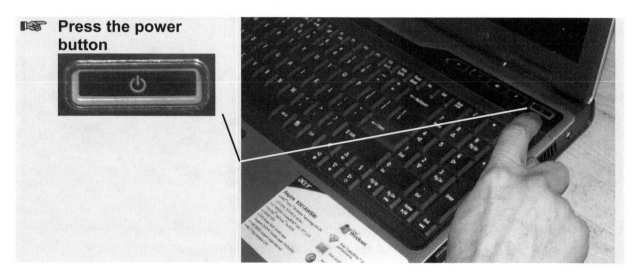

☞ **Press the power button**

The laptop is now turned on. The screen does not need to be turned on separately.

✖️ HELP! I can not find the power button.

If you are unable to locate the power button, consult your laptop's instruction manual or ask the person who sold it to you where the power button is located.

1.3 Starting Windows 7

Windows 7 is automatically started when you turn on your computer.

After a short time, you will see a screen that looks like this:

➥ Please note:

The screenshots used throughout this book may differ significantly from what you see on your computer screen. The appearance of your desktop in *Windows 7* can be customized in many ways. Perhaps someone who recently used your computer added a new desktop background for example. Computer manufacturers can also influence the appearance of your desktop. This will not interfere however with any of the tasks you need to do. You can continue reading.

In the figure below you see two small pictures called *icons* in the center of your screen. There may be more icons on your own screen. Or just one. The icons themselves may look different than the ones you see here. Even the names found under the icons on your screen may be different.

Somewhere on the screen you see an arrow.

This arrow is called the *pointer*.

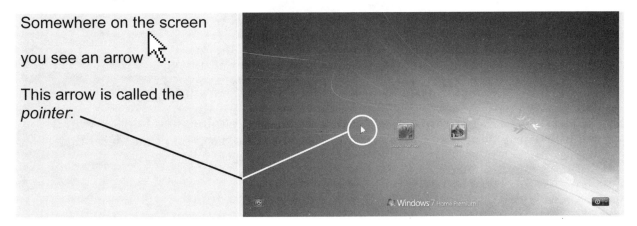

You direct the movement of the pointer on your computer screen by gently moving your mouse. In this chapter you will learn more how to do this.

1.4 Mouse or Touchpad

The pointer can be used as if it were your fingertip. You use it to 'point' to things on the screen such as the icons in the figure above. You can move the pointer in any direction on your computer screen. You can 'click' the items to perform various actions. This is done with a computer mouse:

Your desktop computer will usually be supplied with a computer mouse:

There are many types of designs and options available in computer mice.

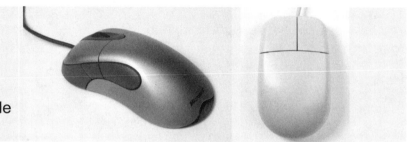

If you are working with a laptop, you can choose whether to operate it with a computer mouse or use the built in touchpad. The touchpad is a sensitive square which reacts when you move your fingertip across it.

Here you see the touchpad for this laptop:

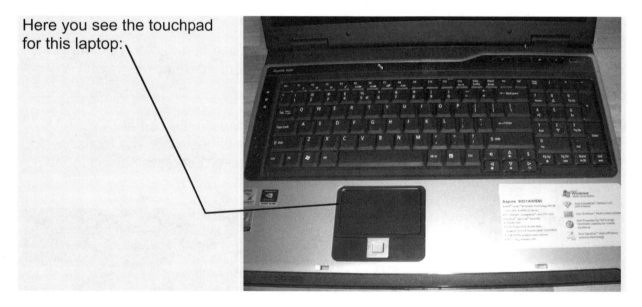

If you are using a laptop for the first time it is good idea to become familiar with a computer mouse. You will then be able to work on a desktop computer later on.

➥ **Please note:**

In this book you will learn how to use a computer mouse.
If you do not yet have a mouse you can purchase one at your local computer store.

💡 **Tip**

To the store
Take your laptop with you when you go to buy a computer mouse at the computer store. The sales representative can then show you how to connect your new mouse to your laptop. Then when you get home you can get started right away.

Here you see a laptop with a computer mouse attached:

💡 **Tip**

Touchpad
Later on, if you want to learn more about using the touchpad to operate your laptop, read the *Tip Working with a touchpad* on page 96.

1.5 How to Hold the Mouse

The mouse sits on your desk or table. The mouse is designed to fit comfortably in the palm of your hand. Here is how to hold the mouse:

Place your mouse beside your keyboard on a clean, smooth surface, such as a mousepad.

Hold the mouse gently with your index finger resting on the left button and your thumb resting on the side.

The mousepad is a surface for enhancing the movement of a computer mouse. It is not absolutely necessary. You can use your mouse on a smooth, clean surface such as the table or desk where your computer is located.

☀ Tip

What's the best way to hold the mouse?

Not like this: **But like this:**

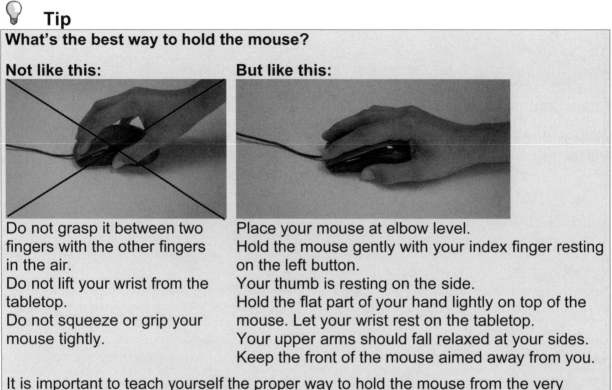

Do not grasp it between two fingers with the other fingers in the air.
Do not lift your wrist from the tabletop.
Do not squeeze or grip your mouse tightly.

Place your mouse at elbow level.
Hold the mouse gently with your index finger resting on the left button.
Your thumb is resting on the side.
Hold the flat part of your hand lightly on top of the mouse. Let your wrist rest on the tabletop.
Your upper arms should fall relaxed at your sides.
Keep the front of the mouse aimed away from you.

It is important to teach yourself the proper way to hold the mouse from the very beginning. You will only have sufficient control of the mouse and be able to move it precisely if you keep it in the palm of your hand.

1.6 Moving the Mouse

You operate the computer almost entirely by using the mouse. The first few times that you use the mouse, it will seem awkward and unfamiliar. Just remember that everyone else had to start from the beginning too. It is a matter of practicing. The more you use the mouse, the more proficient you will become.
To move the mouse, you slide it slowly on your desk surface or mousepad in any direction. As you move the mouse, the pointer on your screen moves in the same direction.

Try it:

Somewhere on the screen

you will see the pointer:

 ⬭➤ **Slide the mouse
    slowly on your desk
    surface or mousepad**

Watch how the pointer
moves with it.

If you run out of room when you move your mouse on your desk surface or mousepad, just pick it up, bring it back closer to you and gently set it down again. Remember: hold the flat part of your hand lightly on top of the mouse. If you grip the mouse too tightly you may inadvertently press one of the buttons. You will learn how to use these buttons later. For now try to move the mouse again:

Somewhere on the screen

you can see the pointer:

 ⬭➤ **Slide the mouse
    slowly on your desk
    surface or mousepad**

When you move the mouse with your hand, the pointer on your screen will move in the same direction.

➥ Please note:

Move the mouse by pivoting your arm at your elbow. Avoid pivoting the mouse with your wrist. This is to guard against possible injury such as *RSI*, repetitive strain injury.

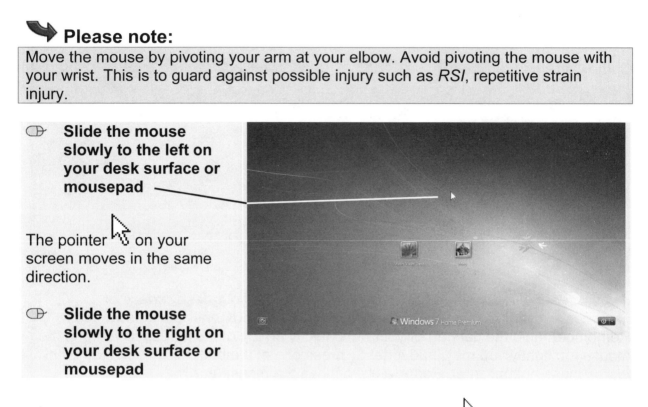

⊂⊅ **Slide the mouse slowly to the left on your desk surface or mousepad**

The pointer ⏵ on your screen moves in the same direction.

⊂⊅ **Slide the mouse slowly to the right on your desk surface or mousepad**

When you move the mouse in different directions, the pointer ⏵ on your screen follows the same movements.

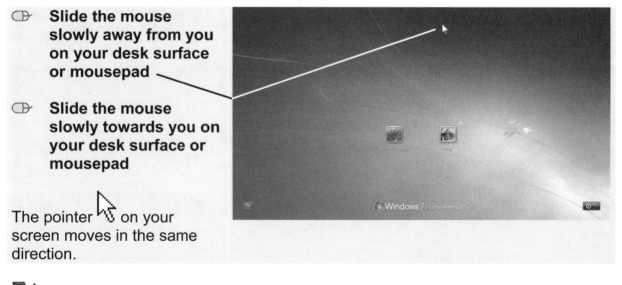

⊂⊅ **Slide the mouse slowly away from you on your desk surface or mousepad**

⊂⊅ **Slide the mouse slowly towards you on your desk surface or mousepad**

The pointer ⏵ on your screen moves in the same direction.

➥ Please note:

If you run out of room when you move your mouse on your desk surface or mousepad, just pick it up, bring it back closer to you and gently set it down again.

⮕ **Slide the mouse slowly in a circle on your desk surface or mousepad**

⮕ **Slide the mouse slowly in a triangle on your desk surface or mousepad**

The pointer on your screen will move in the same direction.

It is a good idea to repeat these exercises a few times until you feel you have sufficient control over your mouse. Then you can continue with the next section.

➥ Please note:

If you run out of room when you move your mouse on your desk surface or mousepad, just pick it up, bring it back closer to you and gently set it down again.

1.7 What Can You Do with the Mouse?

You can use your mouse to interact with objects on your computer screen.
Most mouse actions combine pointing with pressing one of the mouse buttons.
Pointing to an object on the screen means that you move your mouse until the pointer touches that object. Then you can use one of the mouse buttons.
There are four basic ways to use your mouse buttons:

- click (single-click);
- double-click;
- right-click;
- drag.

With these mouse actions you can move objects, select them, open them, edit them, even throw them away. You instruct your computer to perform different tasks by using these mouse actions.
In this chapter you will learn how to point and click with your mouse.

1.8 Pointing

The first thing you need to know is how to point to things with the pointer on the screen. Pointing to an object on the screen means moving your mouse until the pointer touches or hovers above the object. In the previous section you learned how to move the pointer around your computer screen. In the figure below, you see two small pictures, *icons*, in the center of the screen. On your own computer screen you might see more of these icons, or perhaps just one. For the following exercises this does not matter.

☞ Move the mouse

pointer slowly towards the icon

☞ Hold the mouse still as you touch the icon

You will see that the color of the icon changes somewhat.

The mouse pointer is resting now on top of the icon.
Were you unable to do this the first time? Try again.

Remember: hold the mouse gently with your index finger resting on the left button. Your thumb is resting on the side. Hold the flat part of your hand lightly on top of the mouse. Let your wrist rest on the tabletop.

When the pointer touches the icon you can perform your first mouse action. You will need a mouse button to do this. In the next section, you will read about which mouse button to use for this task.

1.9 The Mouse Buttons

Computer mice are available in a wide variety of types and colors. And yet they are all similar: every mouse has at least two buttons.

The most important button is the *left mouse button*:

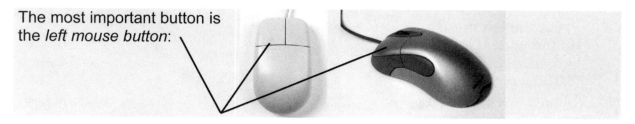

Mouse buttons can be pressed and released. This is called 'clicking'. You can hear a clicking sound when you press one of these mouse buttons.

1.10 Clicking

Clicking is the mouse action that you will use the most. First read how you go about clicking. You do not have to do any clicking yet. Clicking is done like this:

- Point to something with the mouse pointer;
- Hold the mouse gently with your index finger resting on the left button;
- Then press the *left button* on the mouse and immediately release it.

Left button

Now try this yourself:

☞ **Point to an icon**

☞ **Hold the mouse still**

The pointer ⬉ appears to be touching the icon.

You will see that the color of the icon changes somewhat.

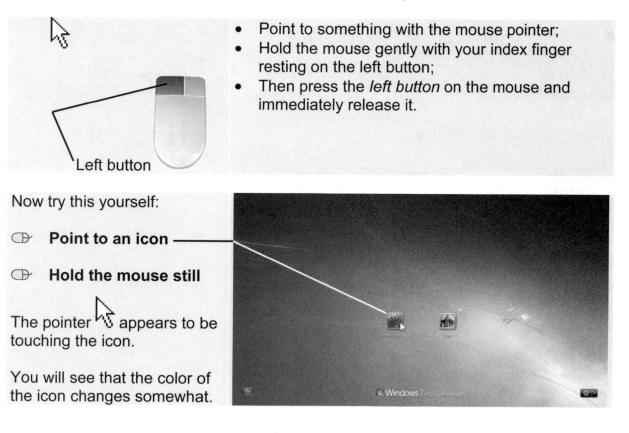

Now *click* the icon using the left mouse button:

Hold the mouse gently with your index finger resting on the left button.

☞ **Press the left mouse button and immediately release it**

You will hear a short clicking sound the instant you press down on the mouse button.

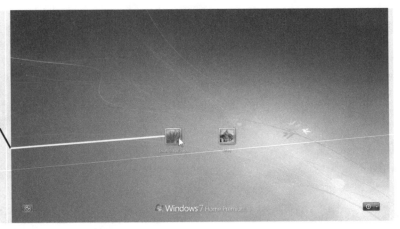

The screen will change when you click the icon.

✖ HELP! When I pressed down on the button, the pointer moved.

This usually means that you have moved the mouse after pointing and before clicking.
Remember:

- Hold the mouse gently with your index finger resting on the left button;
- Your thumb is resting on the side;
- Hold the flat part of your hand lightly on top of the mouse;
- Let your wrist rest on the tabletop.

Then you will not need to look at your hand when you click.

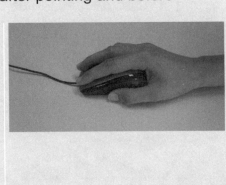

☞ **Try again**

The precise window that appears on your screen will depend on your particular computer. You may see the window shown in the figure below:

If you see this window, you can skip the following steps.

Proceed further on page 37.

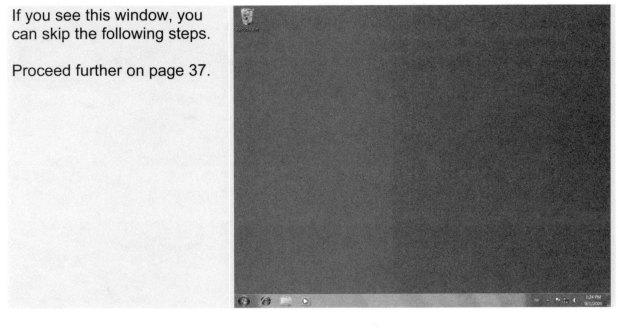

Or you may see this window:

If you see this window, you will need a password in order to continue.

The password is typed in the white area of the box where you see the word

Password

To type the password, it is necessary to use the keyboard of your computer.

Of course you will need to know what the password is beforehand.
If you do not know the password, ask the owner of the computer that you are using what it is.

⌨ Type the password

As you type you will see small black circles appear in the white area of the box: ——————

This is normal. In this way, no one can see what you have typed. This keeps your password hidden from others.

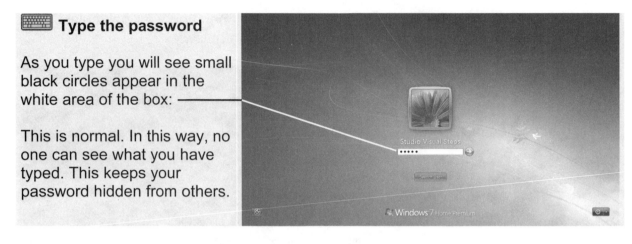

When you have finished typing the password, you can continue.

🖰 **Point to** ➡ ————————

🖰 **Hold the mouse still**

Now you can click ➡.

🖰 **Press the left mouse button and immediately release it**

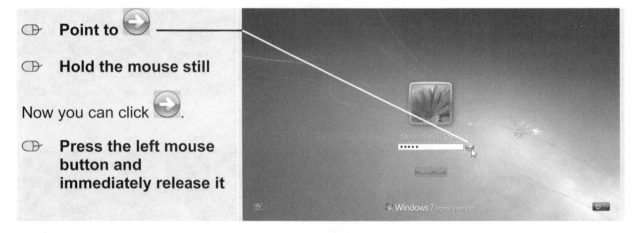

Do not give up if it does not work on the first try and you find yourself moving your mouse accidentally when trying to click. You just need to practice a bit more.

Remember: hold the mouse gently with your index finger resting on the left button. Your thumb is resting on the side. Hold the flat part of your hand lightly on top of the mouse. Let your wrist rest on the tabletop. Then you will not need to look at your hand when you click.
Try it again.

Now you see this window:

HELP! I see a different window.

If you see a different window than the one shown above, it may look like the one shown in this figure:
The picture that you see here is your desktop background. You can personalize your computer with a different background. Remember that *Windows 7* allows you to adjust many settings to suit your own taste. Perhaps someone else has already made a change to your desktop background. You can proceed further on the next page.

1.11 The Desktop

You see the screen shown in the figure below. This screen is called the desktop.

Now take a look at what can be found on your desktop:

This screen shot shows a solid color. The color or picture may be different than the one that appears on your desktop.

Remember that *Windows 7* allows you to adjust many settings to suit your own taste. Perhaps someone else has already done this for you.
Later in the book you will learn how to make these sort of changes yourself.

There is a long horizontal bar at the bottom of your desktop. This bar is called the taskbar:

On the far left side of the taskbar you see this button

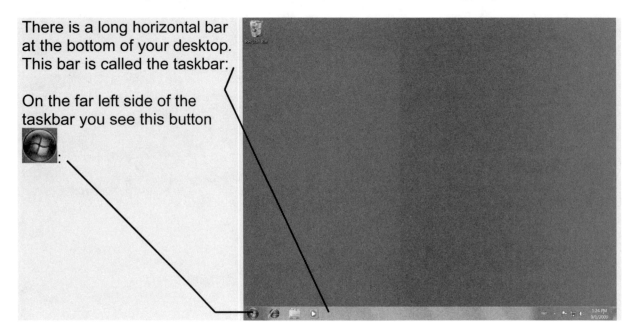

The desktop is the main screen area that you see after you turn on your computer and log on to *Windows*. Like the top of an actual desk, it serves as a surface for your work. When you open programs or folders, they appear on the desktop. Later in this book you will read more about the different kinds of programs and folders.

1.12 Pointing to an Object

When you point to something, a small box often appears that describes the item. Try it:

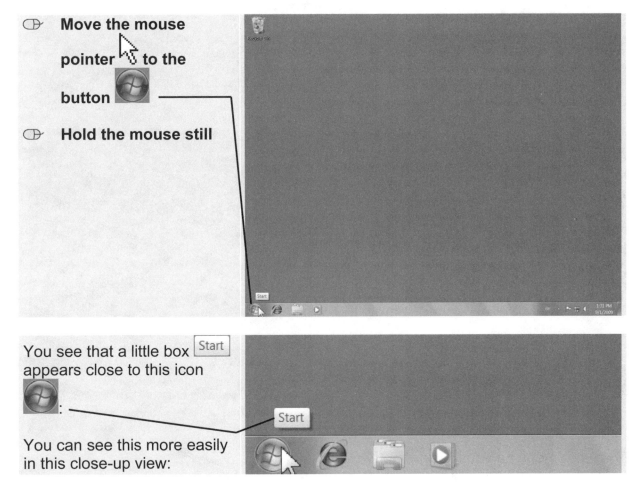

☞ **Move the mouse pointer to the button**

☞ **Hold the mouse still**

You see that a little box appears close to this icon:

You can see this more easily in this close-up view:

Pointing to an object often reveals a descriptive message about it.

1.13 The Start Menu

The Start menu is the main gateway to your computer's programs, folders, and settings. To open the Start menu you will need to click the Start button:

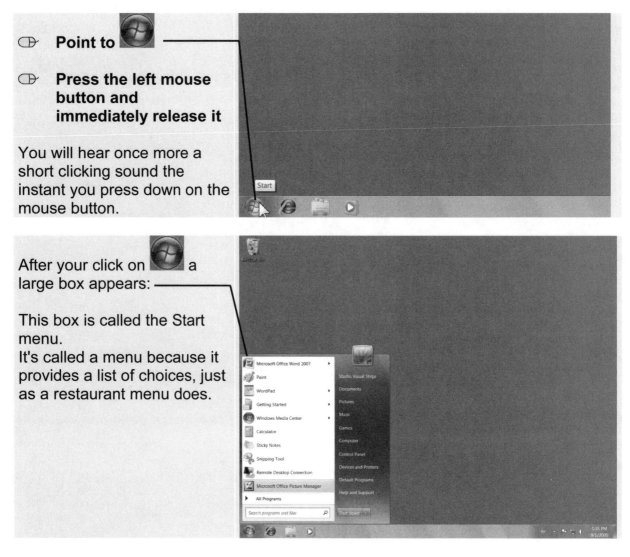

☞ **Point to**

☞ **Press the left mouse button and immediately release it**

You will hear once more a short clicking sound the instant you press down on the mouse button.

After your click on   a large box appears:

This box is called the Start menu.
It's called a menu because it provides a list of choices, just as a restaurant menu does.

The Start menu on your desktop may appear smaller.
Later in this book you will learn how to adjust the size of this box.

This figure shows a close-up of the Start menu:

The large left pane shows a short list of programs on your computer: ──────

Your computer manufacturer can customize this list, so its exact appearance will vary from computer to computer.

Almost everything you do on your computer requires using a program. A *program* is a set of instructions that a computer uses to perform a specific task.
For example, if you want to calculate a number, you use the *Calculator* program.

You are going to start the *Calculator* program. This program is not found in the short list of programs. You can find this program in ▶ All Programs.

1.14 Opening the Calculator Program

You are going to start the *Calculator* program. The Start menu is already opened.
Down near the bottom you see ▶ All Programs:

☞ **Point to**
  ▶ All Programs ──────

You can click now:

☞ **Press the left mouse button and immediately release it**

✖ HELP! The Start menu changed before I clicked.

When you point to long at ▶   All Programs, the Start menu might change before you clicked. If so, you can follow the next step without clicking.

Now another menu appears in the same box. You see a list of programs and a list of folders.

You can easily recognize a folder by this icon 📁.
So what is inside the folders? More programs.

You are going to open the folder called *Accessories*:

👆   **Point to** 📁 Accessories

It automatically turns blue.

👆   **Press the left mouse button and immediately release it**

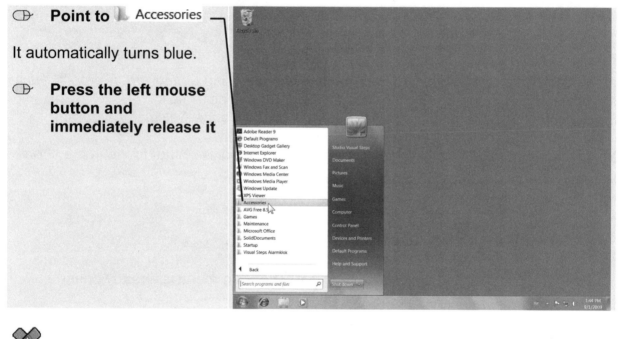

✖ HELP! I opened the wrong folder.

Can you still see the menu, but the wrong folder has been opened?
👆   **Point to** 📁 Accessories

👆   **Press the left mouse button and immediately release it**

The programs that are stored in the 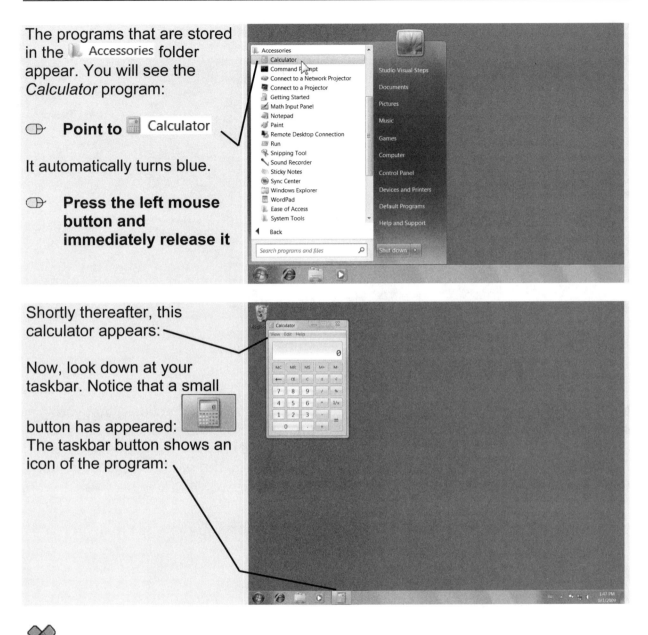 Accessories folder appear. You will see the *Calculator* program:

☞ **Point to** 🖩 Calculator

It automatically turns blue.

☞ **Press the left mouse button and immediately release it**

Shortly thereafter, this calculator appears:

Now, look down at your taskbar. Notice that a small button has appeared:
The taskbar button shows an icon of the program:

HELP! The wrong program appears.

Did you accidentally open the wrong program?

☞ **Point to** ❌ **at the top right corner of the wrong program**

☞ **Press the left mouse button and immediately release it**

The program will close.

☞ **Now go back through the steps above to open the *Calculator***

You have instructed your computer to open the *Calculator* program.

This figure shows the window of the *Calculator* program.

At the top of the window, you see the title bar with a program icon, the name of the program and three buttons on the right:

All of the programs in *Windows 7* use a window such as this and they all work in virtually the same way. This makes them easy to use.

1.15 The Menu Bar

Most programs contain dozens or even hundreds of commands (actions) that you use to work the program. Many of these commands are organized under menus. Like a restaurant menu, a program menu shows you a list of choices. To keep the screen uncluttered, menus are hidden until you click their titles in the *menu bar*, located just underneath the title bar.

This is the menu bar:

☞ **Point to** Help

The word Help changes to the button Help :

You can click this type of button.

➥ Please note:

From this point on in this book you will see this mouse icon ☞ and the word '**Click**' when you are asked to click an item. For example: the instruction

☞ **Click** Help

is the same as

☞ **Point to** Help
☞ **Press the left mouse button and immediately release it**

☞ **Click** Help

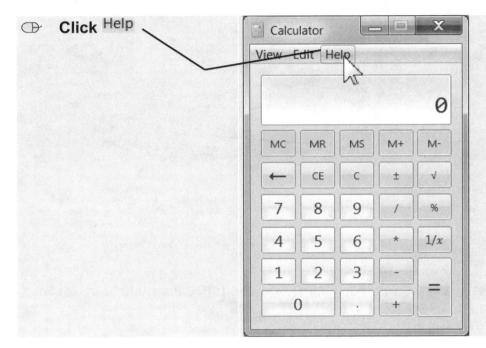

Now a menu appears:

☞ **Click** About Calculator

A second window appears. It floats above the *Calculator* window:

The second window contains information about the program: ————————

At the bottom you see a button that says 'OK'. That means: Okay, I understand.

 **Click** OK

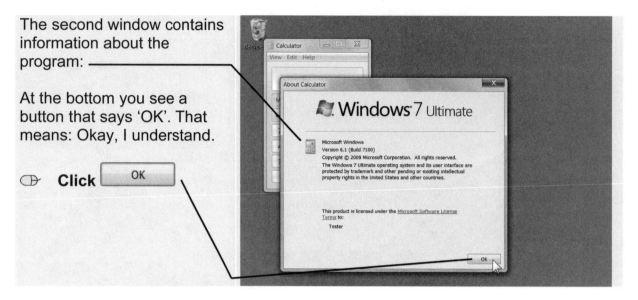

Now the second window is closed.

1.16 Calculate by Clicking

The *Calculator* works just like a real calculator. You can press the buttons by clicking them with the mouse:

Please note:

The instruction ☞ **Click ...** is the same as:

☞ **Point to ...**

☞ **Press the left mouse button and immediately release it**

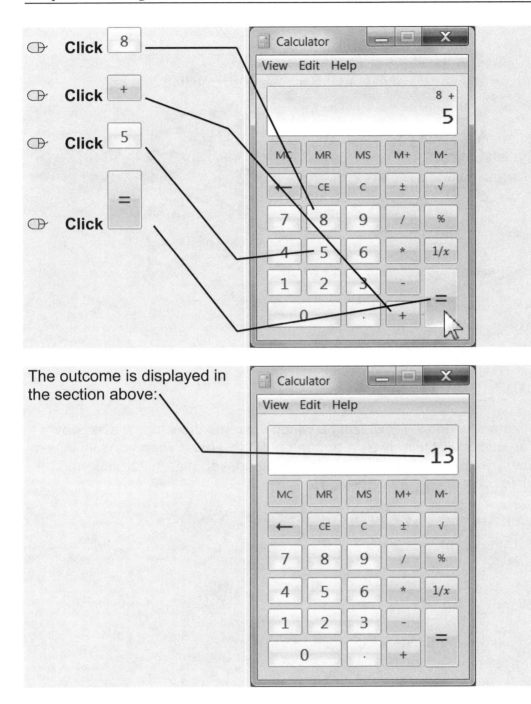

Click 8

Click +

Click 5

Click =

The outcome is displayed in the section above:

Tip

Is it difficult to click on the right spot?
This usually means that you have moved the mouse after pointing and before clicking.
Remember:

- Hold the mouse gently with your index finger resting on the left button;
- Your thumb is resting on the side;
- Hold the flat part of your hand lightly on top of the mouse;
- Let your wrist rest on the tabletop.

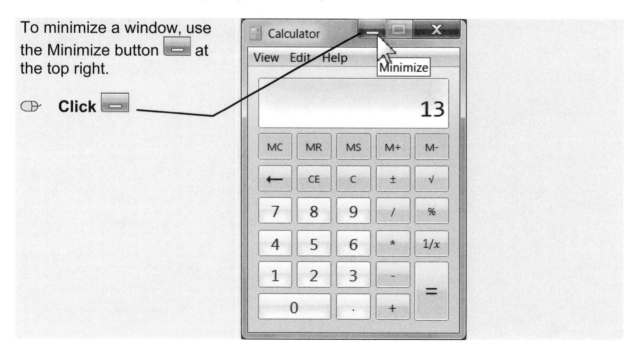

Then you will not need to look at your hand when you click.

Try again

1.17 Minimizing a Window

You can minimize any window. *Minimizing* a window means the window disappears from the desktop and is visible only as a button on the taskbar. When you minimize a program window, you do not close the program; instead, you merely reduce the space the window takes up on your desktop.

To minimize a window, use the Minimize button ▬ at the top right.

⊕ **Click** ▬

The window is minimized and disappears from the desktop:

Next to  you still see the

Calculator button on the taskbar: ——

Remember: you did not actually close the program *Calculator*; you simply reduced the space it takes up on your desktop.

1.18 Starting Another Program

In *Windows 7* you can have more than one program opened at a time.
Take a look:

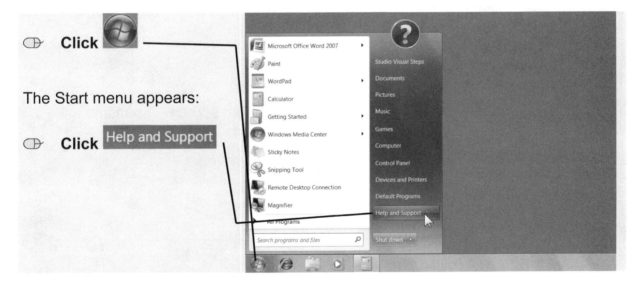

Click

The Start menu appears:

Click Help and Support

Now you see the window for *Windows Help and Support*:

In this figure you see that the window takes up about one half of the surface of the desktop. This may be different on your own desktop.

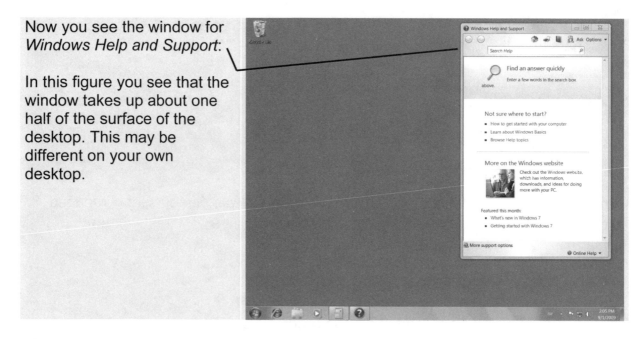

You did not receive a manual with *Windows 7*. All of the information you need is contained in this digital Help system. We will discuss this in more detail later.

1.19 Maximizing and Minimizing

The *Windows Help and Support* window can fill the entire screen. Expanding a window to its largest allowable size is called maximizing.

There is a button ▣ for maximizing the window.

It is in the middle of the three buttons in the upper right corner of the *Windows Help and Support* window:

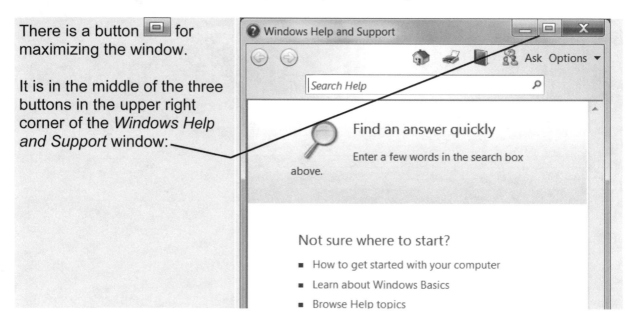

Click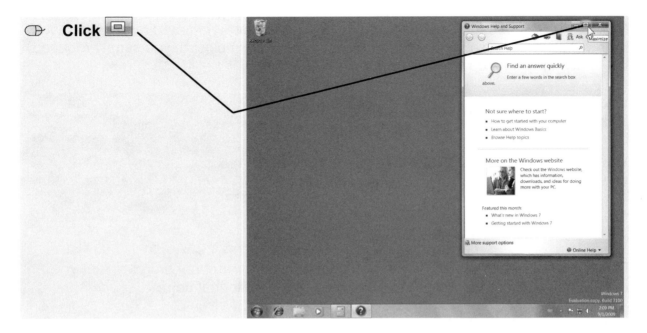

The window changes size. The window now fills the entire screen.

The *Windows Help and Support* window can also be reduced (minimized).

To minimize a window, use the Minimize button at the top right.

Click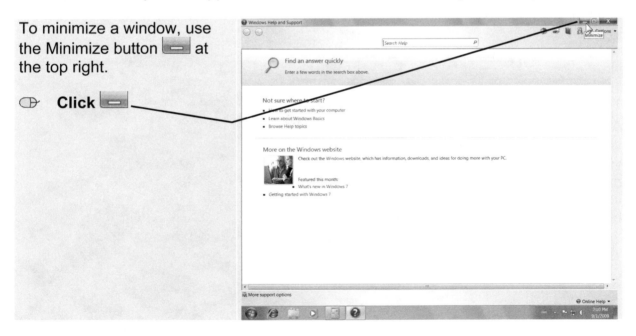

The window will be minimized.

Now you have opened two programs: the *Calculator* and *Windows Help and Support*. Both windows are now minimized. The programs are not closed, you simply reduced the space they take up on your desktop.

If you look down to the taskbar you will see the buttons of the two programs:

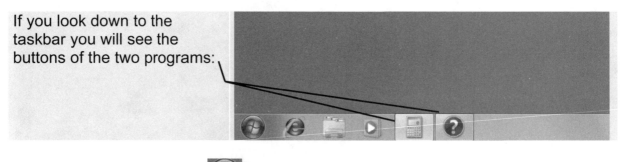

Remember: the bar next to is called the taskbar. For every program that you open a button is created on the taskbar corresponding to that item.

1.20 Making a Window Reappear on the Desktop

To make a minimized window reappear on the desktop, just click its button on the taskbar. The window appears exactly as it was before you minimized it.
Try it:

☞ **Point to**

A small picture appears that shows you a miniature version of the window. This preview is especially useful if you can not identify a window by its title alone.

☞ **Click**

If you have *Windows 7 Starter Edition* or your graphics card is not fast enough, you might not see this miniature.

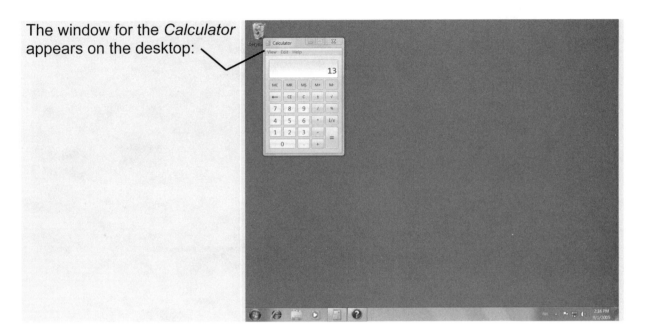

The window for the *Calculator* appears on the desktop:

1.21 Closing a Program

A window can also be definitively *closed*. If you close the *Calculator* window, you close the program.

You can close a window by using this window button :

☞ **Click** X

The window will be closed and the *Calculator* button will no longer be displayed on the taskbar. The program is now closed.

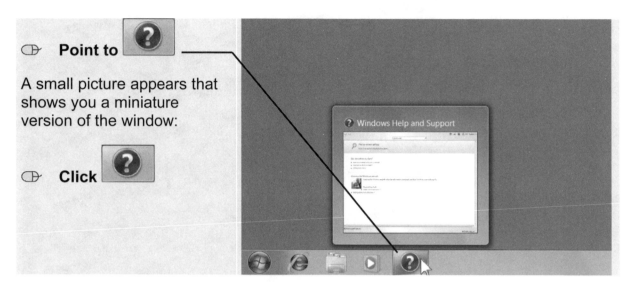

The window *Windows Help and Support* will appear.

1.22 Restoring a Maximized Window to Its Former Size

The window *Windows Help and Support* was maximized. To return a maximized window to its former size, you can use its *Restore button*.

This is the Restore button:

It is in the middle of the three buttons in the upper right corner of the window:

This Restore button appears in place of the Maximize button.

To restore the former size of the window:

☞ **Click**

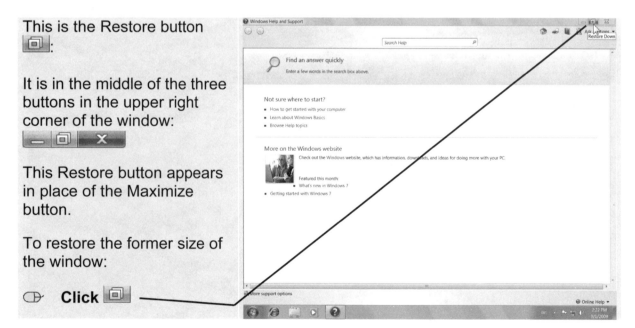

The window is now restored to its former size.

Now you can close this
window:

☞ **Click**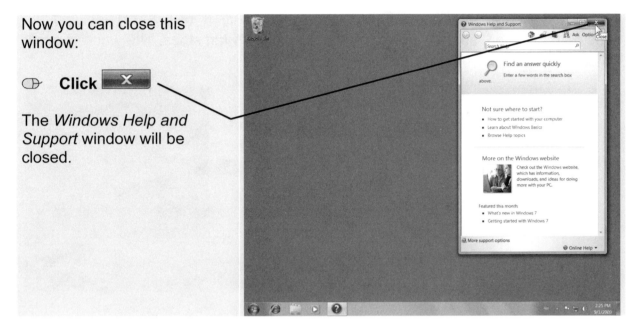

The *Windows Help and
Support* window will be
closed.

Windows Help and Support is now closed and its corresponding button on the
taskbar has disappeared.

1.23 Turning Off Your Computer

When you are done using your computer, it is important to turn it off properly. Not
only to save energy, but also to ensure that your work is saved.
Point to the Start button:

☞ **Click**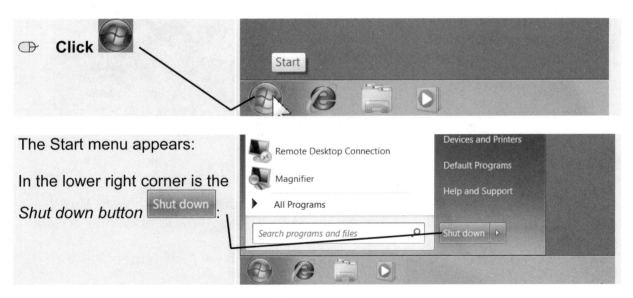

The Start menu appears:

In the lower right corner is the

Shut down button :

When you click this **Shut down** button, your computer switches off. If you still have opened programs, you will be asked to save your work first. After that *Windows 7* turns off the screen, and any noise from the computer's fan stops. The whole process takes only a few seconds. Try it yourself:

☞ **Click** Shut down

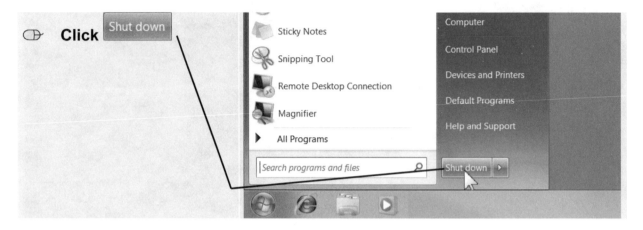

💡 Tip

Leaving your PC on
Do you see the Start menu and you would prefer leaving your computer on? If you click on an empty place on the desktop, the Start menu and the box with the Shut Down option will disappear. Then you can continue.

Your computer screen will turn black immediately. Your computer has now been switched off.

To start your computer:

☞ **Press the power button**

Windows 7 is now closed and the computer has been shut down.

In this chapter you have learned how to turn your computer on and how to shut it down. You have practiced using the mouse and you know how to open and close a program.
The following exercises will help you master what you have just learned.

1.24 Exercises

The following exercises will help you master what you have just learned. Have you forgotten how to do something? Use the number beside the footsteps to look it up in the appendix *How Do I Do That Again?*

Exercise: Opening and Closing

☞ Turn on your computer.

☞ Open the *Calculator*. $\mathscr{C}^5$

☞ Minimize the *Calculator* window. $\mathscr{C}^1$

☞ Open *Windows Help and Support*. $\mathscr{C}^6$

☞ Maximize the *Windows Help and Support* window. $\mathscr{C}^2$

☞ Minimize the *Windows Help and Support* window. $\mathscr{C}^1$

☞ Open the *Calculator* window from the taskbar. $\mathscr{C}^7$

☞ Close the *Calculator*. $\mathscr{C}^4$

☞ Open the *Windows Help and Support* window from the taskbar. $\mathscr{C}^8$

☞ Close the *Windows Help and Support* window. $\mathscr{C}^4$

☞ Turn off your computer. $\mathscr{C}^9$

When you have practiced enough, you can read the *Background Information* and *Tips* on the next page. If you would rather keep working with your computer, you can go on to *Chapter 2 More Use of the Mouse in Windows 7*. The *Background Information* and *Tips* can be read another time.

1.25 Background Information

Dictionary

Desktop	The desktop is the main screen area that you see after you turn on your computer and log on to *Windows 7*. When you open programs or folders, they appear on the desktop.
Icon	A small picture that represents a folder, program, or object.
Menu, Menu bar	Most programs contain dozens or even hundreds of commands (actions) that you use to work the program. Many of these commands are organized under menus. Menus are hidden until you click their titles in the menu bar, located just underneath the title bar.
Mouse actions	Most mouse actions combine pointing with pressing one of the mouse buttons. There are four basic ways to use your mouse buttons: clicking, double-clicking, right-clicking, and dragging.
Program	A set of instructions that a computer uses to perform a specific task, such as word processing or calculating.
Shut down button	The Shut down button turns off your computer: `Shut down`.
Start button	Button that opens the Start menu.
Start menu	The Start menu is the main gateway to your computer's programs, folders, and settings. It is called a menu because it provides a list of choices, just as a restaurant menu does.
Taskbar	The taskbar is the long horizontal bar at the bottom of your screen. The taskbar is usually visible.
Taskbar button	A button representing an open folder or program. These buttons appear on the taskbar.
Title bar	The horizontal bar at the top of a window that contains the name of the window.

- Continue reading on the next page -

Window	A rectangular box or frame on a computer screen in which programs and content appear.
Window buttons	Buttons that are used to manipulate the window: ⬚ ⬚ ✕.
Windows 7	Operating system: the computer program that manages all other computer programs on your computer. The operating system stores files, allows you to use programs, and coordinates the use of computer hardware (mouse, keyboard).

Source: Windows Help and Support

What are the various parts of Windows 7 Desktop called?
The desktop is the main screen area that you see after you turn on your computer and log on to *Windows*. Like the top of an actual desk, it serves as a surface for your work. When you open programs or folders, they appear on the desktop.

Icon:
A small picture that represents a file, folder, program, or other object. For example the *Recycle Bin* icon.

Window:
A rectangular box or frame on a computer screen in which programs and content appear.

Start menu:
The Start menu is the main gateway to your computer's programs, folders, and settings. And as 'Start' implies, it is often the place that you will go to start or open things.

Taskbar:
The long horizontal bar at the bottom of your screen. It contains the Start button and shows which programs or documents are opened.

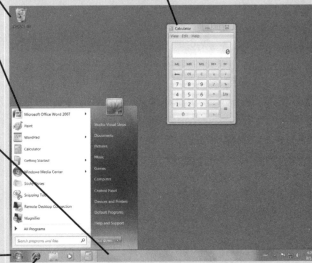

Start button:
Opens the Start menu.

Taskbar button:
Whenever you open a program, *Windows* creates a button on the taskbar corresponding to that item, called a shortcut. The button shows the name of the program.

What's in the Start menu?

The Start menu is the main gateway to your computer's programs, folders, and settings. It is called a *menu* because it provides a list of choices, just as a restaurant menu does. And as 'Start' implies, it is often the place that you will go to start or open things. To open the Start menu, click the Start button found in the lower-left corner of your screen. Or, press the *Windows* logo key on your keyboard. The Start menu appears:

The large left pane shows a short list of programs on your computer:
Your computer manufacturer can customize this list, so its exact appearance will vary. You might notice that over time, the lists of programs in your Start menu change. The Start menu detects which programs you use the most, and it places them in the left pane for quick access.

In the lower left corner is the search box which allows you to look for all kind of things on your computer by typing in search terms:

The right pane provides access to commonly used folders, files, settings, and features:
It is also where you go to log off from *Windows* or turn off your computer.

What are the various parts of a window called?

All of the programs in *Windows 7* are displayed in a window. Most windows have the same basic parts:

Title bar:
Displays the name of the program.

Menu bar:
Contains items that you can click to make choices in a program.

Menu:
A list of commands (choices).

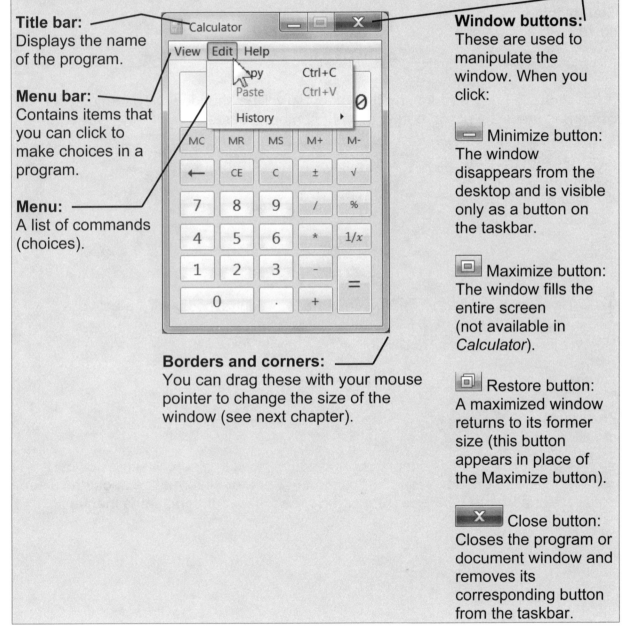

Borders and corners:
You can drag these with your mouse pointer to change the size of the window (see next chapter).

Window buttons:
These are used to manipulate the window. When you click:

Minimize button: The window disappears from the desktop and is visible only as a button on the taskbar.

Maximize button: The window fills the entire screen (not available in *Calculator*).

Restore button: A maximized window returns to its former size (this button appears in place of the Maximize button).

Close button: Closes the program or document window and removes its corresponding button from the taskbar.

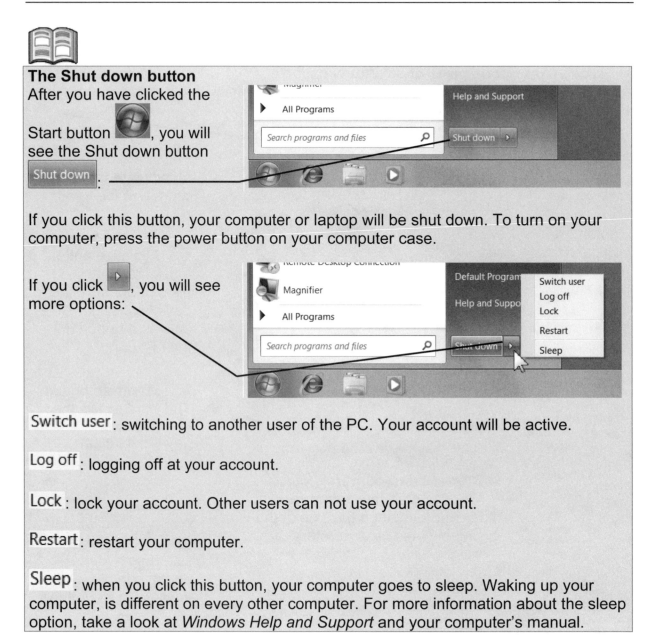

The Shut down button
After you have clicked the

Start button, you will
see the Shut down button

Shut down :

If you click this button, your computer or laptop will be shut down. To turn on your computer, press the power button on your computer case.

If you click, you will see
more options:

Switch user : switching to another user of the PC. Your account will be active.

Log off : logging off at your account.

Lock : lock your account. Other users can not use your account.

Restart : restart your computer.

Sleep : when you click this button, your computer goes to sleep. Waking up your computer, is different on every other computer. For more information about the sleep option, take a look at *Windows Help and Support* and your computer's manual.

1.26 Tips

HELP! I see something else all of a sudden.

Has another image suddenly appeared on your screen?
A moving illustration such as this, perhaps:

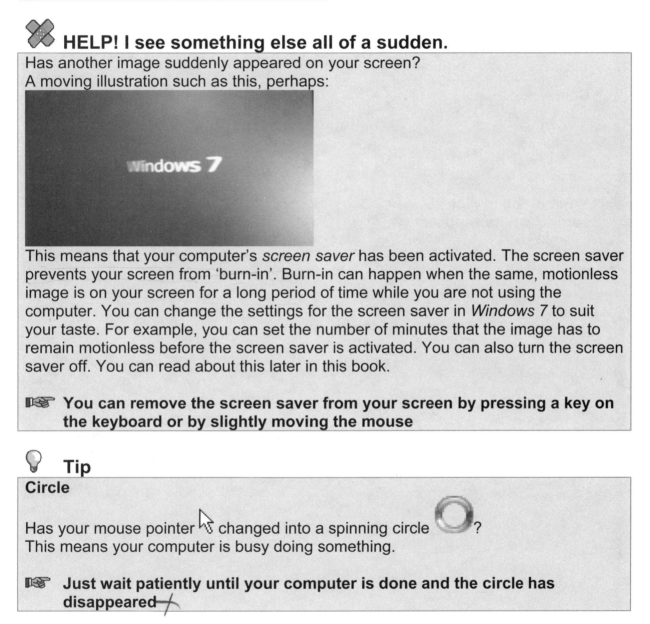

This means that your computer's *screen saver* has been activated. The screen saver prevents your screen from 'burn-in'. Burn-in can happen when the same, motionless image is on your screen for a long period of time while you are not using the computer. You can change the settings for the screen saver in *Windows 7* to suit your taste. For example, you can set the number of minutes that the image has to remain motionless before the screen saver is activated. You can also turn the screen saver off. You can read about this later in this book.

☞ **You can remove the screen saver from your screen by pressing a key on the keyboard or by slightly moving the mouse**

Tip

Circle

Has your mouse pointer changed into a spinning circle ?
This means your computer is busy doing something.

☞ **Just wait patiently until your computer is done and the circle has disappeared**

💡 Tip

Closing windows directly from the taskbar

Windows which are minimized In *Windows* 7 can be closed directly from the taskbar. This is how:

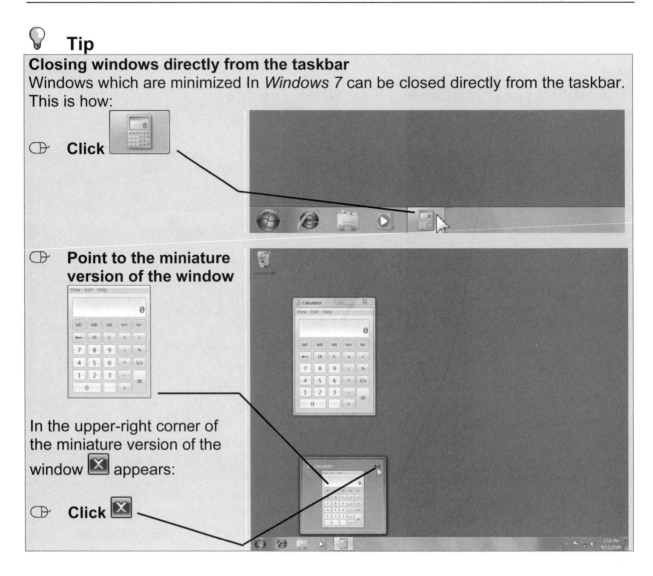

⊕ **Click**

⊕ **Point to the miniature version of the window**

In the upper-right corner of the miniature version of the window ⊠ appears:

⊕ **Click ⊠**

2. More Use of the Mouse in Windows 7

The mouse has become an essential part of the computer. But it is actually a relatively new addition. The mouse did not become a standard part of the PC until *Windows* was introduced.

Before then, only computers made by *Apple* had a mouse, and it had only one button. It quickly became evident that operating a PC had to be made easier so that more people could use it.

This is why the software became increasingly *graphic*: pictures and buttons replaced complicated commands. *Windows 7* is an excellent example of this.

The most important commands can be carried out by using the mouse. Various aspects of *Windows 7* were developed to make it easier to use – there are various kinds of buttons in many sizes on the screen: buttons to press, on and off buttons, buttons that turn and scroll bars. The mouse has also been given more and more functions.

In this chapter, you will learn how to utilize these functions.

In this chapter, you will learn how to:

- drag with the mouse;
- drag a scroll bar;
- use a scroll wheel;
- change the size of a window;
- use the *Windows Help and Support*;
- double-click with the mouse;
- right-click with the mouse.

2.1 Getting Ready

Before you begin:

☞ **Turn the computer (and the monitor) on**

☞ **Open the *Calculator* 🐾5**

The *Calculator* window is
opened:

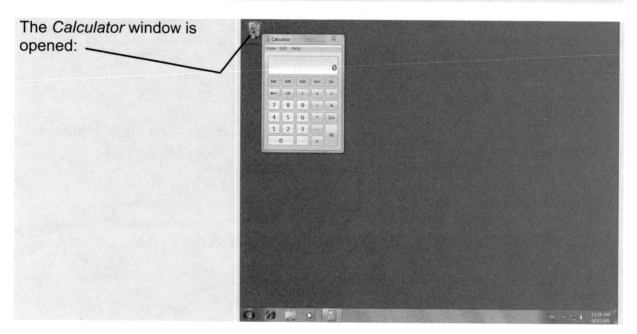

2.2 The Next Three Mouse Actions

In the previous chapter, you learned that there are four basic ways to use your
mouse buttons:

- click (single-click);
- drag;
- double-click;
- right-click.

You have practiced how to click (single-click with the left mouse button) in the
previous chapter. In this chapter, you will learn how to perform the other three mouse
actions.

2.3 Dragging

Dragging is used to move windows and icons around on your desktop.
Dragging is done like this:

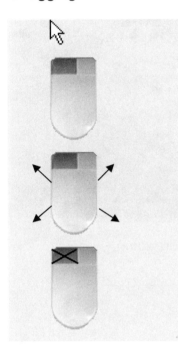

- Point to something with the mouse pointer.

- Press the left mouse button and hold it down.

- Move the mouse.

- Let go of the mouse button when you are done.

For example, you can move the *Calculator* window to another location on the desktop by dragging its title bar. The title bar is the horizontal bar at the top of a window which contains the name of the window. Try it:

☞ **Place the mouse pointer ⌖ on the title bar**

☞ **Press the left mouse button and hold it down**

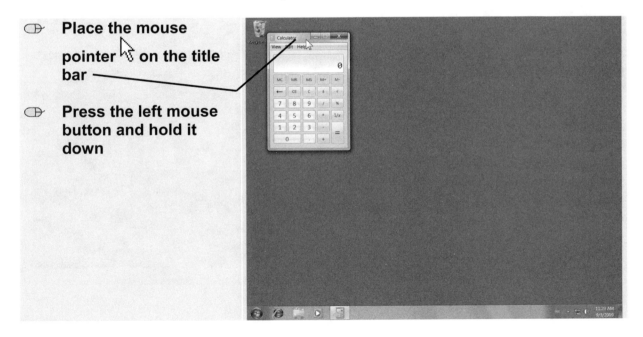

☞ **While holding down the left mouse button, slide the mouse over the tabletop** ─────

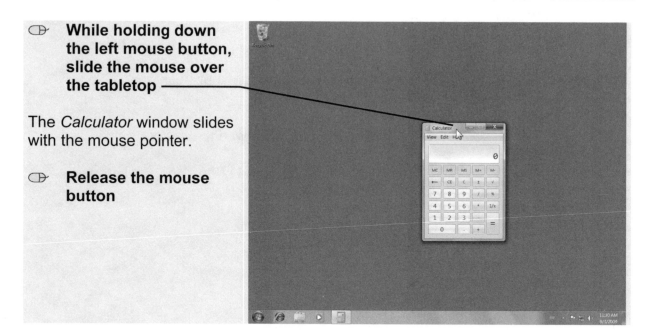

The _Calculator_ window slides with the mouse pointer.

☞ **Release the mouse button**

At the end of this chapter you will find exercises for practicing dragging. Now you can close the _Calculator_ window.

🖙 **Close the _Calculator_ window** ✇⁴

💡 **Tip**

Dragging in Solitaire
A good way to practice dragging, is by playing the popular card game _Solitaire_ on the computer. It is the perfect, handy way to learn to use the mouse.

This _Solitaire_ program comes with _Windows 7_ and it has probably already been installed on your computer.

In _Appendix A Clicking, Dragging and Double-Clicking in Solitaire_ at the back of this book you can read how to start this program and play the game.

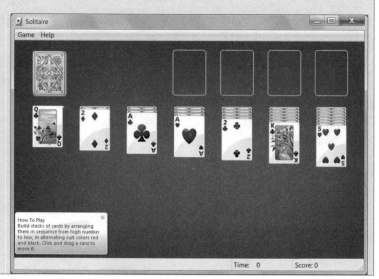

2.4 Dragging with a Scroll Bar

There are many situations in *Windows* where you must *drag* something. You can practice dragging different objects while using the *Windows Help and Support* window.

☞ **Open *Windows Help and Support* ⏍⁶**

This figure shows the *Windows Help and Support* window:

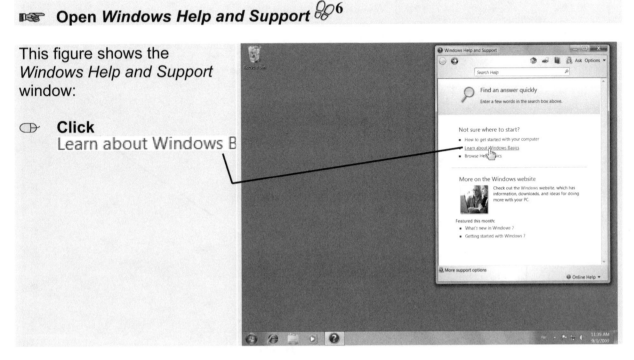

☞ **Click**
    Learn about Windows B

When a document, (web) page, or picture exceeds the size of its window, *scroll bars* appear. The scroll bar allows you to see the content that is currently out of view. This happens in the *Windows Help and Support* window. Part of the content is not fully visible.

Take a look:

In the right-hand side of the window, you see a vertical bar:

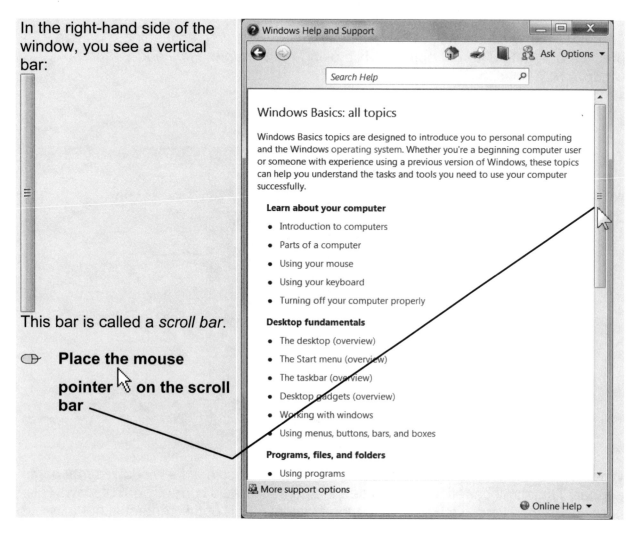

This bar is called a *scroll bar*.

Place the mouse pointer on the scroll bar

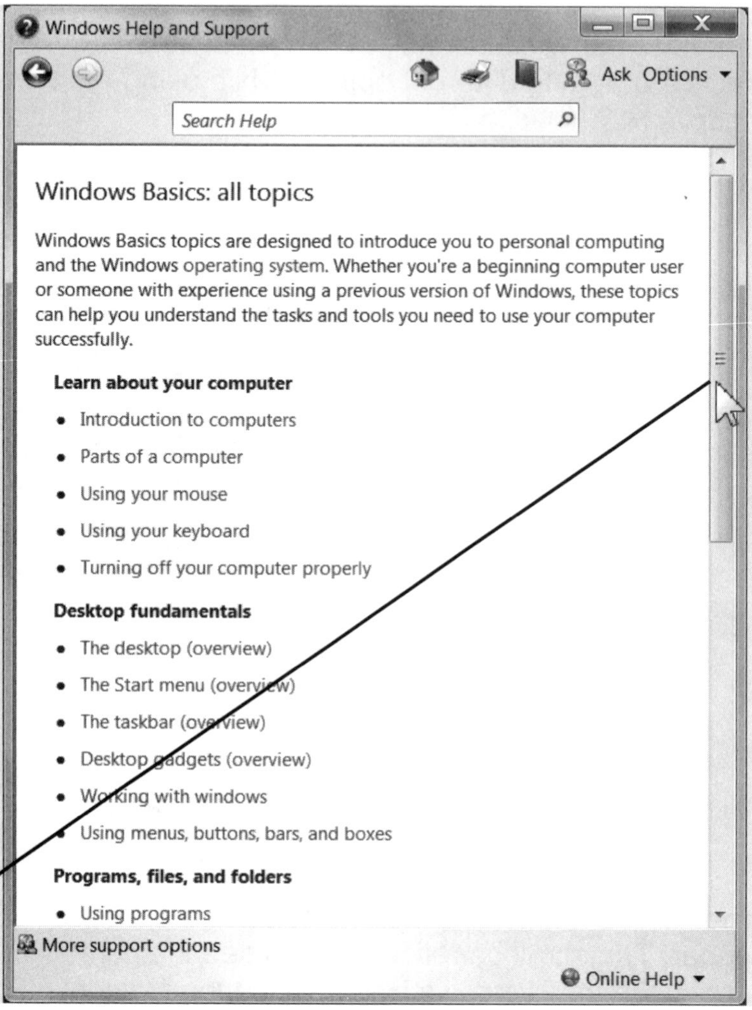

☞ **Press the left mouse button and hold it down**

The scroll bar turns blue.

☞ **Keep pressing the left mouse button, and drag (slide) the mouse pointer down** ──────

The scroll bar will also move down:

☞ **Release the mouse button**

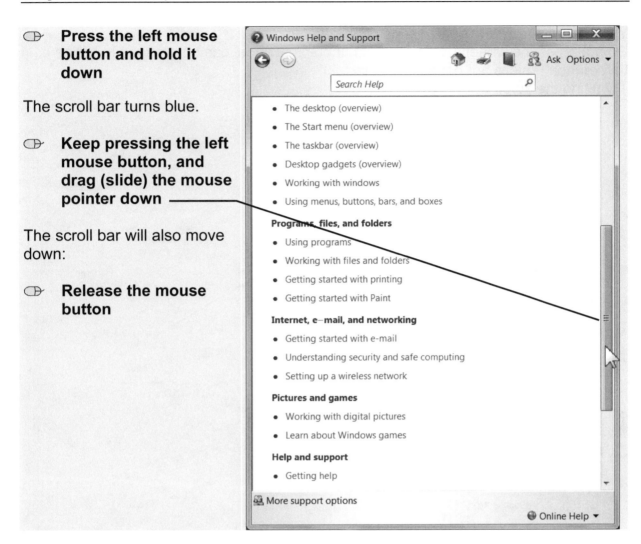

You can use the scroll bar to scroll down the contents of a window, in this case, the topics listed under *Windows Basics: all topics*. These scroll up so that you can read through to the last lines in the list.

2.5 Using the Scroll Wheel of a Mouse

Many mice nowadays include a scroll wheel between the buttons. If you see a scroll bar and your mouse has a scroll wheel, you can use this wheel to scroll through documents and web pages.

The scroll wheel is situated between the left and right mouse button: ──────

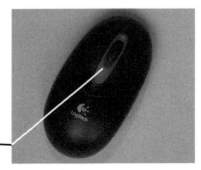

You can roll the wheel gently using your index finger.
Do not press the wheel! On some mice, the scroll wheel can be pressed to act as a third button. This is not necessary here.
Try using the scroll wheel now:

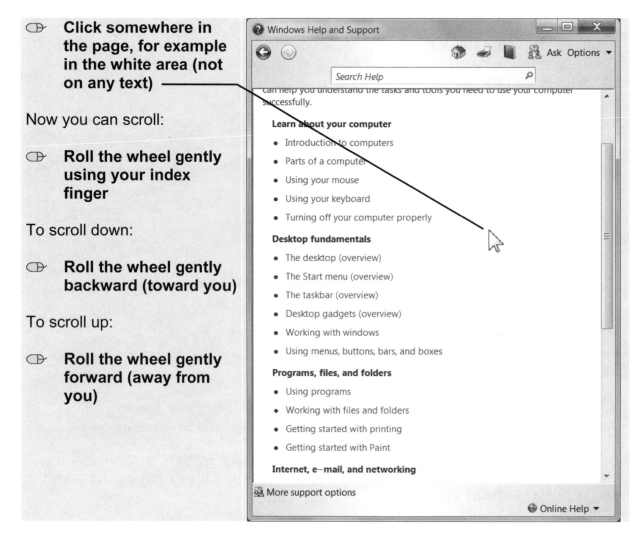

⊂⊅ **Click somewhere in the page, for example in the white area (not on any text)**

Now you can scroll:

⊂⊅ **Roll the wheel gently using your index finger**

To scroll down:

⊂⊅ **Roll the wheel gently backward (toward you)**

To scroll up:

⊂⊅ **Roll the wheel gently forward (away from you)**

You see the page moving up and down and the scroll bar along with it.

2.6 Enlarging and Reducing a Window

When a window is not maximized, you can change its size by dragging the edges of the window's frame with the mouse. Try it:

Place the mouse pointer precisely on the left edge of the window's frame ——————

The mouse pointer changes into a double arrow ⇔:

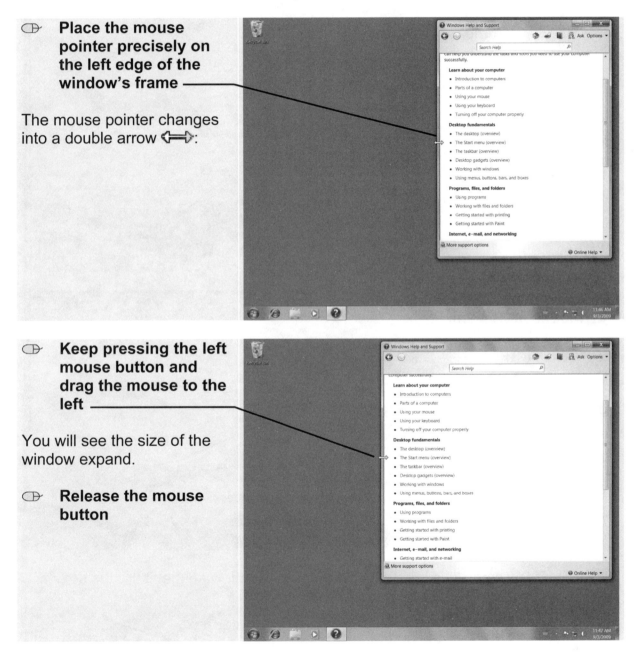

Keep pressing the left mouse button and drag the mouse to the left ——————

You will see the size of the window expand.

Release the mouse button

By dragging with the mouse, you can also change the height of a window.
Remember: this is only possible when the window is not maximized.

☞ **Place the mouse pointer precisely on the bottom edge of the window's frame**

The mouse pointer changes into a double arrow ⇕:

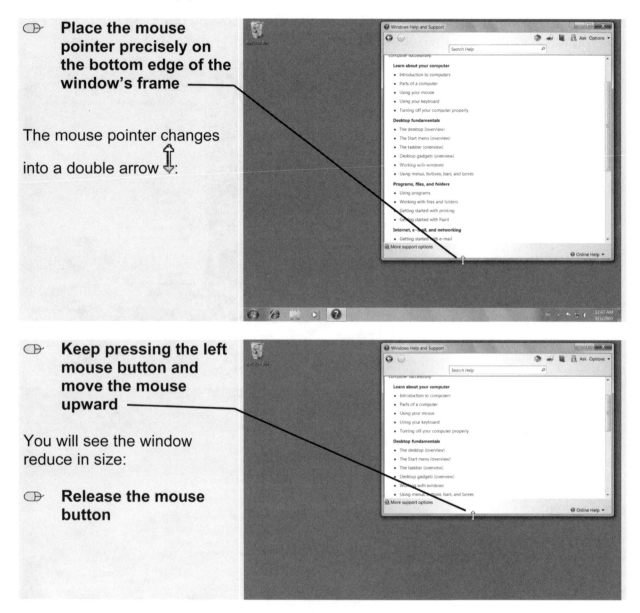

☞ **Keep pressing the left mouse button and move the mouse upward**

You will see the window reduce in size:

☞ **Release the mouse button**

For the next few steps, it is handy to maximize the window so that it fills the screen:

You can see the Maximize button in the upper right corner of the *Windows Help and Support* window:

☞ **Click**

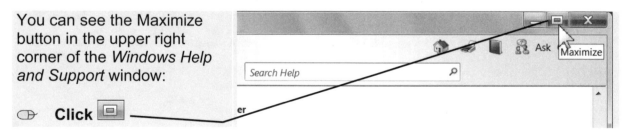

Now the window is maximized and fills the entire desktop:

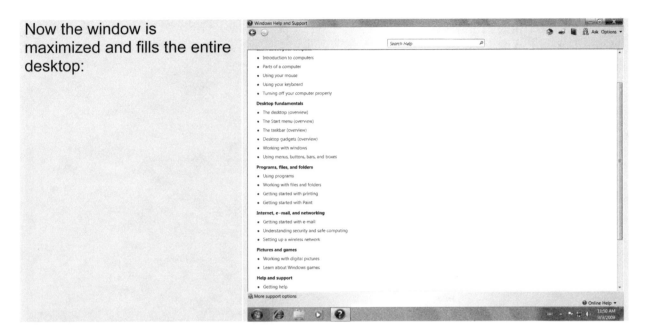

Because you already have the *Windows Help and Support* window open, you can take a closer look at how this program works.

2.7 Back to the Beginning

It is easy to go back to the previous screen of the *Windows Help and Support* window by using the Back and Forward buttons.

At the top left of the window you will find the Back and Forward buttons :

☞ **Click**

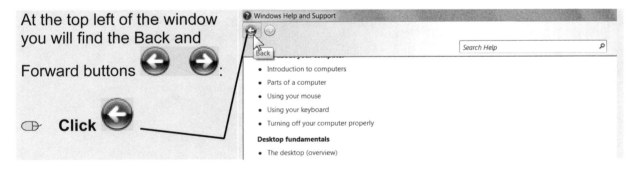

Remember: When you point to something, a small box often appears that describes the item. This is very handy when you are not sure where to click.

You are now back at the beginning of the *Windows Help and Support* program:

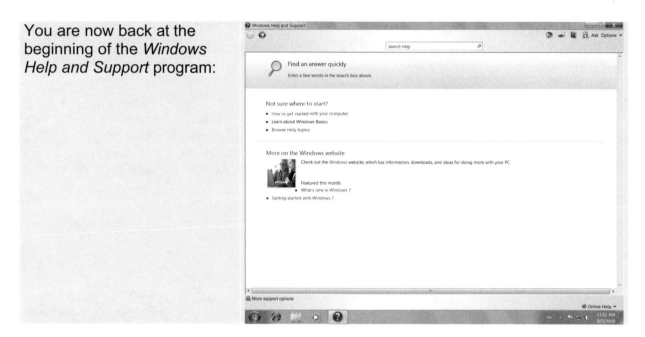

You will see *Windows 7* has many windows with these Back and Forward buttons . You will learn more about these later in the book.

2.8 Using Windows Help and Support

Windows Help and Support is an extensive digital manual for *Windows 7*.

Point to
Learn about Windows Ba

You see the mouse pointer change into a hand:
This hand is a signal that you can click here.

Click
Learn about Windows Ba

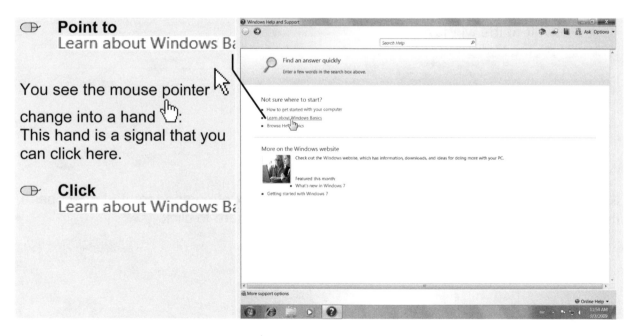

Windows Basics: all topics are designed to introduce you to personal computing and the *Windows* operating system. By clicking the topics, you can find the information you need.

Let's take a look:

⊕ **Click** Using your mouse

The relevant information is now displayed:

You can read the entire article by using the scroll bar or your scroll wheel.
You can also click a topic on the right side of the page:

⊕ **Click**
Pointing, clicking, and dragging

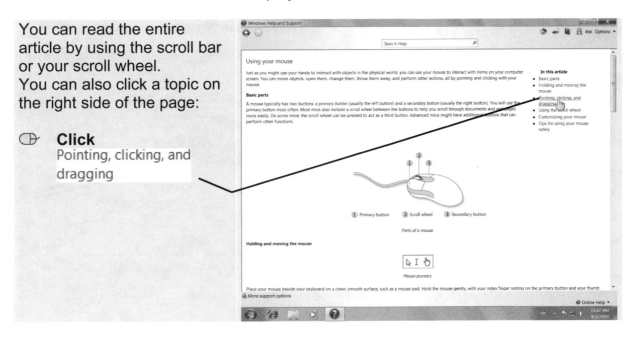

Now information about
pointing, clicking and
dragging appears:

Notice that some of the words
in the text are colored green.
These words can be clicked.

☞ **Click** desktop

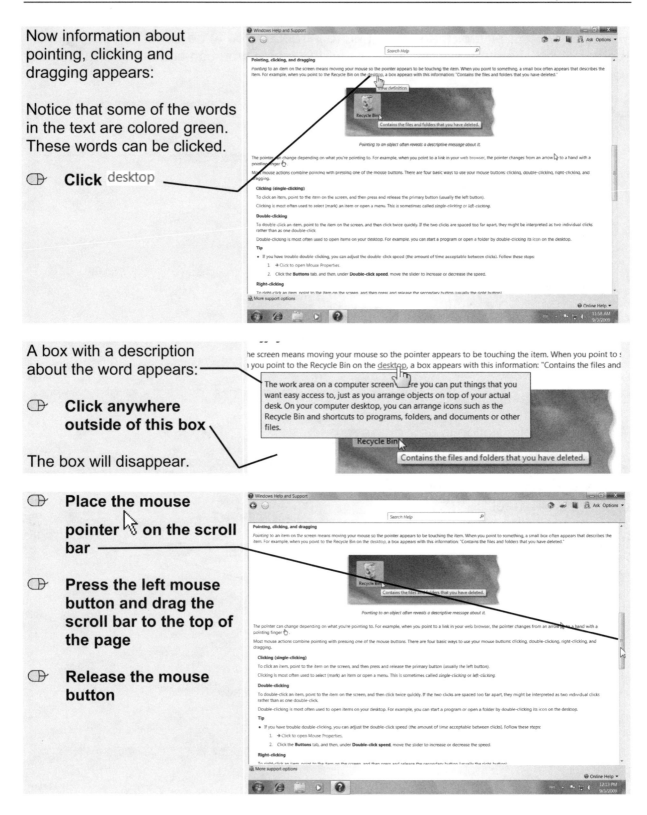

A box with a description
about the word appears:

☞ **Click anywhere
outside of this box**

The box will disappear.

☞ **Place the mouse
pointer on the scroll
bar**

☞ **Press the left mouse
button and drag the
scroll bar to the top of
the page**

☞ **Release the mouse
button**

You now see the top of the page again:

To return to the previous page:

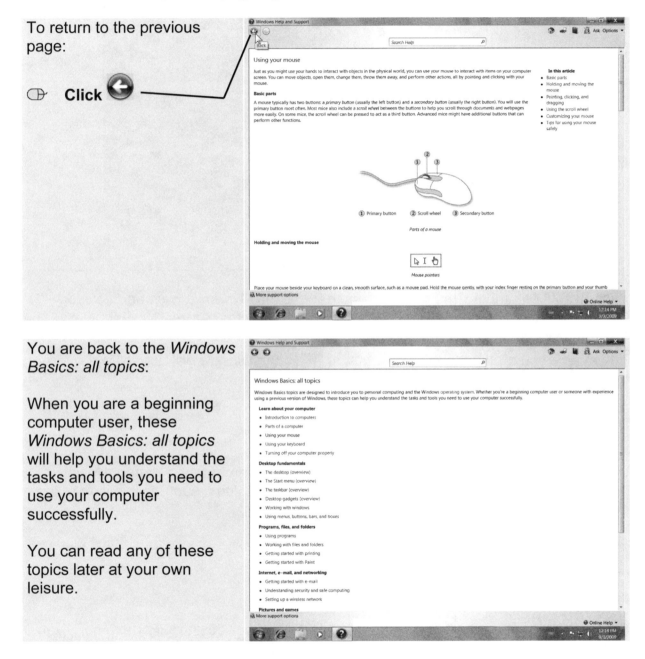

⊕   **Click** ⬅

You are back to the *Windows Basics: all topics*:

When you are a beginning computer user, these *Windows Basics: all topics* will help you understand the tasks and tools you need to use your computer successfully.

You can read any of these topics later at your own leisure.

Now you can close the *Windows Help and Support* window.

☞ **Close the *Windows Help and Support* window** ⸧⸧**4**

Now once again you see the desktop for *Windows 7:*

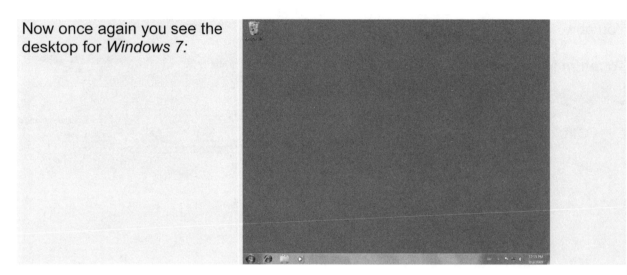

💡 Tip

The previous size of the Help and Support window

Windows 7 'remembers' the size that you gave to the *Windows Help and Support* window. When you start the *Windows Help and Support* program, the window will automatically be maximized.

However, if you click on the Restore button , the window will appear in the size that you gave it the last time you used it.

2.9 Double-Clicking

Until now, you have clicked only once on a word, a command or a button. However, in *Windows 7* you sometimes need to *double-click* on things, such as this icon at the upper left of your desktop:

![Recycle Bin icon]

Double-clicking is most often used to open items on your desktop. For example, you can start a program or open a folder by double-clicking its icon on the desktop.
This is how to double-click:

- Point to something with the mouse pointer.

- Press the left mouse button *twice in rapid succession*.

A program can be quickly started with an icon. Try to double-click an icon.

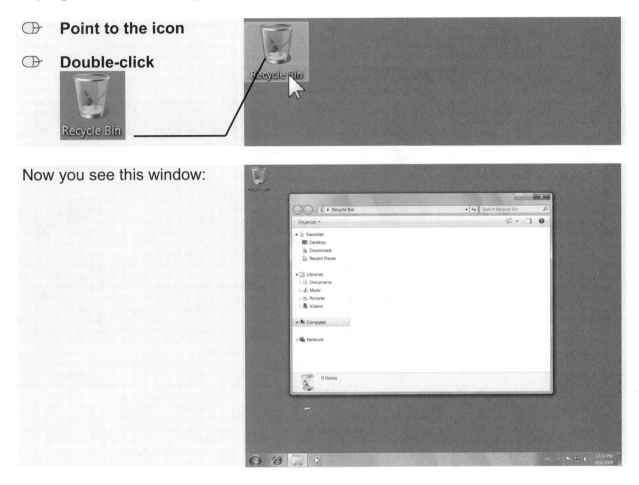

☞   **Point to the icon**

☞   **Double-click**

Now you see this window:

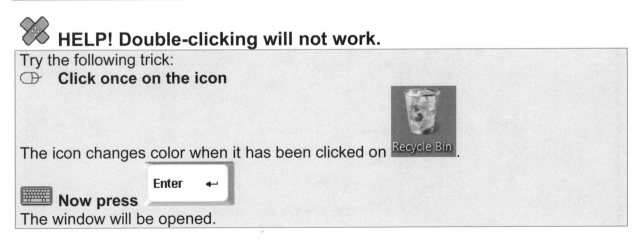

🔖 **Please note:**

When double-clicking, it is important that you *do not move the mouse* between the two clicks. When you do, *Windows* interprets this as two single clicks on two different spots. You might need to try a few times before double-clicking works for you.

✖ **HELP! Double-clicking will not work.**

Try the following trick:
☞   **Click once on the icon**

The icon changes color when it has been clicked on [Recycle Bin].

⌨ **Now press**   [Enter ↵]
The window will be opened.

☞ **Close the *Recycle Bin* window** ✂⁴

Now try again:

☞ **Double-click the *Recycle Bin* icon again**

You see this window again:

2.10 The Many Faces of a Window

You have probably noticed that the screenshots in this book sometimes differ from what you see on your screen. This is in part due to the fact that *Windows 7* can be customized. Now you will open a window where this is very evident:

At the left side of the window:

☞ **Click** Computer

In the right pane of the window you see the various parts of your computer: ⎯⎯⎯⎯

The window that your see on your own computer will probably differ from the one pictured here.

You may have other types of hardware devices.

The manner in which the items are displayed may also be different.

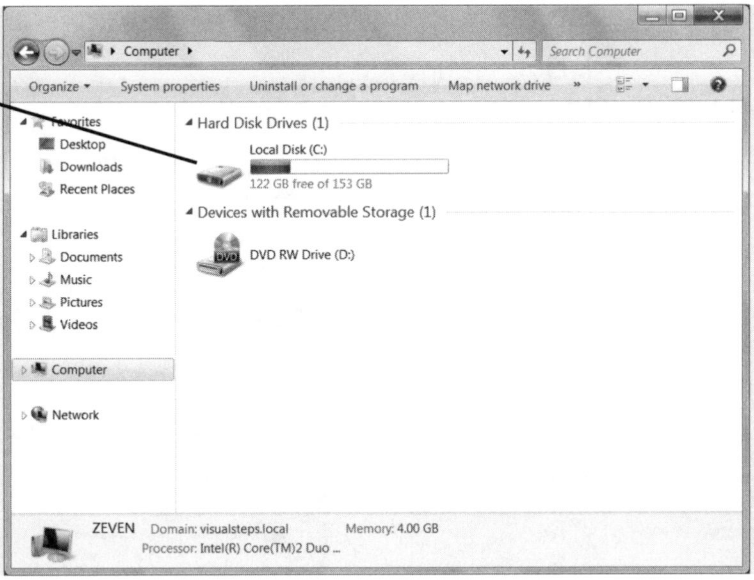

2.11 Changing the View

You can change the appearance of your files and folders in the window.

In the menu bar you see a split button ▦ ▼. Clicking the main part of the button performs a command, whereas clicking the arrow opens a menu with more options.

At the upper right-hand side of the window:

Next to ▦ :

👆 **Click** ▼

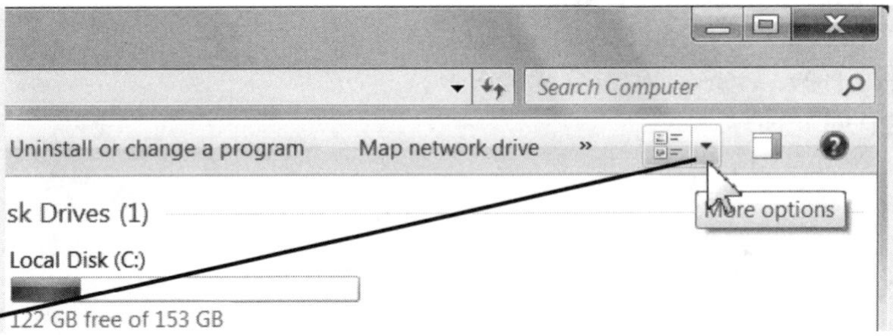

A menu appears with several options:

👆 **Click** ▦ List

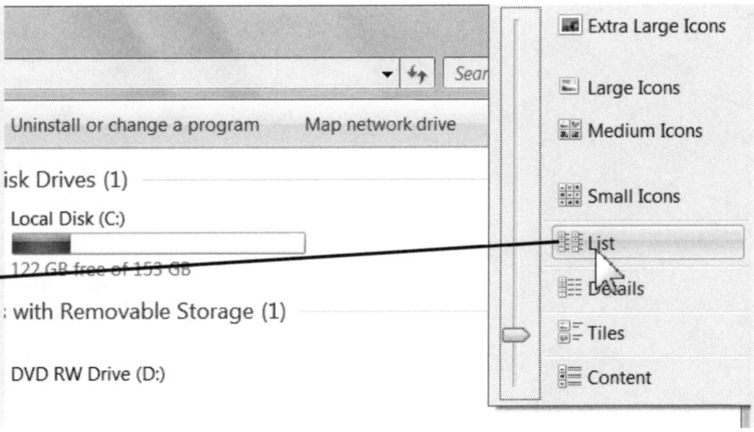

You can see that the window has changed. Now it shows a list with names:

Next to 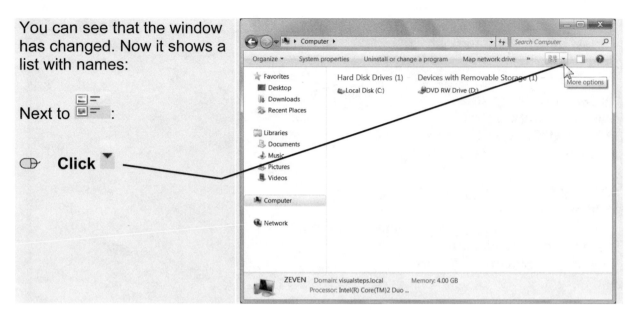 :

👆 **Click** ▼

Instead of clicking, you can also drag the slider ⬭ toward the value that you want:

👆 **Point to the slider** ⬭

👆 **Drag the slider** ⬭ **to** 🖼 Large Icons

In the window you will immediately see a preview of the new view. Now it shows large icons:

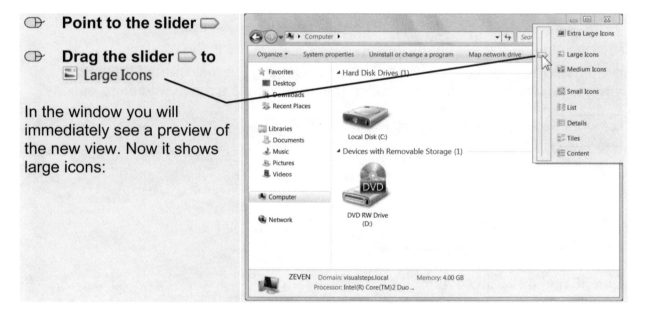

The window has changed again:

Next to :

Click

Click Medium Icons

Now you see the medium icons:

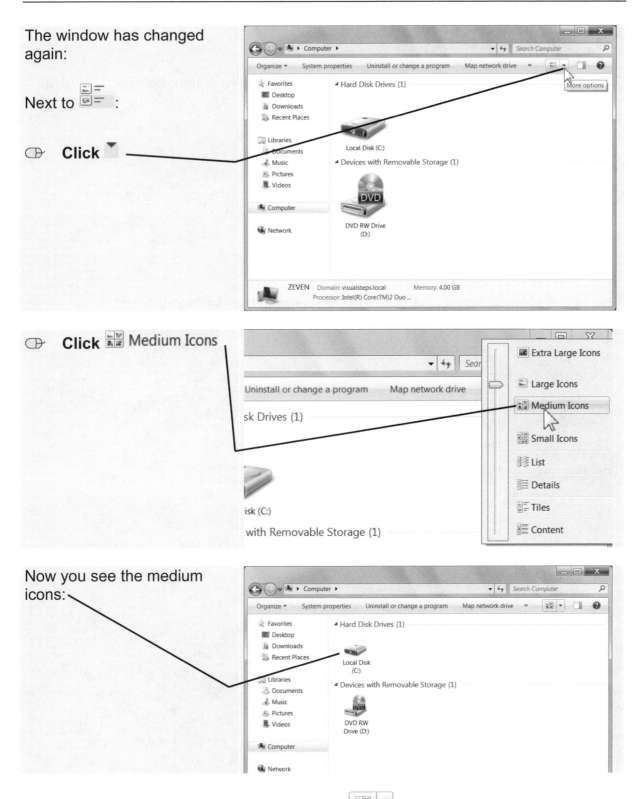

Nearly every *Windows 7* window has a button with which its appearance can be changed. You can use this to choose the appearance that you like best.

2.12 Right-Clicking

The last topic we will discuss in this chapter is the mouse action: *right-clicking.* After all, there is a reason why the mouse has two buttons.
Right-clicking is done like this:

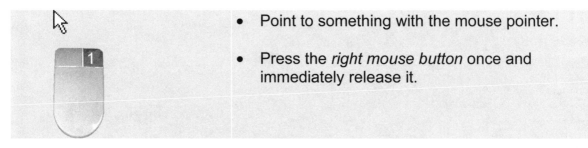

- Point to something with the mouse pointer.

- Press the *right mouse button* once and immediately release it.

This is the same action as the regular click, but with the right mouse button.
However, the right mouse button has an entirely different function, as you will see:

Using the left mouse button, click

Local Disk (C:)

The icon changes colors.

Now use the right mouse button, click

Local Disk (C:)

Now you see a menu next to the mouse pointer with various commands:

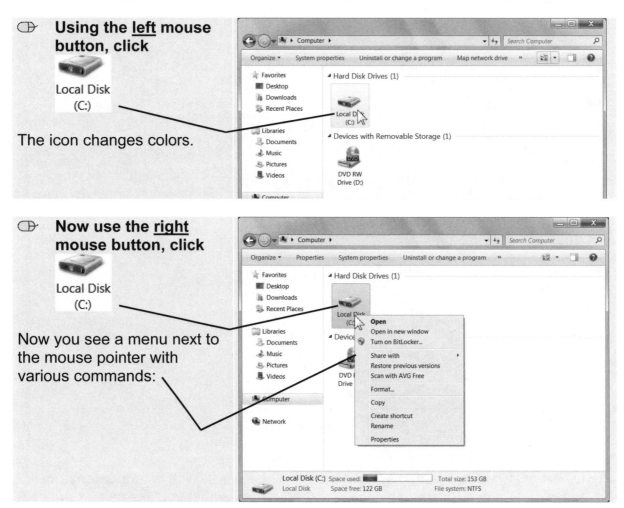

This is how to make this menu disappear:

☞ **Using the <u>left</u> mouse button, click an empty space somewhere on the screen**

You see that the menu has disappeared:

☞ **Close the *Computer* window** ₰₰⁴

You can right-click icons, folders and many other items in *Windows 7*. This will always make a menu appear. These menus can be used to enter commands that are related to the item you clicked. You can right-click the desktop, for example:

☞ **Using the <u>right</u> mouse button, click somewhere on the desktop**

Now you see a menu next to the mouse pointer with different commands:

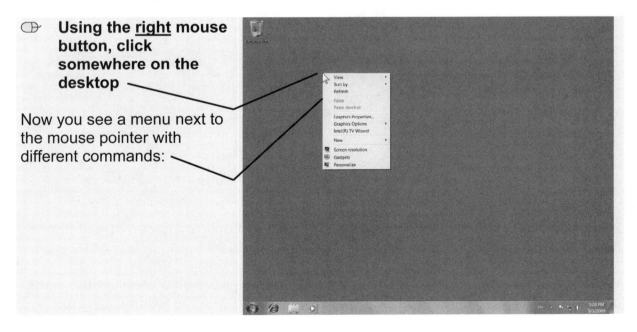

If you want to select a command from a menu of this type, you must use the left mouse button.

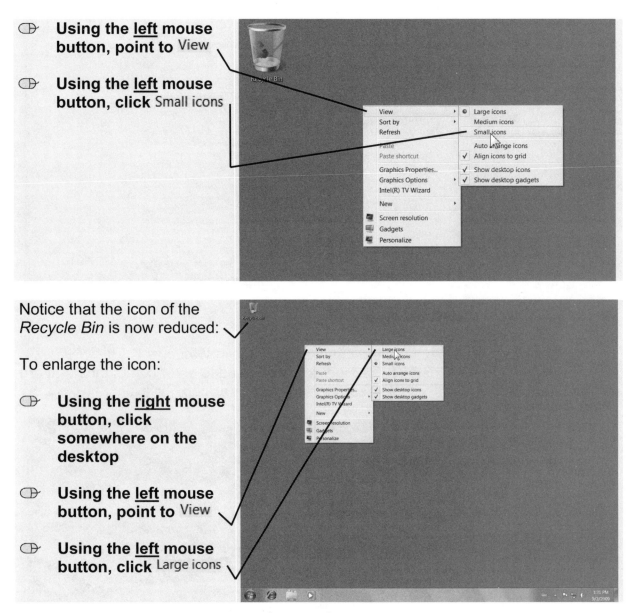

☞ **Using the <u>left</u> mouse button, point to** View

☞ **Using the <u>left</u> mouse button, click** Small icons

Notice that the icon of the *Recycle Bin* is now reduced:

To enlarge the icon:

☞ **Using the <u>right</u> mouse button, click somewhere on the desktop**

☞ **Using the <u>left</u> mouse button, point to** View

☞ **Using the <u>left</u> mouse button, click** Large icons

Right-clicking an item usually displays a *menu*: a list of things you can do with the item.

We have introduced you to all four mouse actions. You have also seen various parts of *Windows 7*. You can practice what you have learned with the following exercises.

2.13 Exercises

The following exercises will help you master what you have just learned. Have you forgotten how to do something? Use the number beside the footsteps to look it up in the appendix *How Do I Do That Again?*

Exercise: Dragging a Window

☞ Open the *Calculator*. 🐾⁵

☞ Drag the *Calculator* window to the middle. 🐾¹¹

☞ Drag the *Calculator* window to the bottom right. 🐾¹¹

☞ Drag the *Calculator* window to the top left. 🐾¹¹

☞ Close the *Calculator* window. 🐾⁴

Exercise: Clicking, Double-Clicking and Dragging

☞ Open the *Recycle Bin*. 🐾¹⁰

☞ Drag the *Recycle Bin* window to the top left of the screen. 🐾¹¹

☞ Close the *Recycle Bin* window. 🐾⁴

☞ Open the *Windows Help and Support* window. 🐾⁶

☞ Maximize the size of the *Windows Help and Support* window. 🐾²

☞ Restore the size of the *Windows Help and Support* window to its the previous size. 🐾³

☞ Close the *Windows Help and Support* window. 🐾⁴

Exercise: Left- and Right-Clicking

☞ Using the <u>right</u> mouse button, click somewhere on the desktop.

☞ Using the <u>left</u> mouse button, click View.

☞ Using the <u>left</u> mouse button, click Medium icons.

☞ Using the <u>right</u> mouse button, click the icon Recycle Bin.

☞ Using the <u>left</u> mouse button, click **Open**.

☞ Close the *Recycle Bin* window. ℰ[4]

Exercise: Using Windows Help and Support

☞ Open the *Windows Help and Support* window. ℰ[6]

☞ Open Learn about Windows Basics. ℰ[20]

☞ Select the topic Introduction to computers and read the information. Do not forget to use the scroll bar.

☞ Go back to the previous page by clicking .

☞ Select the topic Parts of a computer and read the information. Do not forget to use the scroll bar.

☞ Go back to the previous page by clicking .

☞ Select the topic Using your mouse and read the information. Do not forget to use the scroll bar.

☞ Close the *Windows Help and Support* window. ℰ[4]

2.14 Background Information

Dictionary

Back and forward buttons ← →	Buttons you use to go back or forward to a (web) page or screen you have already looked at.
Click	Press and release the primary mouse button (usually the left button). Clicking is most often used to select (mark) an item or open a menu. This is sometimes called single-clicking or left-clicking.
Double-click	Press and release the left mouse button twice in rapid succession. The mouse action that is most often used to open items on your desktop. For example, you can start a program or open a folder by double-clicking its icon on the desktop.
Drag	To move an item on the screen by selecting the item and then pressing and holding down the left mouse button while sliding or moving the mouse. For example, you can move a window to another location on the desktop by dragging its title bar.
Right-click	Press and release the right mouse button. Right-clicking an item usually displays a list of things you can do with the item. For example, when you right-click the *Recycle Bin* on your desktop, *Windows* displays a menu allowing you to open it, empty it, delete it, or see its properties. If you are not sure what to do with something, right-click it.
Scroll bar	When a document, web page, or picture exceeds the size of its window, scroll bars appear to allow you to see the information that is currently out of view. Drag a scroll box up, down, left, or right to scroll the window in that direction.
Scroll wheel	Small wheel between the two buttons of a mouse. If your mouse has a scroll wheel, you can use it to scroll through documents and web pages. To scroll down: roll the wheel backward (toward you). To scroll up: roll the wheel forward (away from you).
Slider ▭	A slider lets you adjust a setting along a range of values. A slider can be dragged.

- Continue reading on the next page -

| **Windows Help and Support** | The built-in help system for *Windows*. It's a place to get quick answers to common questions, suggestions for troubleshooting, and instructions for how to do things. To open it: click the Start button and then click *Help and Support*. |

Source: Windows Help and Support

The parts of the computer

The large cabinet that holds the computer itself is called the computer case or housing:

The case holds the computer's memory and the processor chip that makes everything work.
This computer case also holds the CD drive and/or DVD drive.

Computer case

Every computer has a monitor. The quality of the screen is much better than that of a regular television. Letters and graphic elements are therefore extremely sharp and easy to read.
The size of the computer screen is expressed in *inches*. The minimum size of a computer screen these days is 17 inches. Larger screens measuring 19 or 21 inches or more are becoming more popular.

TFT monitor

Other hardware elements are the keyboard, the mouse, the speakers and the printer.

A portable computer or laptop is a complete system. The case, the keyboard, the mouse, and the display are integrated into a single unit.

The flat display is flipped up when the laptop is being used.

Laptop

How does a traditional mouse work?

The standard mouse is actually relatively simple in terms of technology. Turn the mouse over.
You can see a little ball that rolls as the mouse is moved over the tabletop.

If you take the ball out, you can see three little wheels inside that register the movements of the ball and transmit these to the computer.
When the mouse slides, the ball rolls and the wheels on the inside move.

A variation on this mouse uses an infrared light (LED) or laser light instead of a ball.

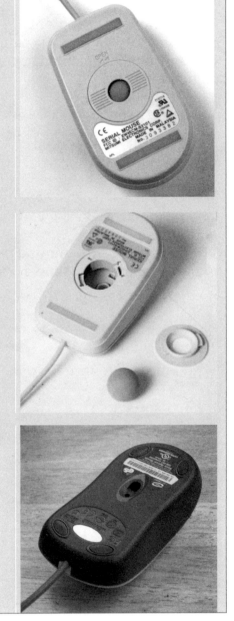

2.15 Tips

💡 Tip

Proper mouse placement
Sometimes the mouse will be too far from you on the tabletop or located at the edge of the mousepad.

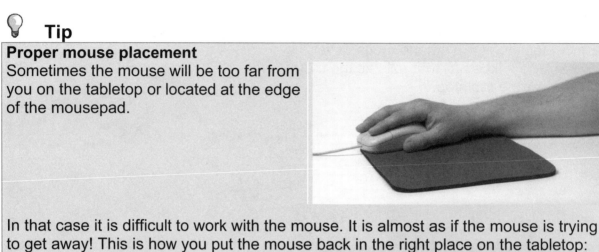

In that case it is difficult to work with the mouse. It is almost as if the mouse is trying to get away! This is how you put the mouse back in the right place on the tabletop:

☞ **First move the mouse pointer to the middle of the screen**

☞ **Now pick up the mouse**

☞ **Put the mouse in the right place**

Tip

Are you left-handed?

Then use the mouse with your left hand. You can switch the settings for the mouse buttons to make your mouse more suitable for left-handed users.

Mouse Properties

| Buttons | Pointers | Pointer Options | Wheel | Hardware |

Button configuration

☐ Switch primary and secondary buttons

Select this check box to make the button on the right the one you use for primary functions such as selecting and dragging.

Double-click speed

Double-click the folder to test your setting. If the folder does not open or close, try using a slower setting.

Speed: Slow ——————●—————— Fast

ClickLock

☐ Turn on ClickLock   Settings...

Enables you to highlight or drag without holding down the mouse button. To set, briefly press the mouse button. To release, click the mouse button again.

OK   Cancel   Apply

You will learn how to change the mouse settings in *Bonus Online Chapter 11 How to Make Working with Your Computer More Pleasant*. Read more about this chapter in *Chapter 9 Bonus Online Chapters and Extra Information*.

💡 Tip

Working with a touchpad

Owners of a laptop can either use a computer mouse or the touchpad in order to move the pointer on the screen, and to click and drag.

A touchpad is used to move the pointer, using motions of the user's finger. It's a substitute for a computer mouse.

Touchpad:

The buttons below or above the pad serve as standard mouse buttons: click (single-click with left mouse button) and right-click (using the right mouse button).
On this laptop these buttons are below the touchpad:

Depending on the model of touchpad, you may also click by tapping your finger on the touchpad.

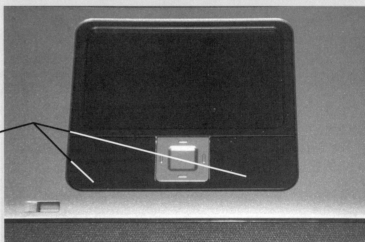

This model has also a special button for dragging the scroll bar of a window:

- Continue reading on the next page -

Some touchpads also have 'hotspots': locations on the touchpad that indicate user intentions other than pointing. For example, on certain touchpads, moving your finger along the right edge of the touchpad will control the scroll bar in a vertical direction for the window that is presently *active*. Moving the finger on the bottom of the touchpad often scrolls in horizontal direction.

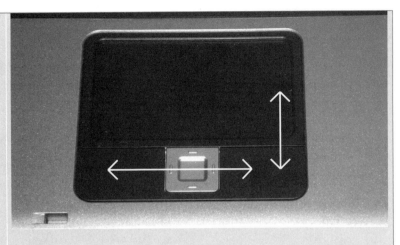

Some touchpads can emulate multiple mouse buttons by either tapping in a special corner of the pad, or by tapping with two or more fingers.

☞ **Read your instruction manual to learn what types of features are available for your specific laptop's touchpad.**

As soon as you have read the information, you can try it:

Moving the pointer

☞ **Put your finger on the right side of the touchpad**

☞ **Slide your finger slowly to the left**

The pointer 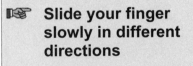 on the screen moves with it.

☞ **Slide your finger slowly in different directions**

The pointer ⬚ on the screen moves with it.

- Continue reading on the next page -

☞ **Put your finger on the touchpad**

☞ **Slide your finger slowly over the touchpad**

☞ **Point to**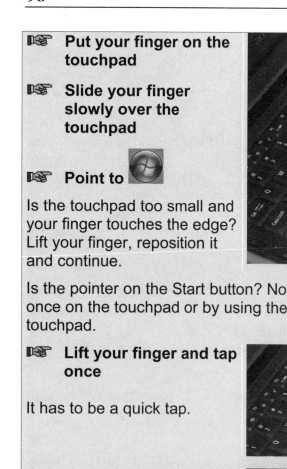

Is the touchpad too small and your finger touches the edge? Lift your finger, reposition it and continue.

Is the pointer on the Start button? Now you can click the Start button by tapping once on the touchpad or by using the special button below, above or beside the touchpad.

☞ **Lift your finger and tap once**

It has to be a quick tap.

Or:

☞ **Lift your finger and press the left button**

The Start menu will appear.

☞ **Point to** ▶ All Programs
☞ **Lift your finger and tap once**
Or:
☞ **Lift your finger and press the left button**

Go on:
☞ **Point to** Accessories
☞ **Lift your finger and tap once**
Or:
☞ **Lift your finger and press the left button**

- *Continue reading on the next page* -

Go on:

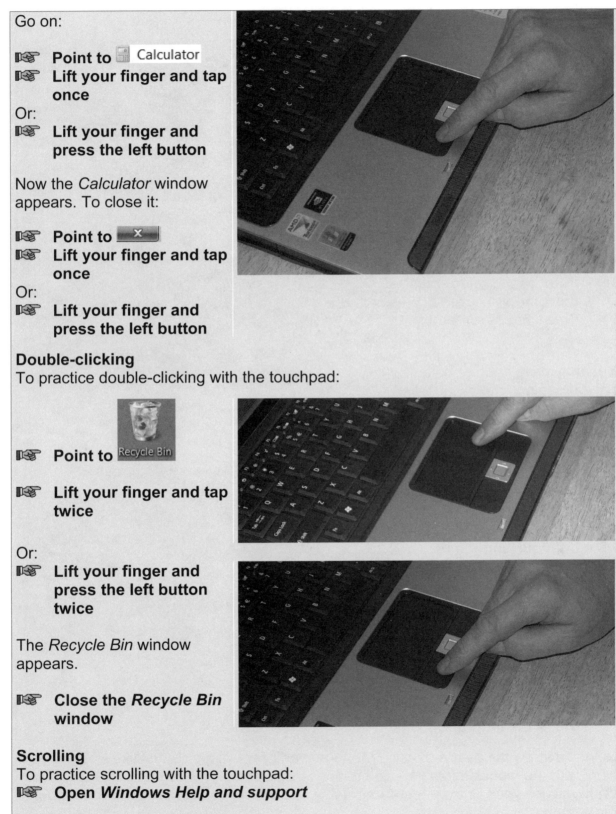

☞ **Point to** 🖩 Calculator
☞ **Lift your finger and tap once**

Or:

☞ **Lift your finger and press the left button**

Now the *Calculator* window appears. To close it:

☞ **Point to** ❌
☞ **Lift your finger and tap once**

Or:

☞ **Lift your finger and press the left button**

Double-clicking

To practice double-clicking with the touchpad:

☞ **Point to** Recycle Bin

☞ **Lift your finger and tap twice**

Or:

☞ **Lift your finger and press the left button twice**

The *Recycle Bin* window appears.

☞ **Close the *Recycle Bin* window**

Scrolling

To practice scrolling with the touchpad:

☞ **Open *Windows Help and support***

- Continue reading on the next page -

There is a scroll bar in this window.

☞ **Point to the arrow** ▾
  below the scroll bar
☞ **Tap once to move the**
  scroll bar down
☞ **Repeat this action**
Or:
☞ **Point to the middle of**
  the window
☞ **Slide your finger over**
  the right scroll area of
  the touchpad

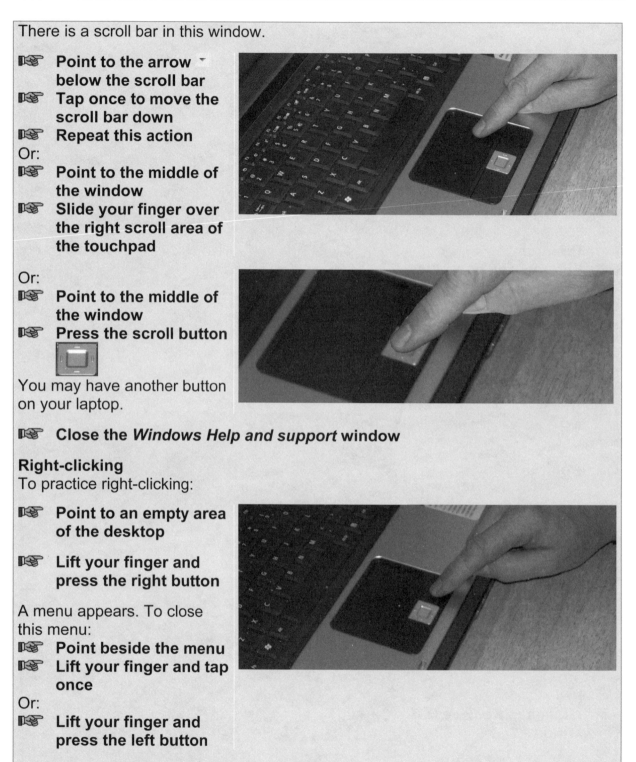

Or:
☞ **Point to the middle of**
  the window
☞ **Press the scroll button**

You may have another button
on your laptop.

☞ **Close the *Windows Help and support* window**

Right-clicking
To practice right-clicking:

☞ **Point to an empty area**
  of the desktop

☞ **Lift your finger and**
  press the right button

A menu appears. To close
this menu:
☞ **Point beside the menu**
☞ **Lift your finger and tap**
  once
Or:
☞ **Lift your finger and**
  press the left button

Now you know the basics of using the touchpad of your laptop. Just like learning to work with the mouse takes time and patience so does learning to use the touchpad. With practice you will soon feel comfortable and have good control over your finger movements.

3. Keyboard Skills

Word processing is the application that made the *Personal Computer* (PC) so popular. It is also the most widely-used application. The typewriter era is long gone, thanks in part to how easy computers have made it to write and produce texts.

As a computer user, it is useful to have good keyboard and word processing skills. These skills are not only needed for writing letters or e-mail messages, for example, but also for various other things. A certain degree of keyboard skill is also necessary, because not everything can be done with the mouse.

Windows 7 has a simple word-processing program that you can use to practice typing. The program is called *WordPad* and was installed on your computer together with *Windows 7*.

In this chapter, you will learn how to:

- open *WordPad*;
- type using the keyboard;
- correct a typing error;
- type capital letters;
- begin a new paragraph;
- type various special characters;
- move the cursor;
- start a new document;
- close *WordPad*.

3.1 Opening WordPad

WordPad is a basic word-processing program that you can use to create and edit documents. You can open it by using the Start button:

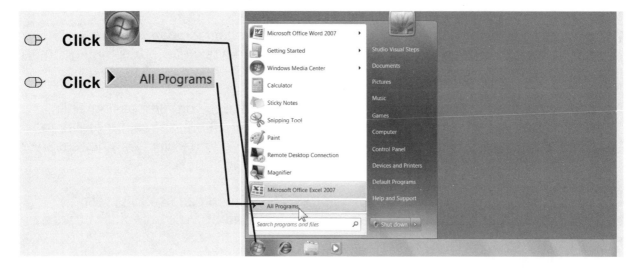

Click

Click ▶ **All Programs**

The *WordPad* program is located in the folder 📁 named *Accessories*:

Click 📁 **Accessories**

Click 📝 **WordPad**

Now you see the empty *WordPad* window:

The text you type will appear in the big white box. This box is like a blank sheet of paper.

At the top left, you will see a short blinking vertical line. This is called the *cursor*.

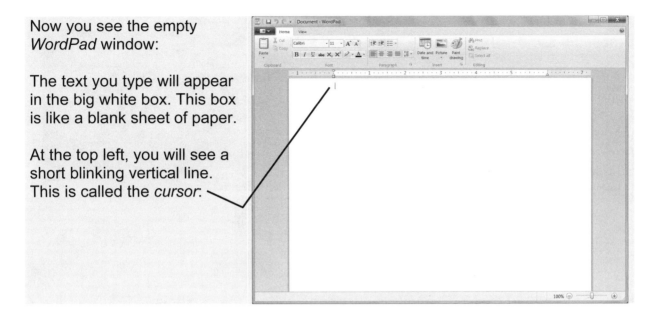

3.2 The Keyboard

A computer keyboard has over one hundred keys. That is much more than the old-fashioned typewriter. When you look at the keyboard, you will see keys for letters and numbers, as well as various other keys. You will learn how to use these keys in this book.

The position of the letters and punctuation marks is still the same as on a typewriter:

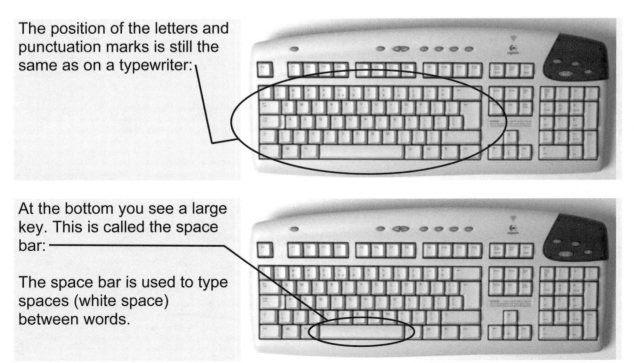

At the bottom you see a large key. This is called the space bar:

The space bar is used to type spaces (white space) between words.

The keyboard of a laptop is almost the same:

Sometimes there are fewer keys on the right-hand side of the keyboard. This does not matter as these keys will not be used while working with this book.

Now you can start typing. The letters will appear where the cursor is:

Type: this is a
first line

3.3 Repeat Keys

The keys on a computer keyboard are repeat keys. This means that if you keep pressing a key, you will automatically see multiple letters appear on the screen. Try it:

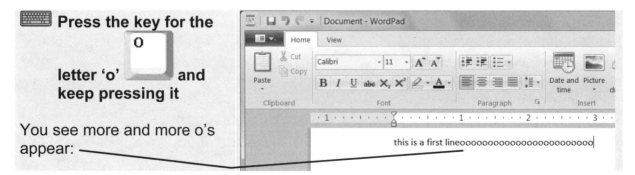

Press the key for the

letter 'o' and
keep pressing it

You see more and more o's appear:

Luckily, it is easy to remove letters you do not need.

3.4 A Typing Error?

In this case, you typed the wrong letters 'o' on purpose. But in the future you may press a wrong key by accident. You can remove wrong letters by pressing the *Backspace key*.

That is a big key, with the left-pointed arrow, sometimes also with the word 'Backspace'.

The Backspace key is usually located at the top right of the keyboard:

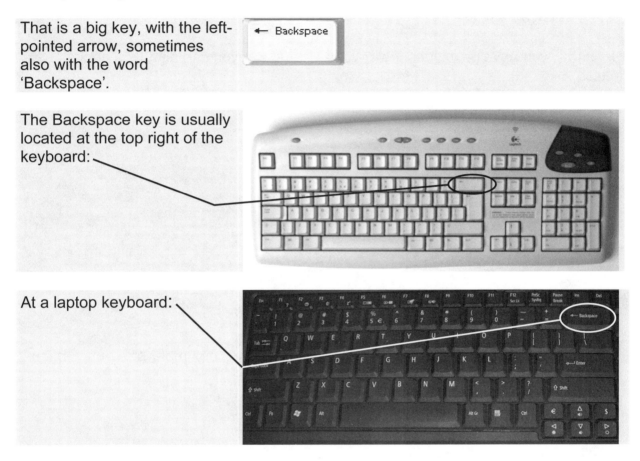

At a laptop keyboard:

The Backspace key is used to remove the letter to the left of the cursor. You can use it now to remove the letters 'o' that you do not need, for example:

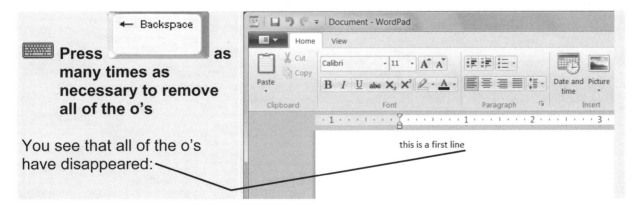

Press as **many times as necessary to remove all of the o's**

You see that all of the o's have disappeared:

Please note:

The Backspace key itself is also a repeat key. Do not press it too long or you will have to retype the text.

3.5 Capital Letters

Until now, you have only typed lower-case letters. But you can also type capital letters.

To do so, you use the large key that says 'Shift':

⇧ **Shift**

There are two *Shift keys*, one on each side of the bottom row of letters:

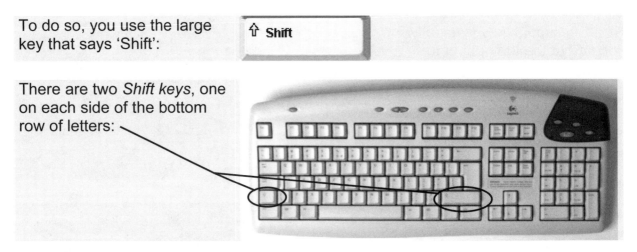

The Shift key is always used in combination with a letter, a number or a punctuation mark.

This is how to type a capital letter:
- press the Shift key and keep it pressed;
- type the letter;
- release the Shift key.

Type: This line is about Amsterdam, the capital of Holland.

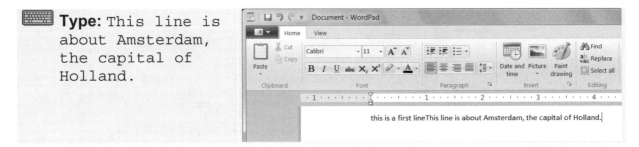

3.6 Words on the Next Line

In word processing programs, the program itself spreads the text over the page. If you type multiple sentences in a row, the text will automatically continue on the next line. Take a look:

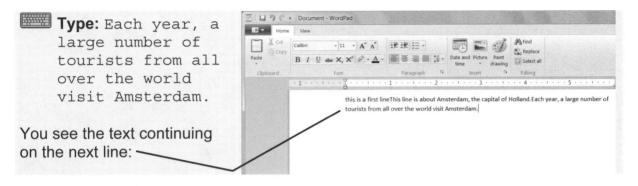

Type: Each year, a large number of tourists from all over the world visit Amsterdam.

You see the text continuing on the next line:

The computer always makes sure that even long sentences will fit nicely on the page. This is done automatically.

3.7 Beginning a New Paragraph

A series of sentences that are grouped together is called a paragraph. A new paragraph starts on a new line.

A new line is made using the *Enter key*:

The Enter key is located on the right side of the keyboard:

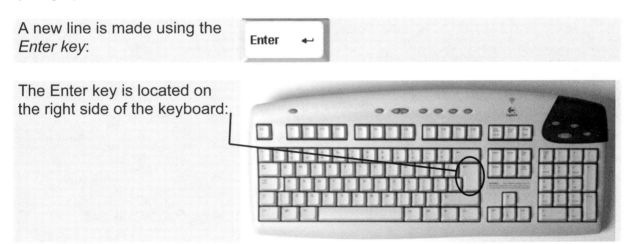

If you press the Enter key, the cursor (the little blinking line) will move down one line.

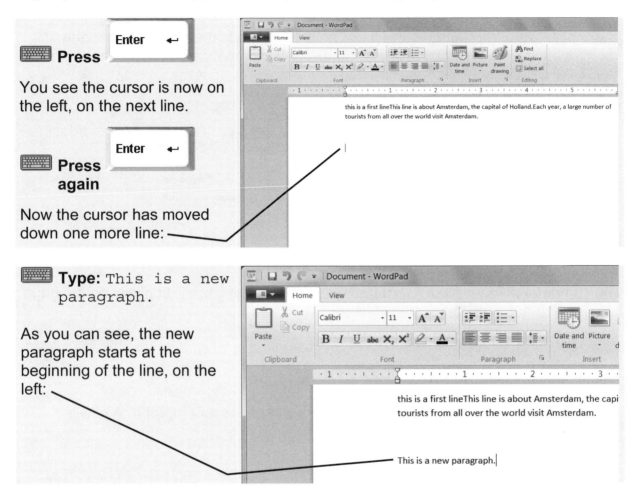

You see the cursor is now on the left, on the next line.

Now the cursor has moved down one more line:

Type: This is a new paragraph.

As you can see, the new paragraph starts at the beginning of the line, on the left:

3.8 Colon or @?

The Shift key is also used to type various other characters.

Examples are: : ? @ * % $ + | } < ! ~ & ^

Many of these characters are located at the top of a key:

The character at the top of these keys is typed using the Shift key, just as you do for capital letters.

Type a space (press the spacebar once)

Type: ! ? : @ +

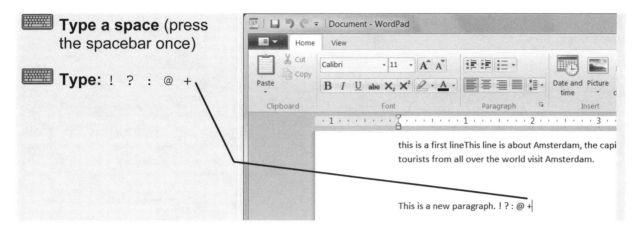

3.9 The Cursor Keys

Everyone makes a typing error now and then. You often do not notice until later, after you have typed more text. To remove the error with the Backspace key, you would have to remove all of the other text as well. Naturally, that is not very convenient. It is better to move the cursor to the place where the error is.

You can move the cursor using the four special cursor keys. These are the keys with the arrows. They are grouped together:

The *cursor keys* are located on the right side of the keyboard:

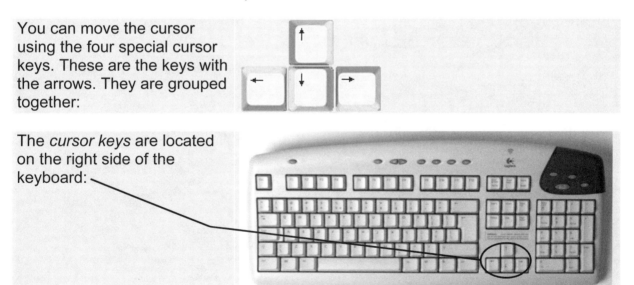

You can use these keys to move the cursor to the left or right, up and down, through the text.

The cursor is blinking next to the +:

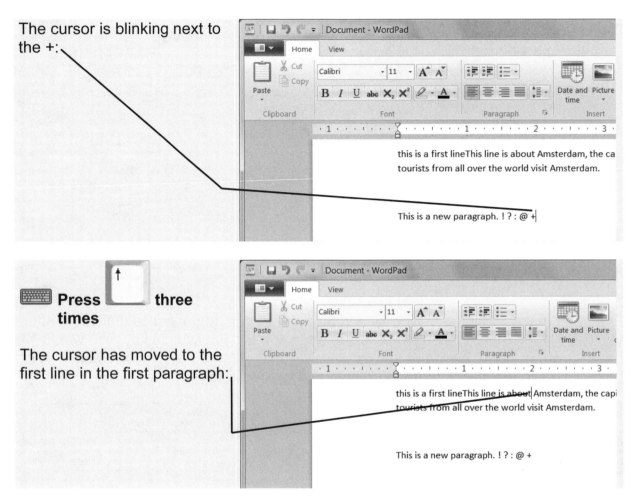

Press ↑ three times

The cursor has moved to the first line in the first paragraph:

If you move to the left or right, the cursor follows through the text:

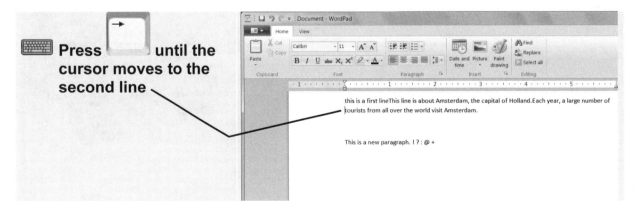

Press → until the cursor moves to the second line

You see the cursor move to the right, through the text, until it jumps to the next line.

3.10 The Beginning and End of the Text

You can use the cursor keys to move the cursor to any position in the text that you want. But you cannot move the cursor over the entire sheet of paper. The text has a beginning and an end. Try it:

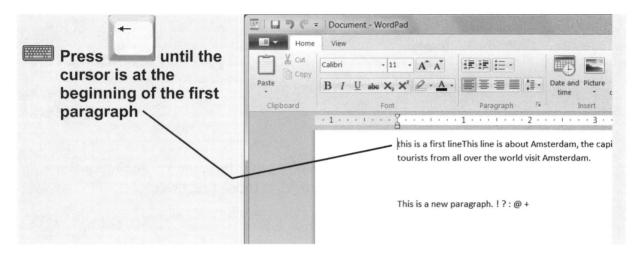

Press ⬅ **until the cursor is at the beginning of the first paragraph**

The cursor will not move any further than the beginning of the text. On some computers, the program may even sound a warning signal.

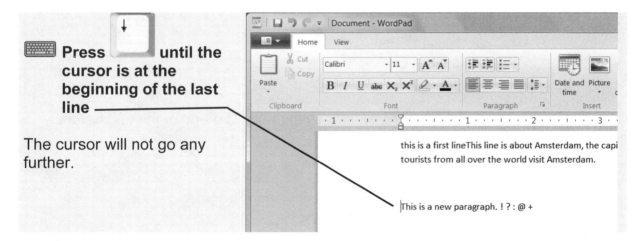

Press ⬇ **until the cursor is at the beginning of the last line**

The cursor will not go any further.

You can not move the cursor any further than the last letter or punctuation mark:

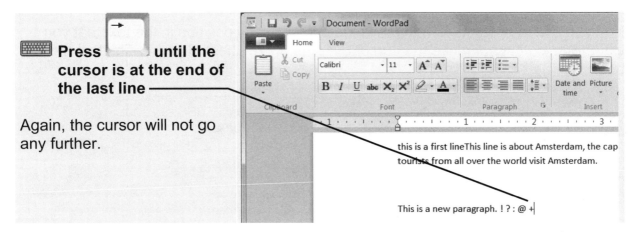

Press [→] **until the cursor is at the end of the last line**

Again, the cursor will not go any further.

As you have seen, the cursor can not be moved further than the beginning or the end of the text you have typed. You can, of course, type more text there.

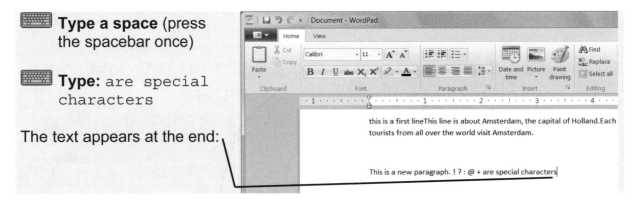

Type a space (press the spacebar once)

Type: are special characters

The text appears at the end:

Of course, you can always add empty lines to the text. The end of the text will then be the last (empty) line:

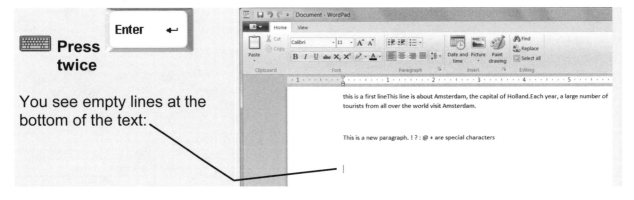

Press [Enter] **twice**

You see empty lines at the bottom of the text:

Now you know how to move the cursor through the text. This is very handy when you want to correct errors or change the text.

3.11 Correcting Mistakes

You can move the cursor to the spot in the text where you want to make a change. For example:

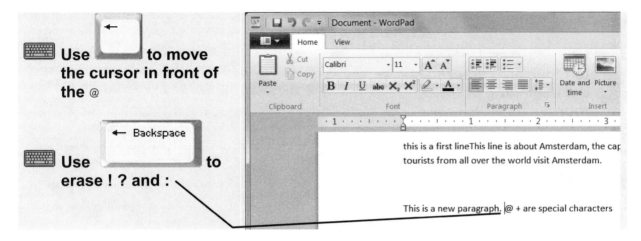

You can also change the first letter of the text into a capital:

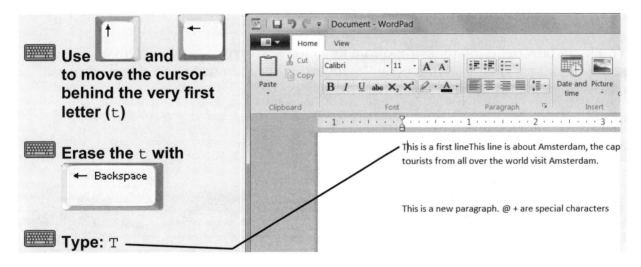

3.12 Removing Empty Lines

You can remove empty lines the same way. Move the cursor to an empty line and press the Backspace key:

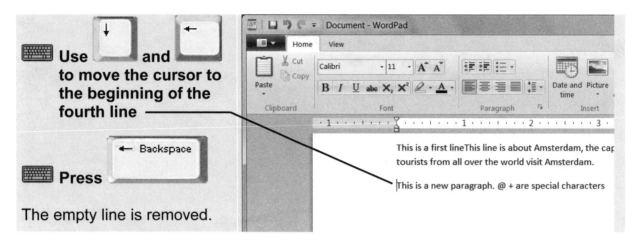

Use ↓ **and** ←
to move the cursor to the beginning of the fourth line ——

Press ← Backspace

The empty line is removed.

This is a first lineThis line is about Amsterdam, the cap
tourists from all over the world visit Amsterdam.

This is a new paragraph. @ + are special characters

3.13 Moving Quickly through Text

You have now used the most important keys for word processing. However, there are some other very useful keys on your keyboard. There are two special keys that will move the cursor through the text even faster.

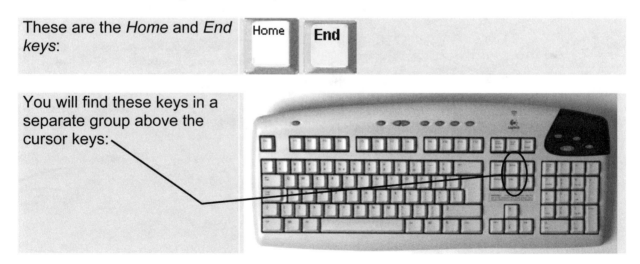

These are the *Home* and *End keys*:

Home   End

You will find these keys in a separate group above the cursor keys:

The Home key is used to move the cursor to the beginning of a line, and the End key is used to move it to the end of a line. In other words: to jump from here to there. Try it:

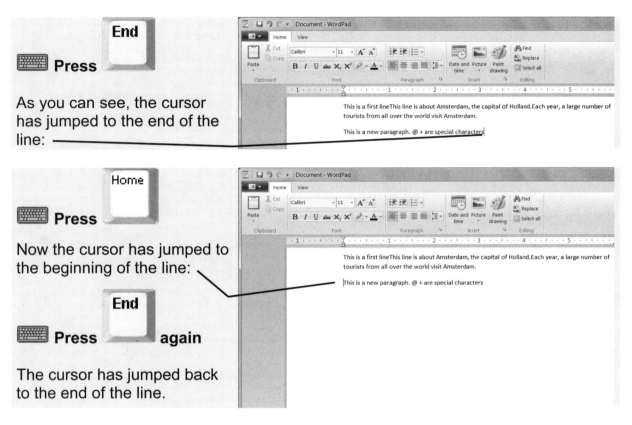

As you can see, the cursor has jumped to the end of the line:

Now the cursor has jumped to the beginning of the line:

The cursor has jumped back to the end of the line.

3.14 Starting a New Document

You have now practiced enough with the keyboard. It is time to start with a new, blank document. This is how:

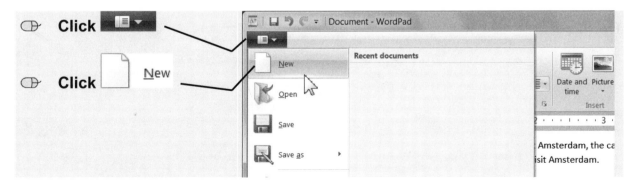

WordPad now asks you whether you want to save the changes to your practice text. You do not need to, so:

☞ **Click** Don't Save

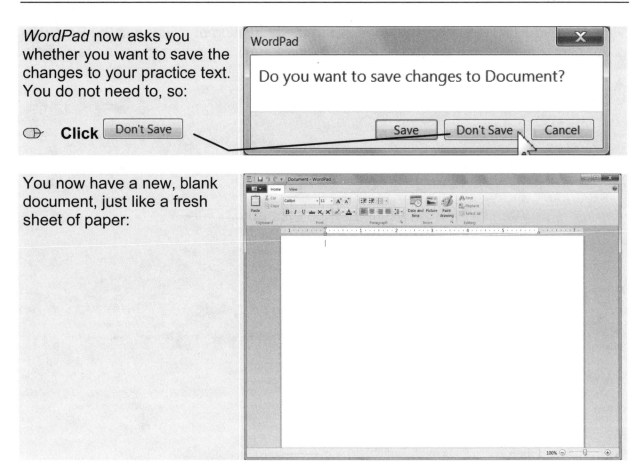

You now have a new, blank document, just like a fresh sheet of paper:

3.15 Accents and Other Special Punctuation

When you look at the keyboard, you will not see any letter keys with accents or other special punctuation such as ç, ñ or é.
But these letters are not difficult to type. You do this by using the keys known as the 'dead' keys, they are the keys commonly used to generate letters with accents:

These are the 'dead' keys:

These keys are used in combination with the letter to which the special punctuation is to be added. For example:

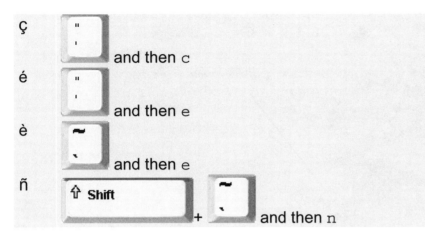

Try it:

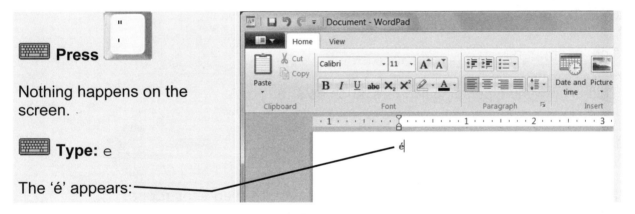

The keys are called 'dead' because nothing happens when you press them. A character does not appear until after you press another key.

Now try to make another letter, such as the 'ñ'. It is a bit more complicated because you have to use the Shift key in order to type the '~'.

HELP! It is not working.

If you are not able to type accents, take a look at *Appendix C Changing Your Keyboard Settings*.

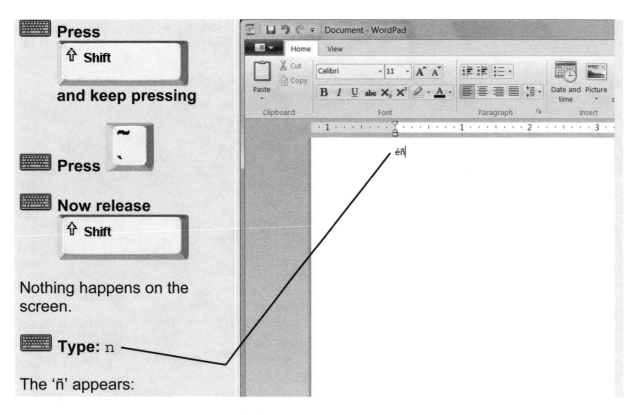

Press

⇧ **Shift**

and keep pressing

Press

Now release

⇧ **Shift**

Nothing happens on the screen.

Type: n

The 'ñ' appears:

This is how you type special letters, such as é, è, ç or ñ.

3.16 Typing Apostrophes

If the key for an apostrophe is dead, how can you type an apostrophe?
This is done using the key together with the space bar. Try it:

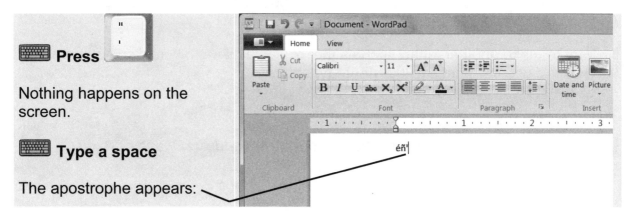

Press

Nothing happens on the screen.

Type a space

The apostrophe appears:

3.17 Closing WordPad

Now you can close the *WordPad* program. This is how:

Click

Click Exit

WordPad once again asks whether you want to save the changes.
You do not need to, so:

Click Don't Save

In the next chapter you will learn how to save a document, such as a letter. For the time being, you do not need to save the practice texts.

3.18 Exercises

The following exercises will help you master what you have just learned. Have you forgotten how to do something? Use the number beside the footsteps to look it up in the appendix *How Do I Do That Again?*

Exercise: Typing Text

☞ Open *WordPad*. 🐾14

☞ Type the following text:
Canberra is the capital of Australia. Canberra is exactly halfway between Sydney and Melbourne, two other large cities.

☞ Now make a new, empty line. 🐾33

☞ Type the following text:
Most people think that Sydney is the capital.

☞ Type the following text:
For a long time, people argued about whether Sydney or Melbourne should be the capital. They finally decided to pick the city in between the two.

☞ In the last sentence, erase the first **the** and type **a** in the same place. 🐾35
They finally decided to pick **the** city in between the two.

☞ This is what the practice text looks like now:

Canberra is the capital of Australia. Canberra is exactly halfway between Sydney and Melbourne, two other large cities.

Most people think that Sydney is the capital. For a long time, people argued about whether Sydney or Melbourne should be the capital. They finally decided to pick a city in between the two.

☞ Move the cursor to the beginning of the line. 🐾31

☞ Move the cursor to the end of the line. 🐾32

☞ Start a new document and do not save the changes. ✂**18**

☞ Close *WordPad*. ✂**15**

Exercise: Corrections

With this exercise, you can practice correcting typing errors.

☞ Open *WordPad*. ✂**14**

☞ Maximize the *WordPad* window. ✂**2**

☞ Type the following text:
```
Many people drink tea in the us. It is not as important
hear as in other contries where a ceremony is made of
drinkingtee, like in japan. They pay much closer attention
to the qality of the te. Other exampels of these countries
are china and Ingland.
```

☞ Correct the following mistakes:
```
Many people drink tea in the US. It is not as important
here as in other countries where a ceremony is made of
drinking tea, like in Japan. They pay much closer
attention to the quality of the tea. Other examples of
these countries are China and England.
```

☞ Start a new text and do not save the changes. ✂**18**

☞ Close *WordPad*. ✂**15**

3.19 Background Information

Dictionary

Cursor	Short blinking line that signals where text will appear.
Cursor keys	Move the cursor left, right, up or down through a text.
Dead key	A key that produces no output when pressed, but which modifies the output of the next key pressed.
Empty line	Line with no text.
Keyboard	The main input device used to communicate with the computer, similar to a typewriter keyboard but with extra function keys.
Paragraph	A paragraph is a section in a piece of writing, usually highlighting a particular point or topic. The start of a paragraph is indicated by beginning on a new line using the Enter key (or hard return) and may include indentation. The paragraph ends by using the Enter key. It consists of at least one sentence.
Repeat keys	Keys that keep giving characters while being pressed.
Space bar	Large key used to type spaces between words.
WordPad	A text editing program you can use to create and edit documents.

Source: Windows Help and Support

Keys

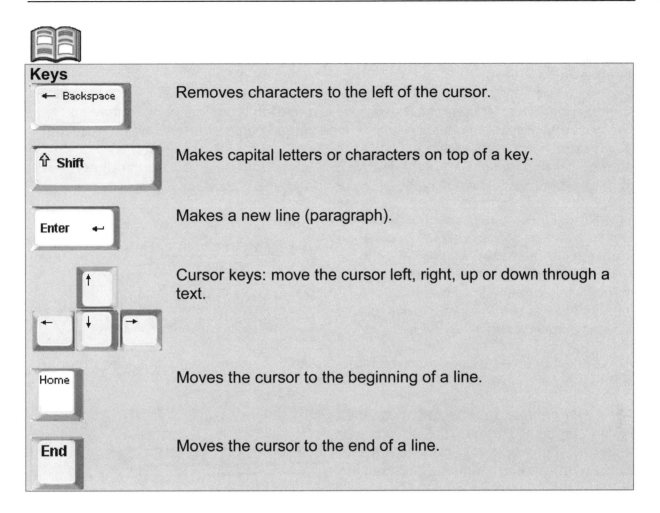

← Backspace	Removes characters to the left of the cursor.
⇧ Shift	Makes capital letters or characters on top of a key.
Enter ↵	Makes a new line (paragraph).
↑ ← ↓ →	Cursor keys: move the cursor left, right, up or down through a text.
Home	Moves the cursor to the beginning of a line.
End	Moves the cursor to the end of a line.

Typing skills

It is certainly not necessary to learn to type like a professional typist in order to work with the computer. Most people have never learned to type, but learn as they go, with two or sometimes four fingers. A time comes when you can quickly find any key and then increase your typing speed.

It is striking that, despite all of the innovations of the computer era, the arrangement of the keyboard is still virtually the same as that of the typewriter.

The normal arrangement used in the United States is still QWERTY. Look at the letters at the top left of the keyboard. A long time ago, the letters were placed in this order to make sure that the typewriter keys would not get stuck even when typing very rapidly.

Apparently, people have become so familiar with this arrangement that they do not want any of it changed.

The keyboard has a separate section for typing numbers. This was designed especially for people who have to enter many numbers and amounts. This section is called the *numeric keypad*.

Some laptops do not have a numeric keypad.

More and more keys are being added. Many of today's keyboards also have special keys used for the Internet. By pressing a single key, for example, you can collect your e-mail.

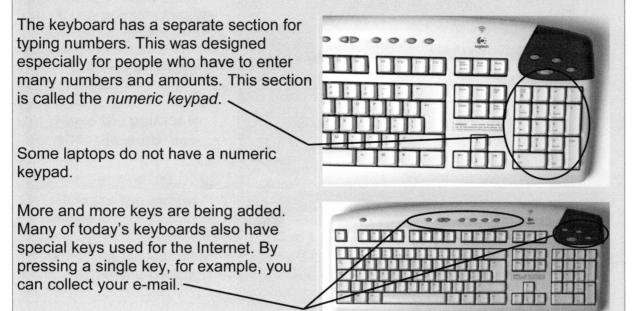

The proper working posture

It is important to arrange your computer properly. This not only makes it more pleasant when you work with your computer, but it also minimizes the risk of various complaints. You will be surprised at the number of hours you will spend working with your PC. A proper working posture is therefore essential. Attention should be devoted to the following:

- You need a table that is sufficiently deep and has the proper height. Your wrists should lie level with the tabletop when typing and using the mouse.
- An adjustable desk chair with arm rests is ideal because you can adjust it to achieve proper support for your back and legs. If your feet do not touch the ground, put something under them to support them - a few thick books, or a small stool or foot rest, for example.
- The keyboard should be directly in front of you. The mouse should be next to the keyboard on the correct side: on the right if you are right-handed and on the left if you are left-handed.

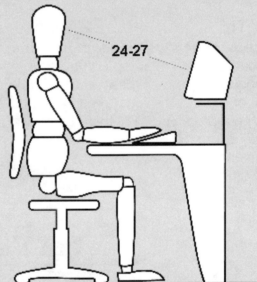

- Place the monitor straight in front of you, at about the same level as your eyes. Do not place the monitor to the left or right because this would force you to constantly strain your neck to turn your head.
- The monitor should be about one arm's length (24 to 27 inches) from your eyes.
- The monitor should not be too low or too high, forcing you to look up or down all the time. If you wear glasses or lenses that are multi-focal (with a special section for reading), having the monitor at the wrong height could force you to use the reading section instead of the 'far-off' section of the lenses. You can always raise the monitor by putting something under it (another thick book?).
- Make sure there is no direct or indirect light shining into the monitor that would make it hard to read.

More ways to customize your computer to make it more pleasant to work with are explained in *Bonus Online Chapter 11 How to Make Working With Your Computer More Pleasant*. Read more about this chapter in *Chapter 9 Bonus Online Chapters and Extra Information*.

3.20 Tips

💡 Tip

Capitals Only
The keyboard has a special key that is used to type capital letters.
This is the key that says *Caps Lock*:

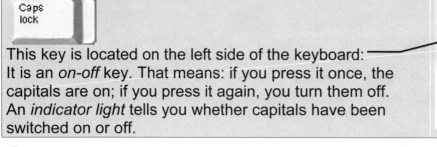

This key is located on the left side of the keyboard: ⎯⎯⎯⎯
It is an *on-off* key. That means: if you press it once, the
capitals are on; if you press it again, you turn them off.
An *indicator light* tells you whether capitals have been
switched on or off.

💡 Tip

Placement of keys on a laptop computer may differ from a desktop keyboard
Keyboards from a laptop computer may differ slightly from those of the desktop
computer. A particular key, for example, the Delete key, may be in a different place.
Most of the descriptions used in this book refer to a desktop keyboard. If you are
using a laptop, you may have to search a bit for the key or key combination being
described.

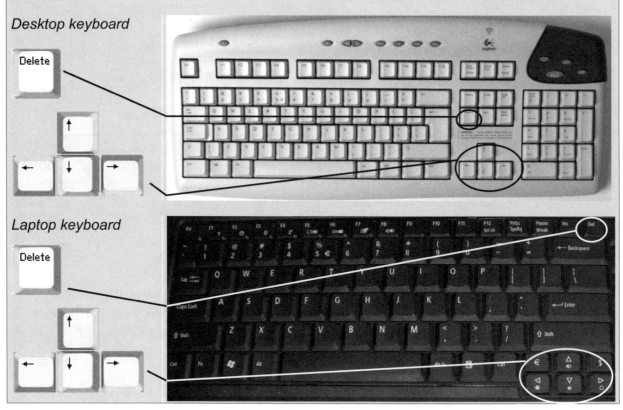

4. Writing a Letter

It is hard to find an office anywhere that still uses a typewriter to type letters.
No messy correction fluid or endless retyping, it is easy these days to produce letters, reports and other documents without errors when using a computer.
Once created, documents or letters can be used over and over again with just a few changes, or sent via e-mail to people on a mailing list.

Writing documents and letters with the computer is also more practical because you can easily change them until they say exactly what you want them to. You can also save a document and work on it again later.

In this chapter, you will start by writing a letter using the computer. This is also done with the program *WordPad*.

In this chapter, you will learn how to:

- write a letter;
- enter the date;
- save a letter;
- open a letter;
- see the print preview;
- print the letter;
- save changes or not save changes.

4.1 Starting a Letter

The easiest way to write a letter is to use the program *WordPad*. You begin by opening this program:

☞ **Open *WordPad*** ✂[14]

You see the empty *WordPad* screen:

4.2 A Larger Font

A *font* is a complete set of characters in a particular size and style of type, including numerals, symbols and the characters of the alphabet.
When you begin typing in *WordPad*, the font size that is automatically used is rather small, and may be unpleasant to work with. This can be easily changed, just like almost everything else in *Windows 7.* When typing a letter, it is handy to start by choosing a font size that is a bit bigger. Here is how you do this:

On the | Home | tab:

⊕ **Click** ˅

⊕ **Click 12**

You will not see anything happen on the screen. But when you start typing, you will see that the text is somewhat larger and easier to read.

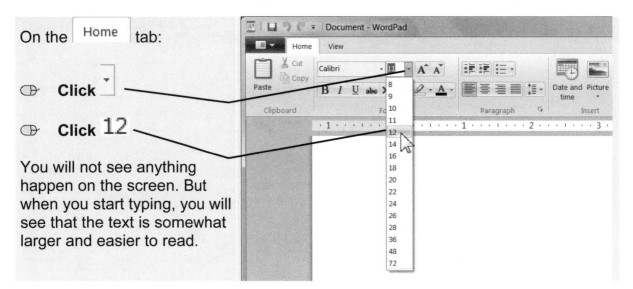

HELP! I do not see the tab Home.

When you do not see the | Home | tab, the *View* tab is selected. You can select the *Home* tab as follows:

☞ **Click** Home

In *Bonus Online Chapter 10 Text Layout*, more information is given about types of fonts and font sizes. You can read more about how to download and open this chapter in *Chapter 9 Bonus Online Chapters and Extra Information*.

4.3 Today's Date

We will begin with an informal letter to someone you know. Naturally, a letter starts with the date. You do not have to type the date yourself. *WordPad* has a command that does it for you.

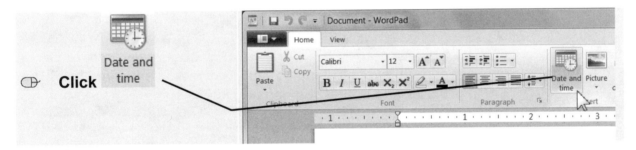

☞ **Click** Date and time

Now you can choose the way you want the date to be written.

☞ **Click the long date notation**

At the bottom of the window:

☞ **Click** OK

Date and Time

Available formats:

8/28/2009
8/28/09
08/28/09
08/28/2009
09/08/28
2009-08-28
28-Aug-09
Friday, August 28, 2009
August 28, 2009
Friday, 28 August, 2009
28 August, 2009
9:55:33 AM
09:55:33 AM
9:55:33
09:55:33

The program automatically inserts the date at the location of the cursor:

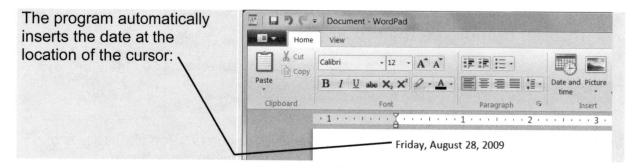

The date in your letter will not be the same as in the illustration. The program inserts today's actual date.

4.4 Undoing

If something goes wrong while you are writing, or if you accidentally press the wrong key, nearly every *Windows* program has a command that will undo it. Try it:

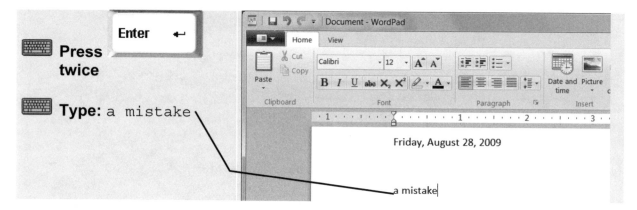

The program always remembers the last thing you did. So you can always *undo* it:

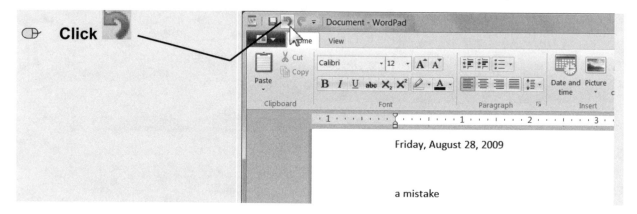

The last line you typed has been removed.

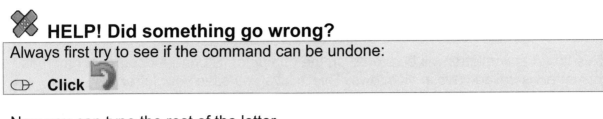

HELP! Did something go wrong?

Always first try to see if the command can be undone:

 Click

Now you can type the rest of the letter.

4.5 Typing a Letter

Please note:

It is important that you type this letter, because this practice letter will be used several times in the rest of this book.

⌨ **Press** | **Enter** ⏎
twice

⌨ **Type:**
Dear name,

This week I started working with Windows 7. This is my first letter typed on the computer.

Sincerely,

Your name

You will save this practice letter on your computer so that you can work on it again later. In daily life, however, you do not necessarily have to save every letter you type. You can also immediately print it and send it.

If you want to save your letter on the computer, you must always tell the computer to do so. If you do not, your letter may be lost. A text is not automatically saved. The text stays in the computer's memory until you stop the program or turn off the computer. The memory that the computer works with is temporary. The text will not be permanently stored until you save it.

4.6 Saving a Document

This first practice letter will be stored on the computer. Storing a document (such as this letter) is called *save* in *Windows*. This is how you save your letter:

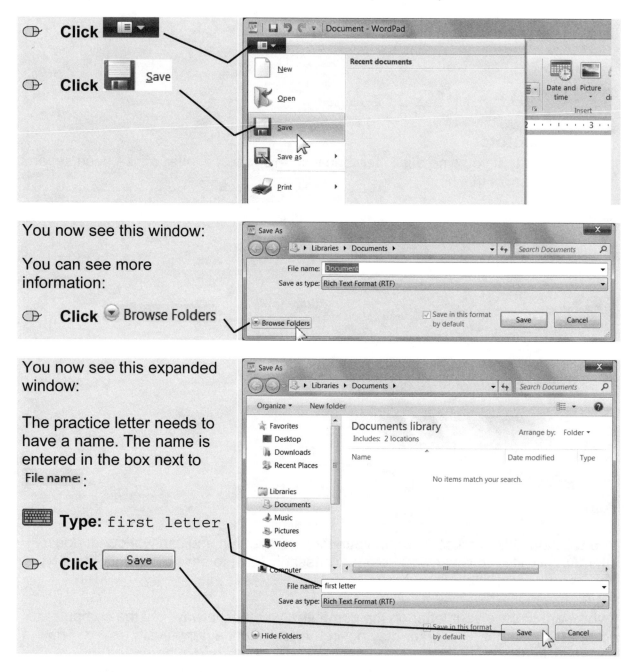

The letter has been saved on your computer's hard disk. How this is done will be explained a bit later.

Now the name of your letter appears at the top of the screen in the title bar:

HELP! The file already exists.

Did this window appear?

Confirm Save As

first letter.rtf already exists.
Do you want to replace it?

Yes   No

If so, you (or someone else) already saved a text with the name *first letter*. You can replace it with your own letter.

Click Yes

4.7 Closing WordPad

Now you must close *WordPad* for the moment. This is done to show you how to retrieve your practice letter so that you can work on it at another time:

☞ **Close *WordPad*** ✂ᵉ¹⁵

Now you can open *WordPad* again:

☞ **Open *WordPad* again** ✂ᵉ¹⁴

You see an empty screen, without your practice letter.

The name *Document* is shown at the top:

Document is the default name for a new text. In order to get your practice letter to appear on the screen, you need to 'open' it first.

4.8 Opening a Document

If you want to use a letter that has been saved on the computer, you must 'open' it first. This is how:

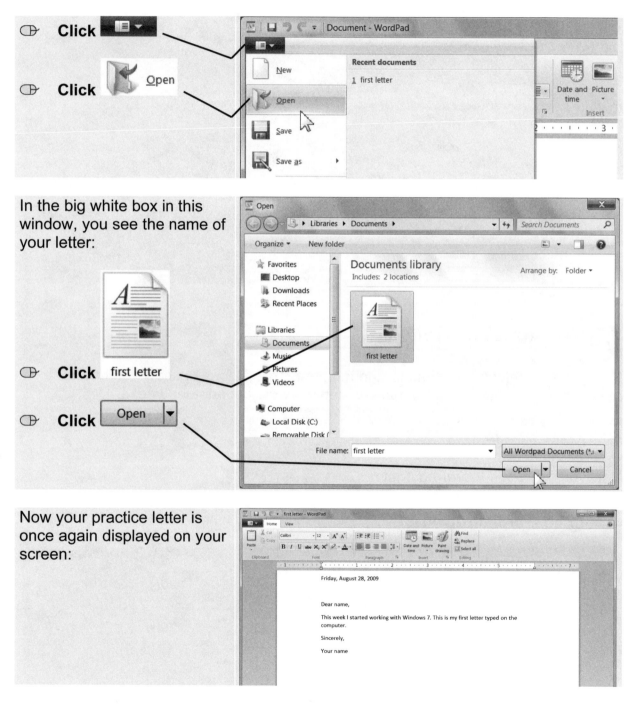

Click

Click Open

In the big white box in this window, you see the name of your letter:

Click first letter

Click Open

Now your practice letter is once again displayed on your screen:

You can continue to work on it now and print it.

4.9 Printing the Letter

When you write a letter, most likely you will want it printed on paper.

Printing is done with a printer:

✖ HELP! No printer?

If you do not have a printer, you can skip this section.

Before you actually print a letter, it is wise to have a preview of what it will look like on paper. *WordPad* has a special command for this:

👆 **Click**

👆 **Place the mouse pointer at**

🖨 Print ▸

👆 **Click**

🔍 **Print preview**
Preview and make changes t
before printing.

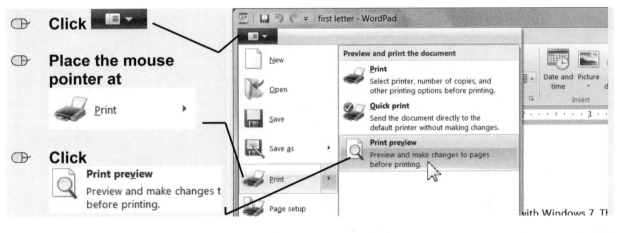

Now this window appears. In the middle is a miniature representation of the page as it will be printed:

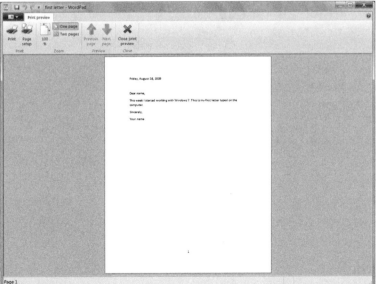

The way the letter is positioned on the page, with the text at the very top left, is not very appealing. You can easily change this by adding some empty lines at the top.

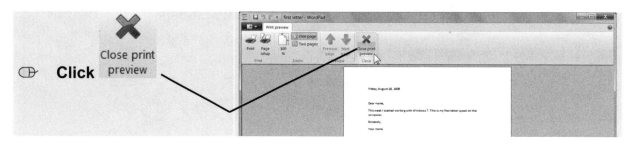

Click Close print preview

Now you can add the empty lines.

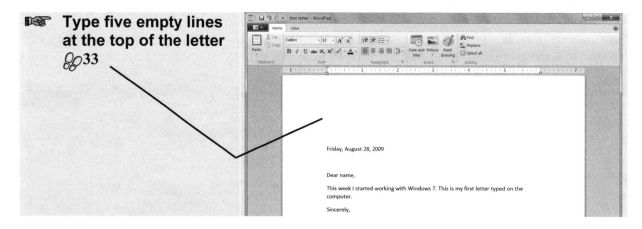

☞ **Type five empty lines at the top of the letter** 🦶33

You can see the results using the *Print Preview:*

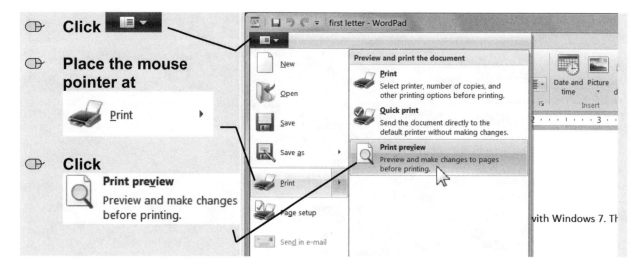

⊕ **Click** [≡▾]

⊕ **Place the mouse pointer at**

    🖨 Print ▸

⊕ **Click**

    🔍 **Print preview**
    Preview and make changes before printing.

Now the letter has moved
down the page a bit:

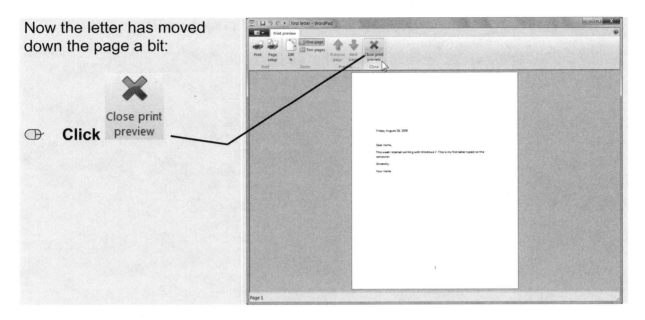

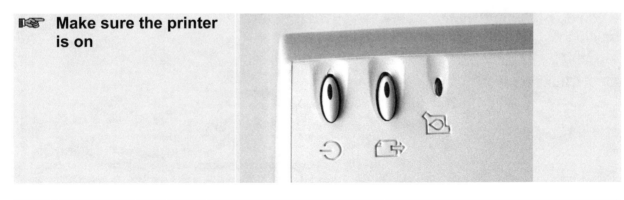

🖰 **Click** Close print preview

You can print the letter the way it is for now. You can do a lot of other things to make the letter look more appealing, for example by using text effects and a different type of font. This will all be explained in *Bonus Online Chapter 10 Text Layout*. You can read more about this chapter in *Chapter 9 Bonus Online Chapters and Extra Information*.

🪝 Please note:

It is important to check if your printer is ready for use before you tell the computer to print anything.

☞ **Make sure the printer is on**

☞ **Make sure there is paper in the printer**

Is everything ready? Then you can tell the computer to print the letter:

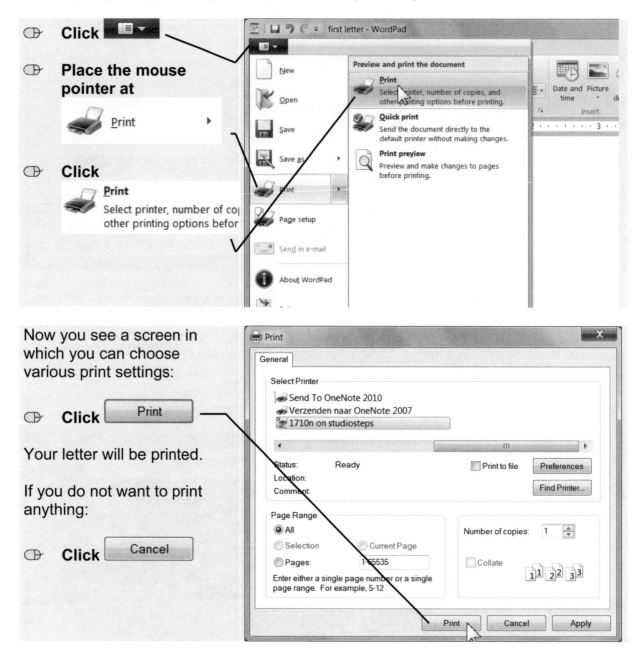

Click ▣▾

Place the mouse
pointer at

Print ▸

Click

Print
Select printer, number of copies
other printing options befor

Now you see a screen in
which you can choose
various print settings:

Click Print

Your letter will be printed.

If you do not want to print
anything:

Click Cancel

4.10 Save Changes?

You can never accidentally lose something you have saved. *Windows 7* always checks to see if something is about to be lost. You should give it a try. Since the last time you saved your practice letter, you have made some changes. You added empty lines to the top of the letter. If you stop now, *WordPad* will warn you:

Click [▤▾]

Click Exit

This week I started working with Windows 7. This is n computer.

WordPad will ask you whether or not the changes should be saved:

In this case, you do want to save them.

WordPad

Do you want to save changes to C:\Users\Studio Visual Steps\Documents\first letter.rtf?

Save   Don't Save   Cancel

Click Save

The changes will be saved and *WordPad* will be closed.

💡 Tip

Saving
To many people, this screen is confusing:

| WordPad   ❌ |

Do you want to save changes to C:\Users\Studio
Visual Steps\Documents\first letter.rtf?

| Save | Don't Save | Cancel |

If you unexpectedly see this screen, you apparently made at least one change. No matter how small, even if the change is simply one space, it is still a change to *WordPad*.

- If you click [Save], the changes will be saved.
- If you click [Don't Save], the changes will not be saved.
- If you click [Cancel], you will return to *WordPad*.

Now you can open your practice letter again to see what happens when you save the changes first yourself.

☞ **Open *WordPad* again** 🦶14

☞ **Open the practice letter** first letter **again** 🦶29

First make a small change to the letter:

At the top of the letter, type `test`

test|

Friday, August 28, 2009

Now you can save this small text change:

Click

Click _Save_

This time you were not asked to select a name. You have already given this document a name: *first letter*.

☞ **Close *WordPad*** ❧15

Did you notice that the screen asking whether to *save changes* has not appeared? That is because you saved the last changes yourself while you were working.

With the next exercise, you can practice saving documents a little more.

4.11 Exercises

The following exercises will help you master what you have just learned. Have you forgotten how to do something? Use the number beside the footsteps to look it up in the appendix *How Do I Do That Again?*

Exercise: Saving Changes

☞ Open *WordPad.* ᵎ⁴

☞ Type the following short letter:

Date

Dear Sirs,

With this letter I want to thank you for your excellent service.

Sincerely,

Your name

☞ Save this letter and name it *exercise 1.* ²⁶

☞ Start a new letter. ¹⁶

☞ Open the *exercise 1* letter again. ²⁸

☞ Add the line printed in bold letters below:

Date

Dear Sirs,

With this letter I want to thank you for your excellent service. **I would also like to inform you that the appliance works perfectly.**

Sincerely,

Your name

☞ Print the letter. ¹⁹

☞ Start a new letter, and while doing so have the changes saved. ¹⁷

4.12 Background Information

Dictionary	
Font	A complete set of characters in a particular size and style of type, including numerals, symbols, punctuation and the characters of the alphabet.
Open	Command to find and retrieve a document which has been saved on a hard drive, CD-ROM or other memory device.
Print	Command to produce a copy of the document on paper with the help of a printer.
Print Preview	A feature that allows the user to view on the computer screen the document as it will appear on the printed page.
Save	Command to store a file on a memory device such as a hard drive or USB stick for future use.
Undo	Command to undo the last thing you did in a program.

Source: Windows Help and Support

File types
WordPad in *Windows 7* can only open the following file types: .rtf, .docx, .odt, .txt.

Printers

The printer most commonly used in the home is called an *inkjet* printer.
This type of printer prints characters by spraying very small, precise amounts of ink onto the paper.

Many of these printers can also make color prints. These printers have not only a cartridge with black ink, but also another cartridge with at least three colors. Any color imaginable can be copied by mixing the various colored inks. Each type of printer has different cartridges.

Inkjet printer

Inkjet printers can print on regular paper as well as on special types of paper, depending on the quality of print you want. You can get special photo paper to print photos, for example.

Laser printers are often used in the office sector. They are a non-impact printing device which operates in similar fashion to a photocopier, in which a laser draws the image of a page on a photosensitive drum which then attracts *toner* (an extremely fine-grained powder) on to the paper, where it is subsequently bonded by heating.

Laser printers are known for high quality prints, good print speed, and a low cost-per-copy. Laser printers are available in both color and monochrome varieties.

Laser printer

A recent development is the *photo printer*, which uses special photo paper to print digital photographs.

You can connect this kind of printer to the computer, but there are also models that can print directly from a digital camera's memory card. In this case, the camera's memory card fits into a card reader that is built into the printer.

Photo printer

Saving on the computer

The computer has a certain amount of *working memory.* This working memory consists of chips in which the information is temporarily saved.

When you turn the computer off, however, the memory is emptied. This is why you also need to be able to save information more permanently.

That type of memory exists in various types: the computer's *hard disk* or an external hard disk, but also *USB sticks* (*USB memory sticks*), *CD-recordable/-rewritable* and *DVD-recordable/-rewritable* and *blu-ray disk.*

Hard disk

USB stick

External hard disk

CD-r / CD-rw

DVD-r / DVD-rw

Blu ray disk

The most important saving method uses the hard (disk) drive on your computer. The hard disk is a small, sealed box that has been built into your computer.

Hard disk

Inside a computer case

Case (housing)

In this box, a small disk rotates. The disk is magnetic, making it possible to save information on it.

You determine what is saved on the hard drive. You can save documents on it, or drawings, or computer programs. You can copy, move or delete files from the hard drive.

Where to save?

Every desktop computer in use today contains one or more hard disk drives. In addition, many computers will have a CD drive and/or a DVD drive that can read and write (if the drive is a 'burner') CDs and/or DVDs. You can also save your work to a USB stick. USB sticks connect to the PC's USB ports.

In the *Computer* window, you can see which items your PC contains. In this example, it contains the following items:

Local Disk (C:)
123 GB free of 153   Hard disk

DVD RW Drive (D:)   DVD RW drive

LACIE (F:)
290 GB free of 298   External hard disk

Removable Disk (
953 MB free of 96   Removable disk

Windows gives every memory device a letter for a name.
- The hard disk drive always gets the letter **C**. (If there is a second hard disk, it will get the letter **D**.)
- The CD or DVD drive gets the next letter of the alphabet. In the example above, that's **D**. If there are two such drives, the next one will be named **F**.
- The next device gets the letter **G**, and so forth.

In the window above, you see that the letter **F** has been given to a removable disk. In this example, that is a USB stick inserted into the computer. But it could also be an external hard disk connected to the PC, or a digital camera's memory card.

Please note: Other items or devices may be present on your computer. The letters you see on your screen will belong to different devices.

You usually save your work on your computer's hard drive. If you want to take your work with you to another computer, or if you want to make a backup copy of a file, then you can save your work onto a floppy disk, a USB stick or a memory card. Another option for saving your work is to burn it onto a CD or DVD.

CD and DVD

These days, computers come standard with a CD player, DVD player or blu ray player, which you can use to read CDs, DVDs or blu ray disks.

CD-roms, DVD-roms and blu ray disks are the media for distributing computer programs. A CD can hold a large number of files, and a DVD or blu ray disk can contain even more.

You can even put files on a CD, DVD or blu ray disk yourself. You do need a different type of device for this, however: a CD writer, DVD writer or blu ray writer. This kind of device can 'write' onto a special kind of blank disk. This disk is recordable (r).
They can be bought in your local electronics, office supply, and discount department stores.

The CD rewriter and DVD rewriter are two other devices for reading and writing files to CDs or DVDs. Disks used in these devices are re-recordable (rw), they can be erased and recorded over numerous times without damaging the medium. They are a little more expensive however and in the case of DVD-rw may not be compatible with certain DVD players.

You can not play DVDs or blu ray disks in a CD-drive, but the other way around works just fine.

4.13 Tips

💡 **Tip**

Regularly save your work
If you work for a lengthy period of time, you should regularly save your work. It is also wise to save your work first before making large changes. If anything goes wrong, you then have a spare copy that has been saved.

💡 **Tip**

When not to save changes?
When you close a program window, the computer shows you this question:

WordPad   [X]
Do you want to save changes to C:\Users\Studio Visual Steps\Documents\first letter.rtf?
Save   Don't Save   Cancel

You can click on [Don't Save] if:
• you do not want to save the text;
• the version of the text that you saved earlier is better than the current version. In that case, it would be a waste to replace it.

💡 **Tip**

Rules for file names
What rules apply to naming a text?

File name: [   ] ▼

A file name may not:
• be longer than 255 letters or numbers, including spaces;
• contain one of the following characters: \ / : * ? " < > . |

⚲ Tip

Did something go wrong with your printer?
When this happens, be sure to check:
- whether the printer is turned on;
- whether the printer has paper;
- whether something else is wrong, such as an empty ink cartridge or a jammed piece of paper. If necessary, consult the printer manual.

Did you fix what was wrong?
Then *WordPad* will try again and the printing will start automatically.

⚲ Tip

Quick Access Toolbar
At the top of the window, you will see various buttons. This area is called the *Quick Access Toolbar*. You can use the buttons to enter a command with a single mouse click: .

These buttons have the following functions:

    Save a document

Undo

Redo

When you click ▼ next to the Quick Access buttons, you will see more commands:

When you click one of the commands, it will be added to the Quick Access Toolbar.

Customize Quick Access Toolbar	
	New
	Open
✓	Save
	Send in e-mail
	Quick print
	Print preview
✓	Undo
✓	Redo
	Show below the Ribbon
	Minimize the Ribbon

For example:

    Create a new document

Open a document

Print the text

See the Print Preview

💡 Tip

Line Spacing
In *WordPad* the default line spacing is standard 1.15. This means there is always some space between the text lines. You can change the line space as follows:

👆 **Click** 📝

👆 **Click** 1.0

By default, *WordPad* also adds a 10 pt space after a paragraph. This is how you change this setting:

👆 **Click** 📝

👆 **Click**
Add 10pt space after paragra|

Now there is no more space between the lines:

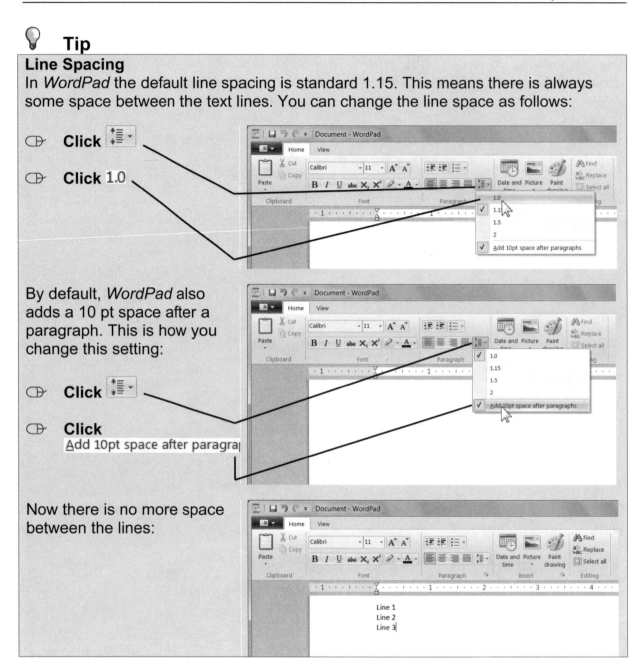

5. Word Processing

It is very easy to modify a text using your computer. You can select a word, copy it and move it somewhere else, move sentences or paragraphs, or save the text for future use.

Because so many people use word processing programs, many standard letters (*templates*) exist. It is easy to make your own template. You might start by creating a simple, new document about a certain subject, like an invitation. You add a place for a name and other bits here and there to make the invitation more personal. The recipient's name is inserted and the invitation is printed. The recipient of such an invitation will think you have written a unique and a personal message, but most of the document was typed just one time.

This chapter primarily focuses on word processing. You will discover how easy it is to change sentences: sometimes all you have to do is click and drag with your mouse.

In this chapter, you will learn how to:

- move the cursor with the mouse;
- select a single word or paragraph;
- delete a word;
- move a word or paragraph;
- split a paragraph and paste it back together.

5.1 The Cursor and the Mouse

☞ **Open *WordPad* 📎14**

You can move the cursor with the cursor keys on the keyboard, or by using the mouse. In order to practice this, type the following words to a popular nursery rhyme.

⌨ **Type:** mary had a little lamb

⌨ **Press** Enter ↵

⌨ **Type:** its fleece was white as snow

⌨ **Press** Enter ↵

⌨ **Type:** and everywhere that mary went

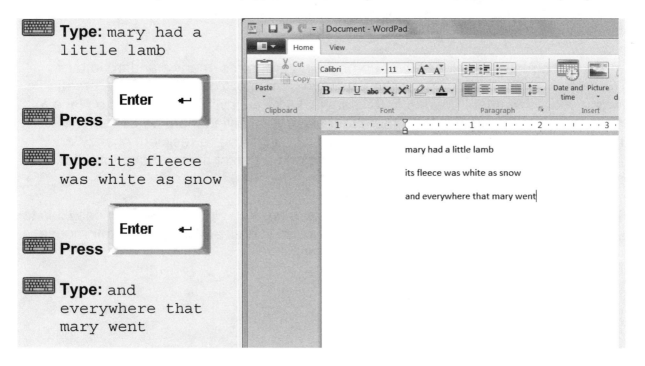

When you slide your mouse pointer over text, the pointer changes its appearance

from an ↖ (arrow) into this I. When you click the mouse somewhere in the text, the cursor will move immediately to that spot.

🖱 **Move the mouse pointer I to the right side of the word** little

🖱 **Click with the mouse**

You will see that the cursor appears after the word 'little':

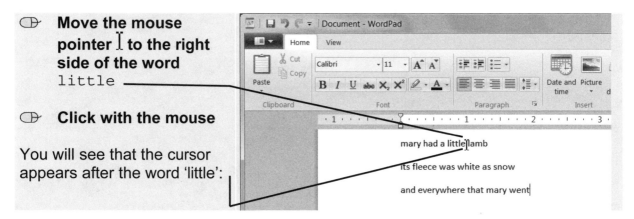

Now you can delete the word 'little' using the Backspace key:

☞ **Delete the word**
little ✂️**34, 35**

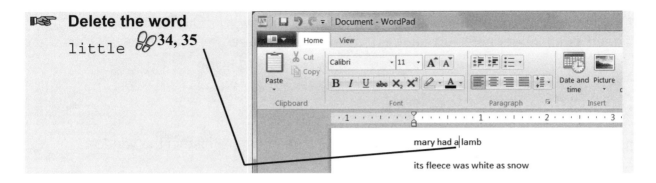

5.2 Selecting a Word

Using the Backspace key to delete a word is not very efficient. There are faster ways to delete a word or even an entire paragraph all at once.
In order to do so, you must first *select* the portion that you want to delete. Selecting is done with the mouse.

☞ **Move the mouse pointer Ⅰ to the word** fleece

☞ **Double-click with the mouse**

You see the word 'fleece' turn blue:

This means that the word has been *selected*.

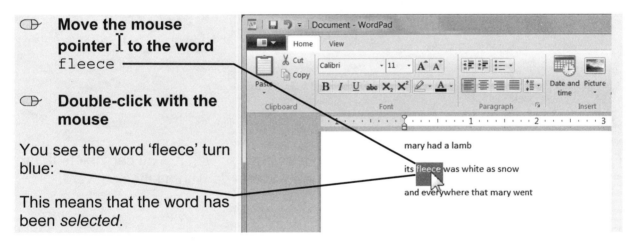

You can select a different word in the same way.

☞ **Move the mouse pointer Ⅰ to the word** everywhere

☞ **Double-click with the mouse**

You see that the word 'everywhere' has now been selected:

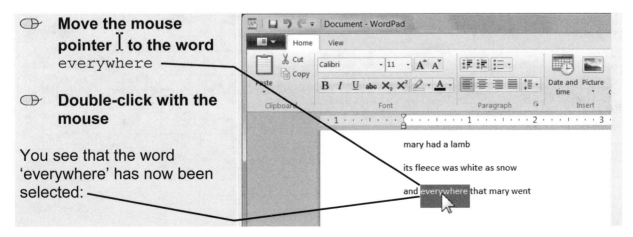

As you can see, this method allows you to select one word at a time. The word 'fleece' is no longer selected after you select 'everywhere'.

5.3 Undoing a Selection

It is very easy to undo a selection. Simply click somewhere else in the window:

☞ **Move the mouse pointer I somewhere in the window**

☞ **Click with the mouse**

You see that the word is no longer selected:

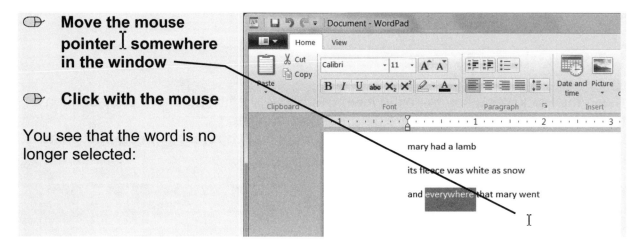

5.4 Deleting a Word

Once you have selected a word, you can do many things with it. You can delete it, for example. Later, you will see some more things you can do with a selected word.

Deleting is done with the Delete key:
(Sometimes it only says *Del.*)

The Delete key is in the group of keys above the cursor keys:

On a laptop computer, this key is often positioned somewhere else, for instance in the top right-hand corner.

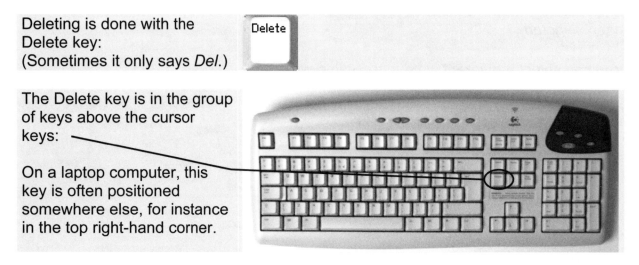

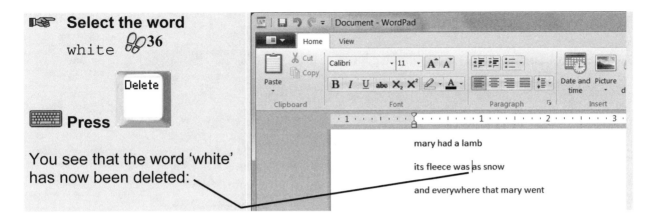

5.5 Dragging a Word

You can drag a selected word to another place in the text. To practice this, first type the last line of the nursery rhyme. The words are in the right order now, but will not be after this exercise.

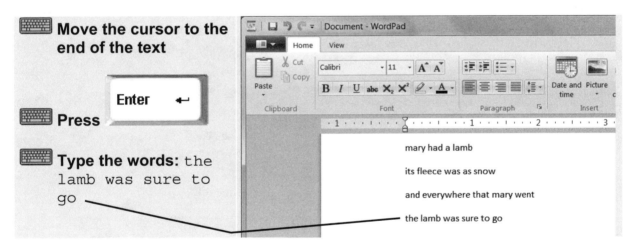

Before you can drag a word, you must select it:

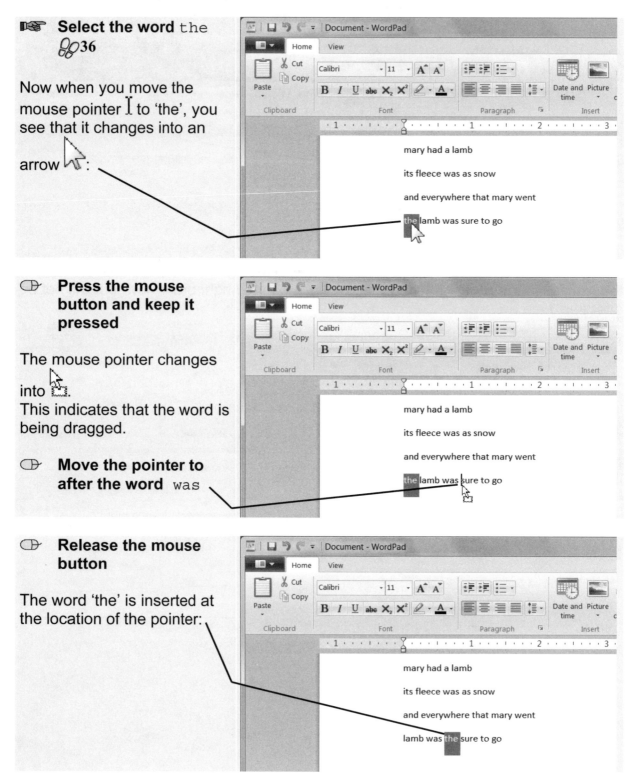

☞ **Select the word** the
&&36

Now when you move the
mouse pointer I to 'the', you
see that it changes into an

arrow :

**Press the mouse
button and keep it
pressed**

The mouse pointer changes

into .
This indicates that the word is
being dragged.

**Move the pointer to
after the word** was

**Release the mouse
button**

The word 'the' is inserted at
the location of the pointer:

Learning to drag words will take some time. At the end of this chapter, you will find an exercise to practice dragging. You need to save the text for this:

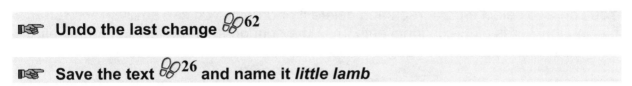

☞ **Undo the last change** 🐾**62**

☞ **Save the text** 🐾**26 and name it *little lamb***

5.6 Typing Over a Word

If you want to replace one word with another, it is not always necessary to delete the word first. You can simply type over a word that has been selected. Try it:

☞ **Select the word** go
🐾**36**

⌨ **Type:** walk

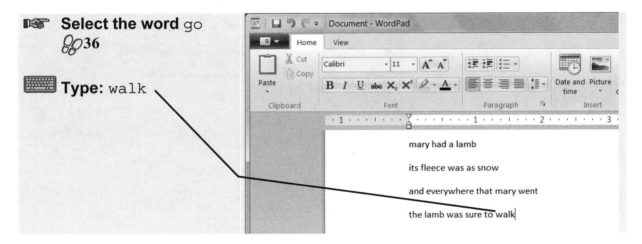

As you can see, the selected word is replaced by the new word you typed.

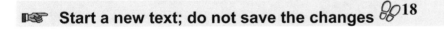

☞ **Start a new text; do not save the changes** 🐾**18**

Now you have an empty screen again, without text.

5.7 Selecting a Paragraph

You can also select a paragraph and delete it or drag it. You can easily practice by placing the words of the national anthem in the right order. Type the first four lines. They have been put in the wrong order on purpose:

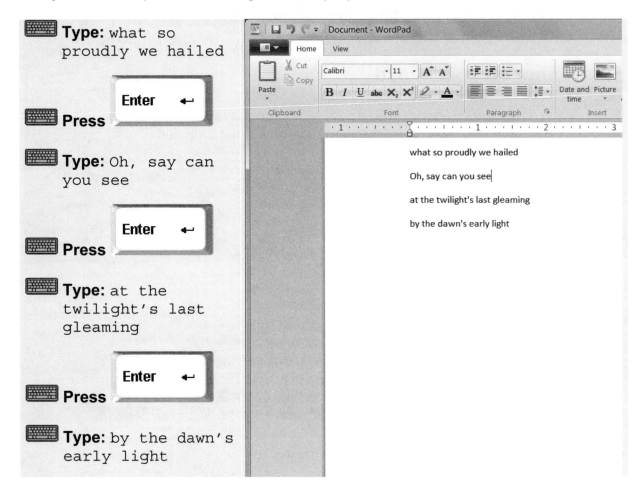

The start of a paragraph is indicated by beginning on a new line (using the Enter key). The paragraph ends by using the Enter key. A paragraph can be a group of sentences, one sentence alone or even just one line of text. In the text above every line is a paragraph.

It is easy to select a paragraph. Double-clicking with the mouse selects a word. Triple-clicking selects the paragraph:

Move the mouse arrow I to the second paragraph

Click three times with the mouse

You see that the second paragraph is now selected:

If triple-clicking does not work the first time, just try it again.

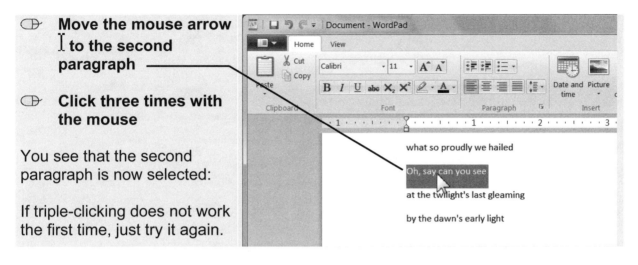

5.8 Dragging a Paragraph

Dragging a paragraph is done the same way as dragging a word. You can point to the selected paragraph and drag it to the place where it should be:

Move the mouse arrow to the selected paragraph

Press the mouse button and keep it pressed

The mouse pointer changes into .

Move the mouse arrow to the front of the top paragraph

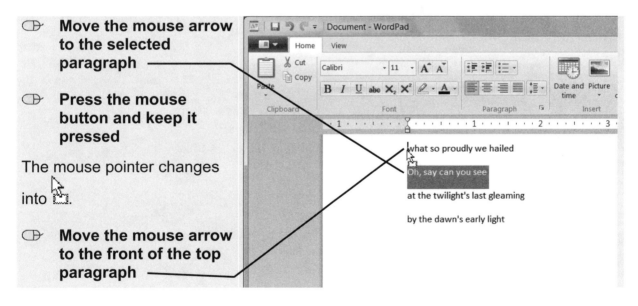

☞ **Release the mouse button**

The paragraph is entered at the top:

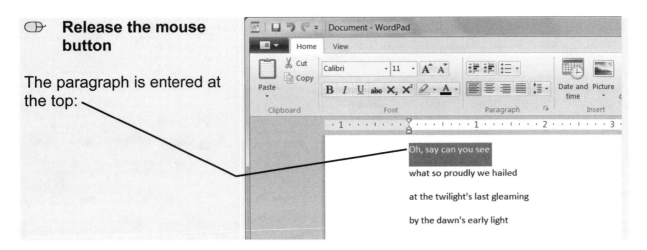

Dragging paragraphs will be easier once you give it some practice. See the relevant exercise at the end of this chapter. There you can put the entire anthem in the right order. You will be saving the text for this purpose shortly.

5.9 Mini Word Processing

Now you have learned the most important actions in word processing. Actually, *WordPad* is not the only program where these actions are useful. These same actions can be used in various other situations in *Windows 7*, for example when you are saving a document. Take a look:

☞ **Click**

☞ **Click** *Save*

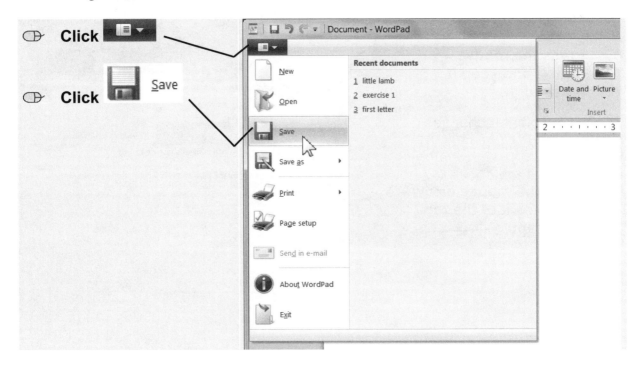

You now see this window:

In the box next to File name: , a tentative name is already shown, namely Document :

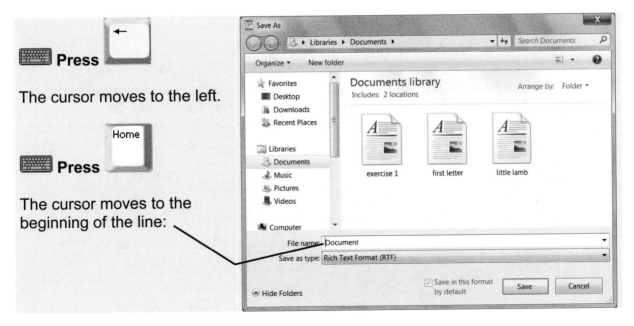

This box acts like a kind of mini word processor. You can use all of the actions that you learned in *WordPad* in these boxes as well. Examples are:

- if the word is selected, you can delete it using the Delete key;
- if you press the cursor keys, the cursor will move through the word;
- if the word is not selected, you can add letters or delete them.

Go ahead and try:

Press

The cursor moves to the left.

Press Home

The cursor moves to the beginning of the line:

As you can see, the cursor acts the same way it does in *WordPad*. Selecting is also done the same way:

In the box next to File name: :

👆 **Double-click on the word** Document

The word 'Document' is selected. You can start typing right away.

⌨ **Type:** Anthem

👆 **Click** Save

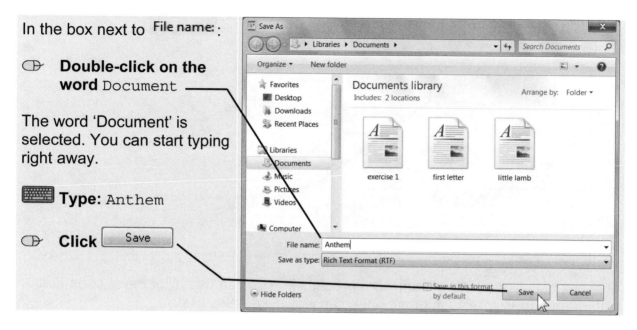

The text is saved as *Anthem.rtf*.

☞ **Start a new text** 👣16

Now you have an empty screen again, without text.

5.10 Splitting and Pasting Paragraphs

You have already seen that you can make empty lines (in fact empty paragraphs) by pressing the Enter key. You can also split a paragraph the same way. Sometimes this will happen accidentally when you press the Enter key. It is useful to know that you can *undo* this.

⌨ **Type:** The Everglades are in Florida.

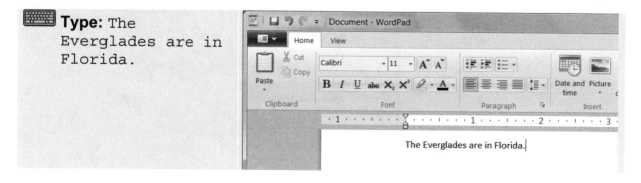

Move the pointer to the word `are`

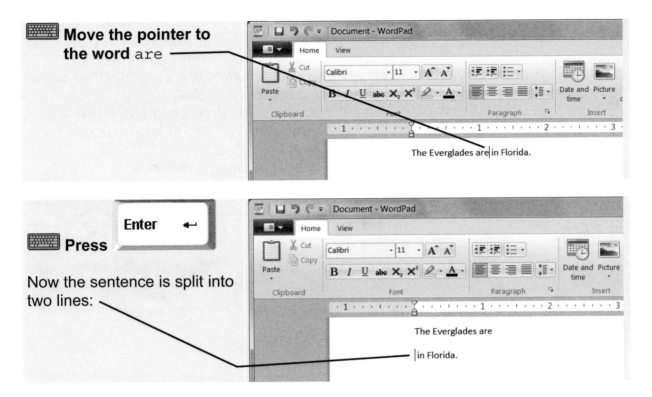

Press Enter

Now the sentence is split into two lines:

Both lines are in fact separate paragraphs. The bottom paragraph can easily be pasted back to the top paragraph using the Backspace key. In this instance, the cursor is still in the right place, at the beginning of the line.

Press Backspace

Now the sentence is pasted back together:

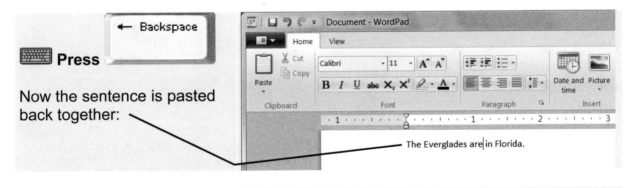

☞ **Start a new text, do not save the changes** ⚸18

5.11 Copying, Cutting and Pasting

Windows has three very useful commands: *copying, cutting* and *pasting.* Once you have copied or cut something, you can paste it somewhere else.
You can copy or cut in one program, and paste into a different program. A text created in an e-mail program can be pasted in a letter in *WordPad*, for example.

You can practice doing this in *WordPad*. Type the following three lines:

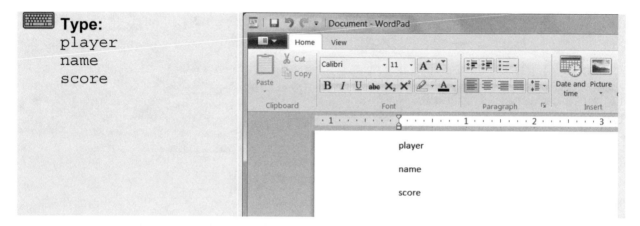

A portion of text, such as a word, is easy to copy and paste somewhere else in the text. But before you can copy something, you must select it first. Remember this rule:

➥ **Please note:**

Select first ... then act.

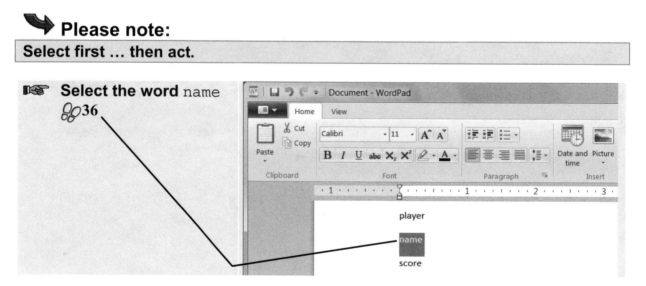

At the `Home` tab:

⊕ **Click** Copy

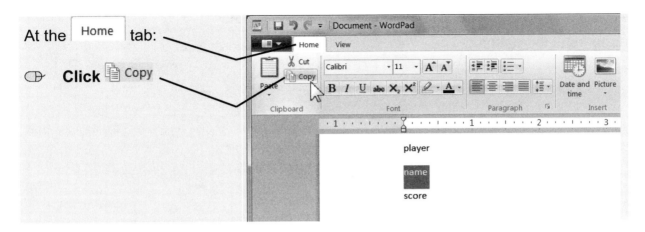

You can not see anything happening, but the word 'name' has now been copied to the *Clipboard*. *Windows Clipboard* is a temporary storage area.
You can paste the word 'name' somewhere else. The cursor is used to indicate where to paste.

Move the cursor to the end of the last line

☞ **Make an empty line at the bottom**
33

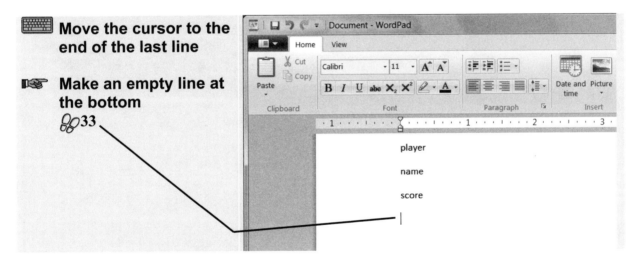

Now you can paste the word*:*

⊕ **Click**

Please note: do not click
Paste
.

The word 'name' now appears at the bottom:

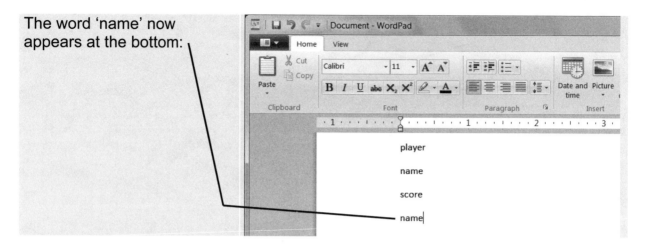

A word that you *select* and *copy* can be pasted as many times as you want. Take a look:

Click 📋 **again**

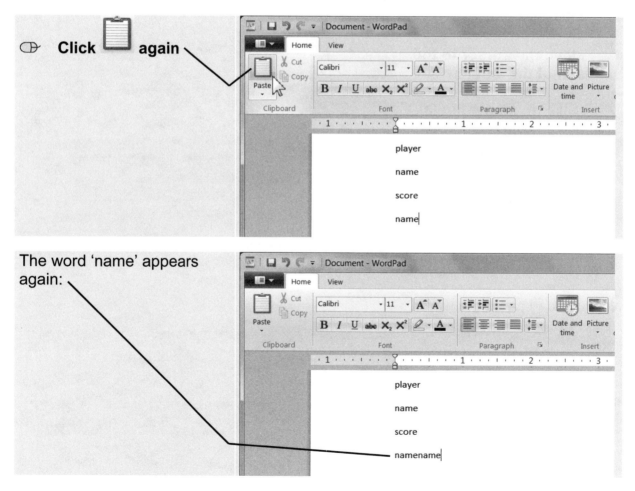

The word 'name' appears again:

➥ **Please note:**

You can only paste the last text you copied. Each time you copy a text, any previously copied text is removed from the computer's memory.

You can also *cut* a word and paste it somewhere else. Give it a try, but remember the rule:

➥ **Please note:**

Select first … then act.

☞ **Select the word**

player ✂36

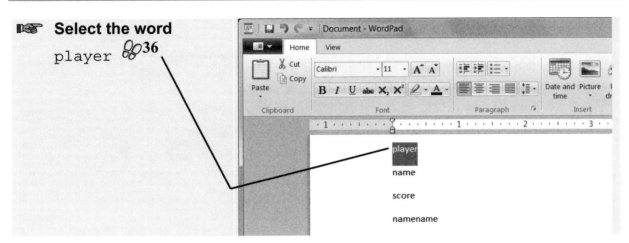

Now you can cut the word 'player':

⊖ **Click** ✂ Cut

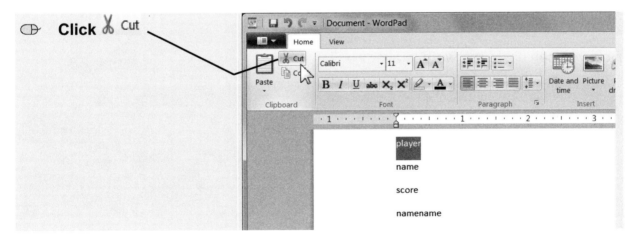

Now the word 'player' has disappeared:

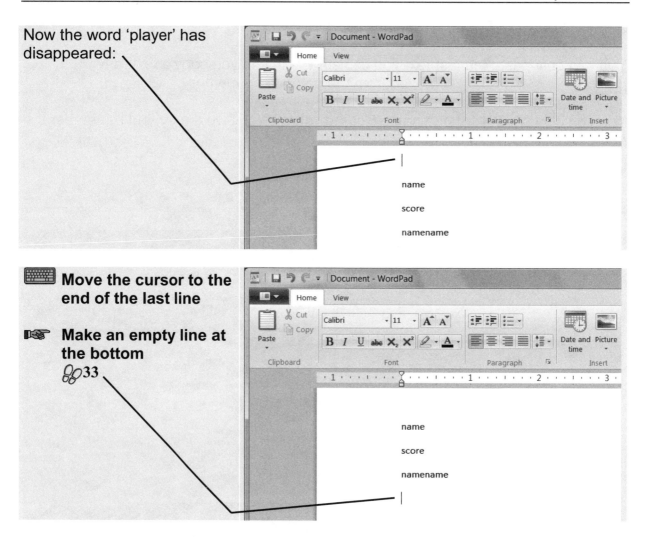

⌨ **Move the cursor to the end of the last line**

☞ **Make an empty line at the bottom**
👣33

Now you can paste the word 'player':

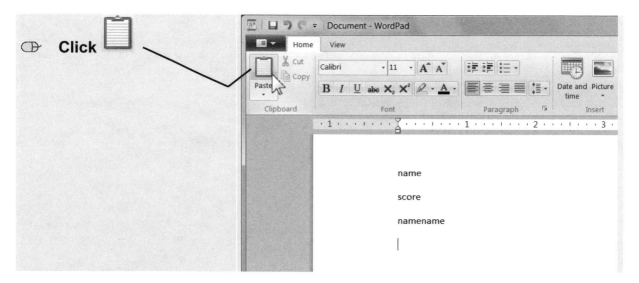

⊕ **Click** 📋

The word 'player' appears at the bottom:

In this way you see how easily words or sentences can be moved. First select, then cut, then paste your selection somewhere else. Please note that in this example, you'd have to type a space in the middle of the pasted word 'namename'.

🖐 Please note:

You can only paste the last text you cut. If you cut a new text, the text you cut previously will be lost. You can always *undo* your last step, if you do not want to lose that portion of text.

☞ **Start a new text, do not save the changes** 👣**18**

With the next exercises you can practice what you have learned in this chapter.

5.12 Exercises

The following exercises will help you master what you have just learned. Have you forgotten how to do something? Use the number beside the footsteps to look it up in the appendix *How Do I Do That Again?*

Exercise: The Song

This exercise will help you practice deleting and dragging words and attaching portions of text to one another.

☞ Open the document with the name: 📄 little lamb . 𝒬𝒬²⁹

☞ Select the word 'that'. 𝒬𝒬³⁶

mary had a lamb

its fleece was as snow

and everywhere that mary went

the lamb was sure to go

☞ Delete the word 'that'. 𝒬𝒬³⁵

☞ Select the word 'sure'. 𝒬𝒬³⁶

mary had a lamb

its fleece was as snow

and everywhere mary went

the lamb was sure to go

☞ Drag the word 'sure' and position it after the word 'lamb':

mary had a lamb

its fleece was as snow

and everywhere mary went

the lamb sure was to go

Now you can put the song on a single line:

☞ Attach the four paragraphs to make a single line. 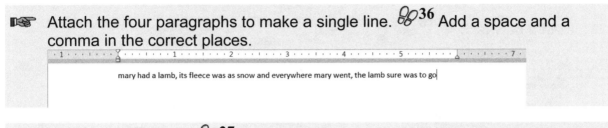[36] Add a space and a comma in the correct places.

> mary had a lamb, its fleece was as snow and everywhere mary went, the lamb sure was to go

☞ Save this document. [27]

Exercise: The National Anthem

This exercise lets you practice dragging lines of text.

☞ Open the document with the name: 📄 Anthem . [29]

☞ Drag the paragraphs so that they are in the correct order:

> Oh, say can you see
>
> by the dawn's early light
>
> what so proudly we hailed
>
> at the twilight's last gleaming

☞ Now add the following four paragraphs:
```
through the perilous fight
whose bright stars and broad stripes
were so gallantly streaming
o'er the ramparts we watched
```

☞ Now drag these paragraphs so that they are also in the correct order:

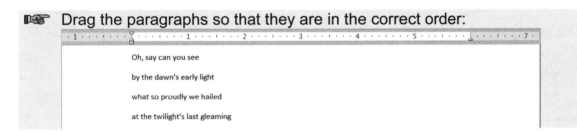

> Oh, say can you see
>
> by the dawn's early light
>
> what so proudly we hailed
>
> at the twilight's last gleaming
>
> whose brought stars and broad stripes
>
> through the perilous fight
>
> o'er the ramparts we watched
>
> were so gallantly streaming

☞ Save the document. ✎²⁷

☞ Start a new text. ✎¹⁶

Exercise: Copying and Pasting

☞ Type the following three lines (paragraphs):
two
three
points

☞ Select 'points'. ✎³⁶

☞ Copy the word 'points'. ✎²¹

☞ Move the cursor after the word 'two' ✎³⁰ and type a space.

☞ Now paste the word: 'points'. ✎²²

☞ Move the cursor after the word 'three' ✎³⁰ and type a space.

☞ Now paste the word 'points' here. ✎²²

two points

three points|

points

☞ At the bottom, select the word 'points'. ✎³⁶

☞ Cut the word 'points'. ✎²³

two points

three points

|

☞ Close *WordPad*, you do not need to save the changes from above. ✎¹⁵

5.13 Background Information

Dictionary	
Copy	Command to duplicate a selected portion of a document, so that it can be inserted somewhere else.
Cut	Command to remove a selected portion of a document, so that it can be inserted somewhere else.
Delete	Action that removes a selected portion of a document.
Paste	Command to insert a previously selected portion of a document which had been copied or cut.
Select	Action with the mouse that highlights a portion of a document.

Source: Windows Help and support

Word processing programs
Until now, you have worked with *WordPad*. It is a simple program that is more than sufficient for learning the basic principles of word processing. Its big brother is called *Microsoft Word*. This is a highly-detailed program that offers numerous functions.

You can make virtually anything you want with *Microsoft Word*: letters, minutes of meetings, folders, posters, flyers, cards, and other types of printed matter. The program has many functions for designing the layout of these items. It is very easy to make tables, for example.

The program also has some extra *tools* such as an excellent spelling and grammar checker that you can turn on before you start typing. Then while you are typing, it alerts you when spelling and grammatical errors occur.

Microsoft Word is available as a separate program, but is usually sold as part of the *Microsoft Office* package. This package has a number of programs, including the popular spreadsheet *Excel* (a program for making calculations).

5.14 Tips

 Tip

Correcting on-screen?
Many people find it difficult to correct texts on their screens since it is easy to overlook typing errors. They often print their work first so that they can add corrections on paper. However, nearly every word processing program, such as *Microsoft Word*, has an excellent spelling checker that will find most of the typing errors for you and offer suggestions for improvement.

 Tip

Did something go wrong?
Always try to undo what went wrong first:

⊕ **Click** ↺

In almost all cases you can undo the last action you performed. In some programs you even can undo more than one action.

 Tip

Selecting by dragging
You can select not only a whole word or an entire sentence, but any section of text you want:

⊕ **Move the cursor to the beginning of the section you want to select**

one two three Ɩour five

six seven eight nine|

⊕ **Keep pressing the mouse button and drag the mouse to the right**

one two three four Ɩive

six seven eight nine .

You will see that the letters are selected one after the other:

⊕ **Keep pressing the mouse button and drag the mouse downward**

one two three four five

six seven eight nine

This makes it possible to select multiple words or lines: .

It takes some practice, but soon you will be able to select any portion of the text that you want.

💡 Tip

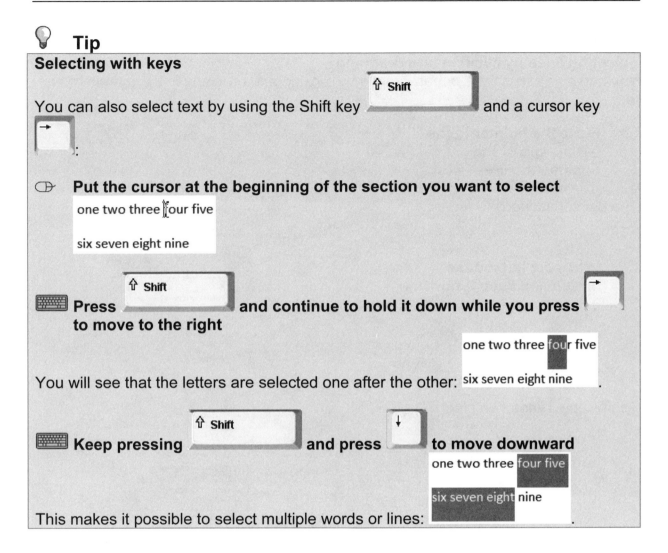

Selecting with keys

You can also select text by using the Shift key ⬆ Shift and a cursor key ➡ :

👉 **Put the cursor at the beginning of the section you want to select**

one two three |four five

six seven eight nine

⌨ **Press** ⬆ Shift **and continue to hold it down while you press** ➡
to move to the right

You will see that the letters are selected one after the other: one two three four five
six seven eight nine .

⌨ **Keep pressing** ⬆ Shift **and press** ↓ **to move downward**

one two three four five
six seven eight nine

This makes it possible to select multiple words or lines: .

Tip

Selecting lines by clicking and dragging

You can also select lines or paragraphs by clicking and dragging in the margin of the text:

⊕ **Place the pointer in the left margin of the document**

The pointer changes to an arrow:

⊕ **Press the left mouse button and keep it down**

⊕ **Drag the mouse downward**

The selected lines turn blue:

⊕ **Release the mouse button**

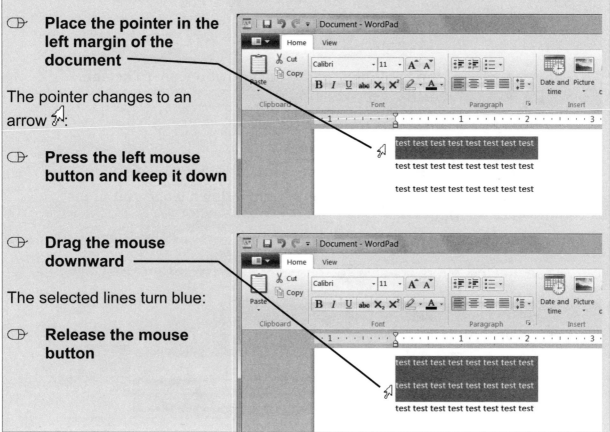

6. Libraries, Folders and Files

In this chapter you will learn how to work with *libraries*, *folders* and *files*. A *file* is the generic name for everything saved on the computer. A file can be a program, a data file with names, text you have written, or a photo. Actually, everything that is on the hard disk of your computer is called a file.

A *folder* is little more than a container in which you store files. If you put thousands of paper files on someone's desk, it would be virtually impossible to find any particular one when you needed it. That is why people often store paper files in folders inside a filing cabinet. Arranging files into logical groups makes it easy to locate any particular file. Folders on your computer work exactly the same way.
Not only do folders hold files, but they also can hold other folders. A folder within a folder is usually called a *subfolder*. You can create any number of subfolders, and each subfolder can hold any number of files and additional subfolders.
In this chapter, you will also learn how to work with *libraries*. You can link folders and files to a library. Subsequently, the folders and files will be displayed in the library. This way, you can easily find your files on your computer.

When it comes to getting organized, you do not need to start from scratch. *Windows 7* comes with a handful of common folders and libraries that you can use as anchors to start organizing your files. Here is a list of some of the most common folders you can use to store your files and folders: *My Documents, My Pictures, My Music, My Videos, My Downloads*. The common libraries are *Documents*, *Pictures*, *Music* and *Videos*. In the previous chapters you have already saved some of your work using the *Documents library*.
Using a folder window, you can work with files and folders that are on the hard disk of your computer. You can delete, copy and move files or folders there.
Perhaps at one time you will want to copy a text or another file to a USB memory stick. You can do that in this folder window as well.

In this chapter, you will learn how to:

- use the folder window and add a new folder;
- move and copy a file to another folder, copy and delete files;
- change the name of a file or folder;
- empty the *Recycle Bin*;
- create a new library and delete it;
- copy a file to a USB memory stick;
- work with a library.

6.1 Opening Your Personal Folder

Your *Personal folder* is a folder that contains your *My Documents*, *My Pictures*, *My Music, My Contacts* folders, as well as other folders. The *Personal folder* is labeled with the name you use to log on to your computer. The *Personal folder* is located at the top of the Start menu. Take a look:

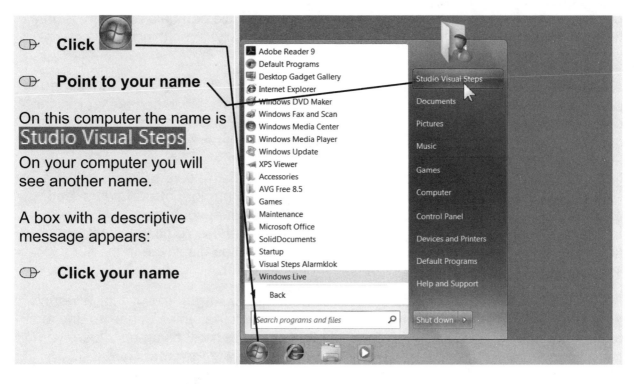

Click

Point to your name

On this computer the name is Studio Visual Steps.
On your computer you will see another name.

A box with a descriptive message appears:

Click your name

Windows Explorer will now be opened:

Now you see this window with all your folders:

This window is called a *folder window*.

The content of the *Personal folder* can be slightly different on every computer.

6.2 Changing the Display of the Folder Window

There are several ways to view your folders in the folder window. Take a look at the display settings of your folder window:

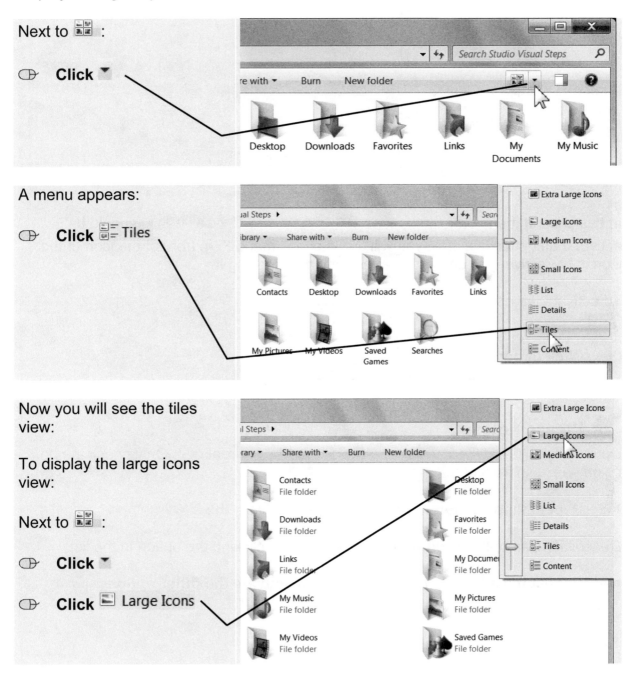

Next to ⊞ :

☞ **Click** ▾

A menu appears:

☞ **Click** ⊞ Tiles

Now you will see the tiles view:

To display the large icons view:

Next to ⊞ :

☞ **Click** ▾

☞ **Click** ⊡ Large Icons

Click Organize ▾

A menu appears:

Point to ☐ Layout

A second menu appears:

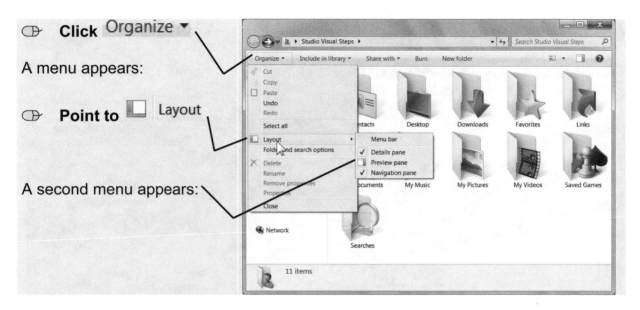

In this second menu only the options Details pane and Navigation pane should be active. If an option is active, you will see a check mark ✔ in front of the icon. If the icon is not active, you can activate the option by clicking it.

To activate the option
Details pane:

Click (if necessary)
Details pane

🢂 Please note:

Do not click Details pane if you see a check mark ✔ in front of it. Only check the box if you see ☐ in front of it.

☞ **Repeat these actions (if necessary) to activate the** Navigation pane

Deactivating an option is done in a similar way, by clicking the option in the list.

☞ **Repeat the actions (if necessary) to deactivate the other options**
Preview pane

Now the folder window on your computer should look the same as the window below:

You are going to open a folder. This is how you do it:

⊕ **Double-click**

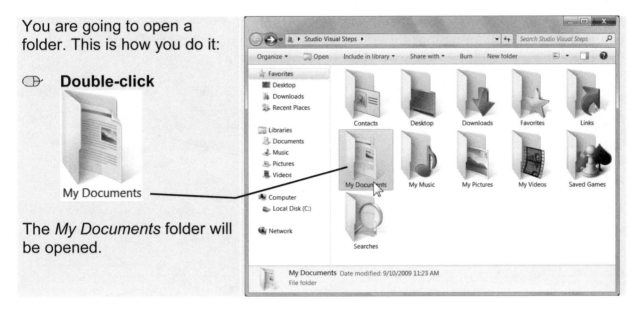

My Documents

The *My Documents* folder will be opened.

6.3 Understanding the Different Parts of a Folder Window

In addition to showing the contents of the folder, a folder window has specific areas that are designed to help you navigate around the folders on the hard disk of your computer, or work with files and folders more easily. Take a look now:

Navigation pane:
It shows all the folders on your computer.

Notice how the *address bar*
⯈ Studio Visual Steps ⯈ My Documents
identifies the folder you are currently using:

The files in this folder are shown as icons in the file list:

When you select a file, you can see information about it in the *details pane*, here:

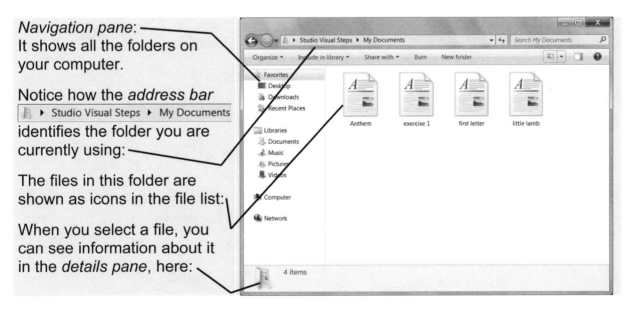

By using the navigation pane on the left side, you can quickly navigate to any folder on your computer. When you click a folder in the navigation pane, you will see the contents of the folder you clicked displayed in the *file list*.

🩹 HELP! I see a different view.

You might see a different view when you navigate through the windows. In every window you can select a different view. To select the settings for the view you see in this book, do as follows:

Next to ⊞⊞ :

⊕ **Click** ▼

⊕ **Click** ▣ Large Icons

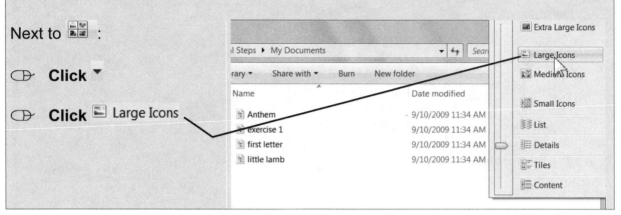

6.4 The My Documents Folder

Windows 7 has a special folder where you can save all of your text documents. This folder is called *My Documents*. You have already saved some of your work in the *My Documents* folder in the previous chapters.

The address bar of the folder window shows your current location on the computer:

📁 ▸ Studio Visual Steps ▸ My Documents

You will now see the content of the *My Documents* folder:

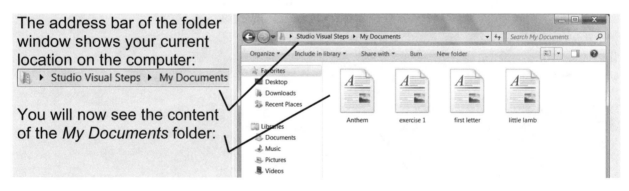

There are at least four files in the *My Documents* folder: your practice texts.

Look closely at these files:

Each file is represented by an icon:

Anthem   exercise 1   first letter   little lamb

6.5 File and Folder Icons

Windows 7 represents files and folders as icons. You may see one or more of the following folder icons:

A folder.
A folder may contain other (sub)folders or files, but it can also be empty.

You may see one or more of the following file icons:

A text file created with the *WordPad* program or with *Microsoft Word*.

A music file.

A photo file.

A video file.

   The library.

The different default libraries on your computer.
Read more about libraries in *section 6.17 Libraries*.

These are only a few examples. There are many, many more icons because each program uses its own file icons.

6.6 Creating a New Folder

A folder is a container that helps you organize your files. Every file on your computer is stored in a folder, and folders can also hold other folders. Folders located inside other folders are often called *subfolders*.
You can add new folders yourself. This can be handy, for example, to keep your letters separate from all your other documents. In this exercise, you will create a new folder inside the *My Documents* folder.

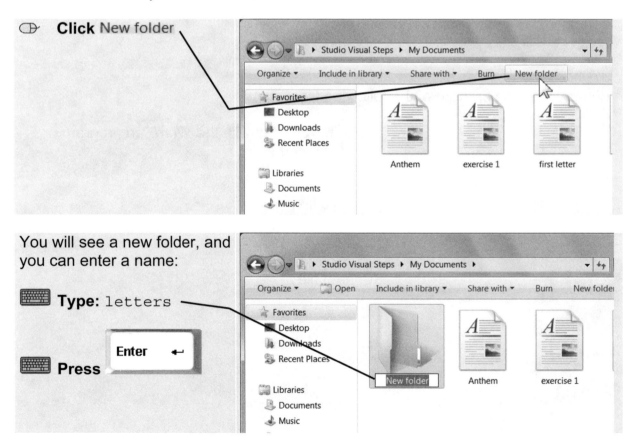

Click New folder

You will see a new folder, and you can enter a name:

Type: letters

Press Enter ↵

Now you have created a new

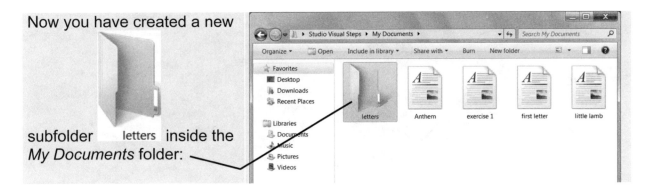

subfolder   letters inside the
My Documents folder:

You can use this *letters* folder to save a letter that you have written in *WordPad*, for example.
To do so, you can minimize the *My Documents* folder window and then start the *WordPad* program.

☞ **Minimize the *My Documents* folder window** 🐾¹

6.7 Saving to a Folder

As an exercise, you will first write a letter in *WordPad* and then you will save it in the

subfolder you just made,   letters .

☞ **Start *WordPad*** 🐾¹⁴

Add some 'content' to your letter, type the following short sentence:

⌨ **Type:**
   letter to be saved

letter to be saved

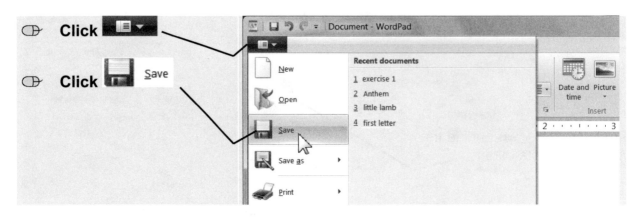

Click

Click ☐ Save

You will now see the *Save As* window:

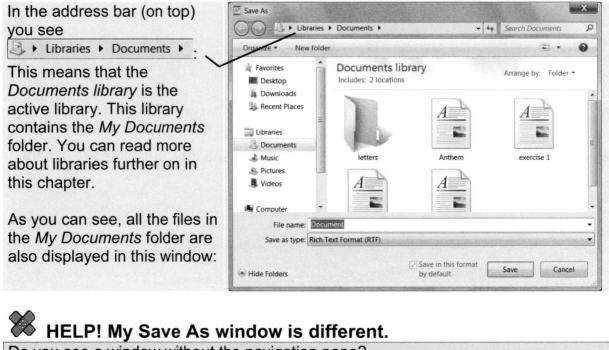

In the address bar (on top) you see
☐ ▸ Libraries ▸ Documents ▸ .
This means that the *Documents library* is the active library. This library contains the *My Documents* folder. You can read more about libraries further on in this chapter.

As you can see, all the files in the *My Documents* folder are also displayed in this window:

✖ HELP! My Save As window is different.

Do you see a window without the navigation pane?

Click 🔽 Browse Folders

You want to save your new letter in the   letters   subfolder. First, you will need to open the *letters* subfolder. It is easiest to do this when the *Documents library* window is already opened:

Double-click   letters

Now the *letters* folder will be opened. Notice that the folder name *letters* now appears in the address bar to the right of *Documents.* The file list is currently empty.

In the lower part of the window, a file name is already shown: Document. That is the *default* name the program always shows. This is how you change the name:

Next to File name::

Click Document

Delete the name ☝35

Type: note

Then:

Click Save

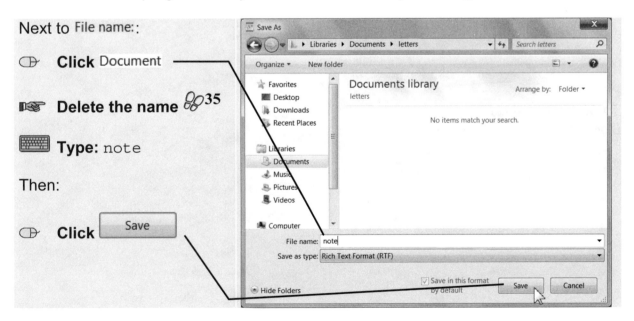

Now the *note* file has been saved to the *letter* folder.

☞ **Close the *WordPad* program** 🦶**15**

Now you can reopen the *My Documents* folder window, to verify that your file has been saved to the *letters* subfolder.

☞ **Open the *My Documents* folder window with the button on the taskbar** 🦶**25**

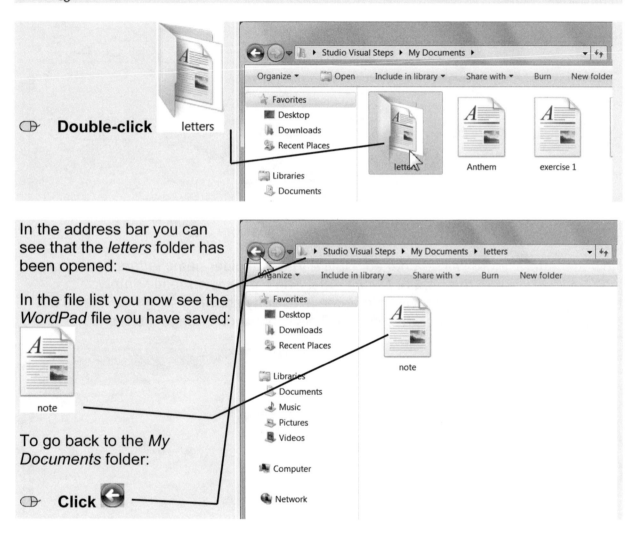

Double-click letters

In the address bar you can see that the *letters* folder has been opened:

In the file list you now see the *WordPad* file you have saved:

note

To go back to the *My Documents* folder:

Click ⬅

6.8 Copying Files

You can also copy files. For example, you can make a second copy of a letter that you want to change slightly. To practice, you can copy your practice texts.

Now you see the files in the *My Documents* folder:

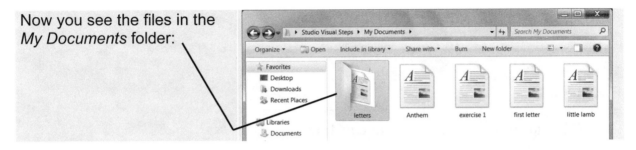

You can now copy one of the practice texts, but remember the rule: select first, then act.

Please note:

Select first ... then act.

Selecting a file is easy: simply click its icon or name.

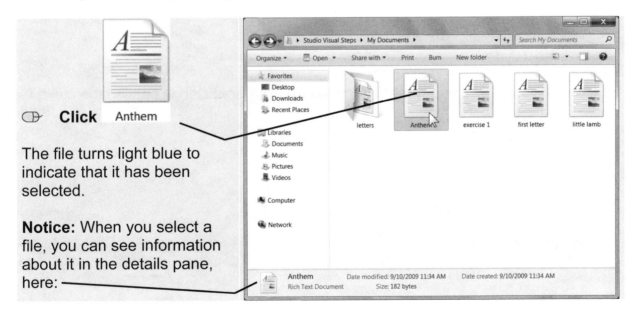

Click Anthem

The file turns light blue to indicate that it has been selected.

Notice: When you select a file, you can see information about it in the details pane, here:

✖ **HELP! There is a blue box around the name.**

Do you see a light blue box around the name? Has the mouse pointer changed into ⊥?

For example:

Anthem

☞ **Click somewhere else in the window**
☞ **Try again**

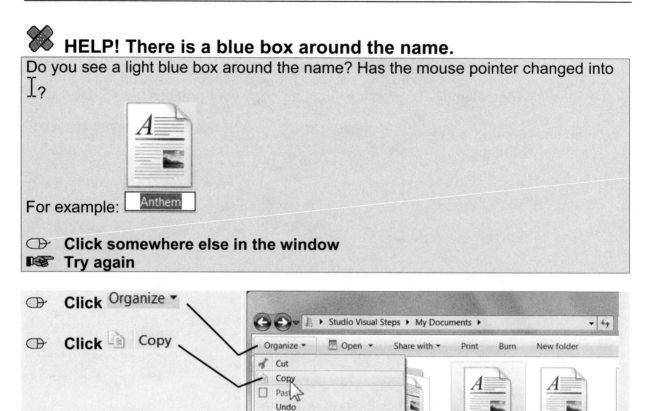

☞ **Click** Organize ▾

☞ **Click** 📄 **Copy**

Windows 7 now knows you want to copy the file. The next step is pasting the copied

file into the   letters   folder:

To open the *letters* folder:

☞ **Double-click** letters

Now you will see the content of the *letters* folder:

👆 **Click** Organize ▾

👆 **Click** ☐ Paste

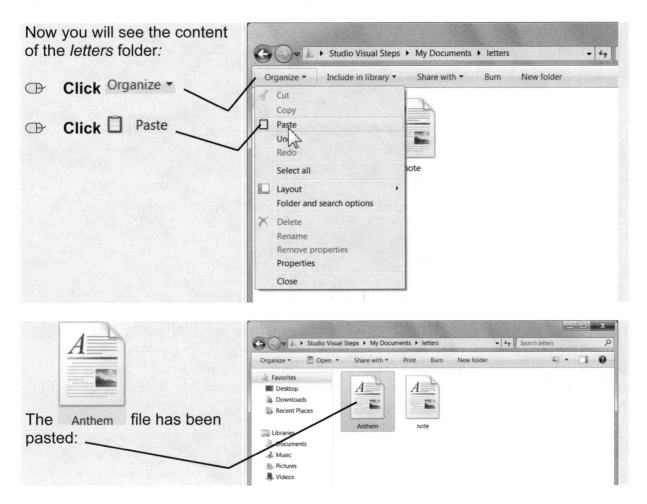

The Anthem file has been pasted:

There are more ways to copy a file. For example by using the right mouse button. Try it:

👆 **Right-click** Anthem

A menu appears:

👆 **Click** Copy

Right-click a blank area of the folder window ——

A menu appears:

Click Paste

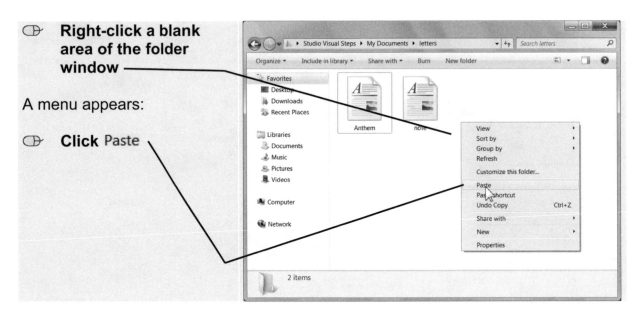

Now there is a copy named Anthem - Copy of the file in the same folder. Notice that the word 'Copy' has been automatically added to the name. This is because files with duplicate names are not allowed inside the same folder. Even though the content of the file is the same, the name of the file has to be different if it is located in the same folder.

Click

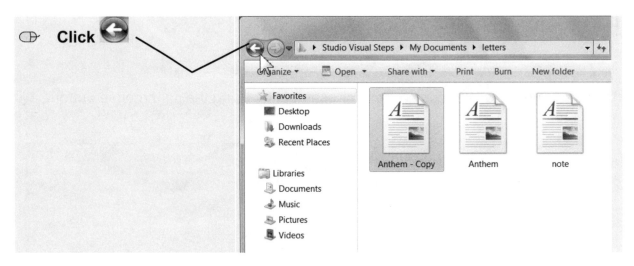

Remember: in the address bar of the window you can see which folder is opened:

▶ Studio Visual Steps ▶ My Documents ▶ letters

6.9 Moving a File

You can also cut a file and paste it into another folder. The file will then be moved to the destination folder.

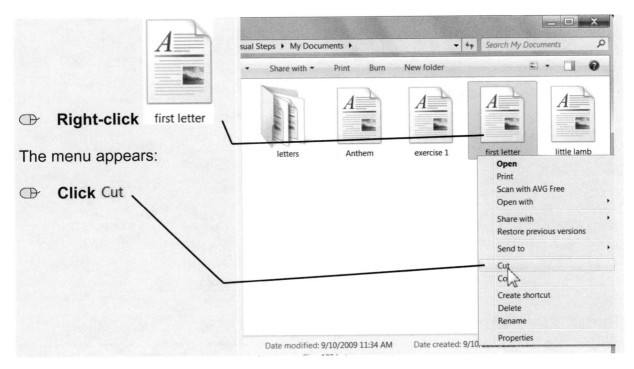

Right-click first letter

The menu appears:

Click Cut

You are going to paste the file into the *letters* folder:

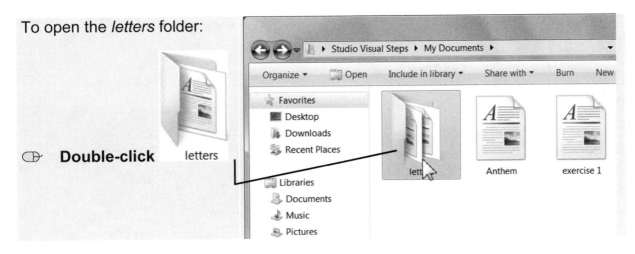

To open the *letters* folder:

Double-click letters

Now you see the folder *letters*:

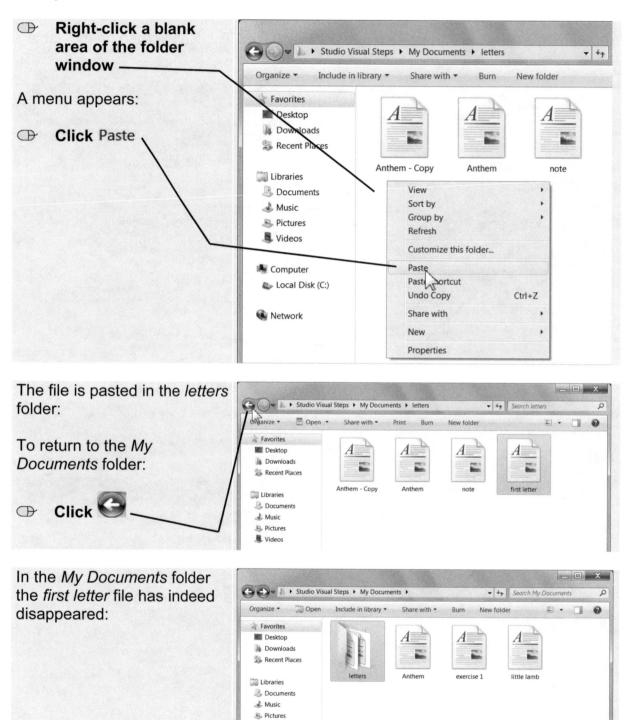

☞ **Right-click a blank area of the folder window** ———

A menu appears:

☞ **Click** Paste

The file is pasted in the *letters* folder:

To return to the *My Documents* folder:

☞ **Click** ⬅

In the *My Documents* folder the *first letter* file has indeed disappeared:

6.10 Dragging and Dropping Files

The easiest way to move files to another folder is by *dragging and dropping*.
Try it:

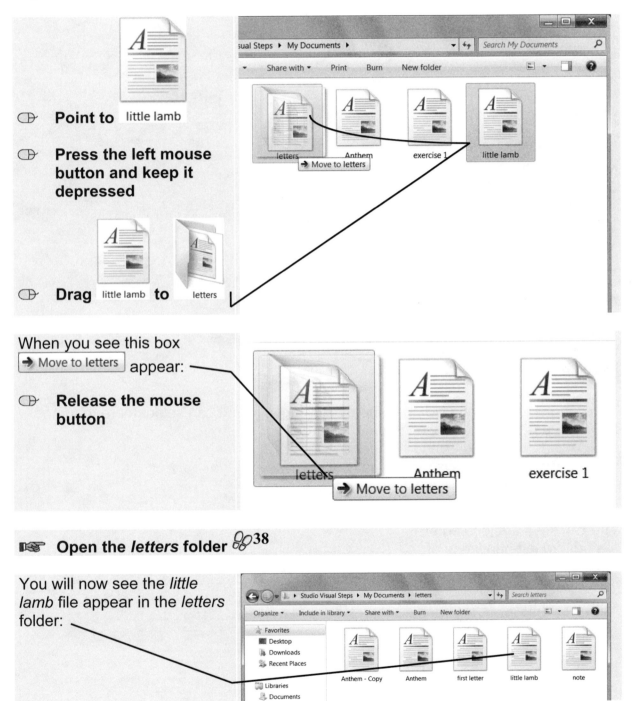

☞ **Open the** *letters* **folder** 🐾38

You will now see the *little lamb* file appear in the *letters* folder:

6.11 Selecting Multiple Files

You can also copy more than one file at a time. To do this, you must select the files first. Go ahead and try:

⊕ **Click**   Anthem

The file is light blue, so you know it has been selected.

⊕ **Click**   first letter

The *first letter* file is now selected, but *Anthem* is no longer selected:

You can select only one file at a time by clicking. But you can select more than one file if you use a special key on your keyboard:

The *Control key*. It always shows the abbreviation 'Ctrl':

Ctrl

The Ctrl keys are located at the bottom left-hand side of the keyboard:

Use one of these keys.

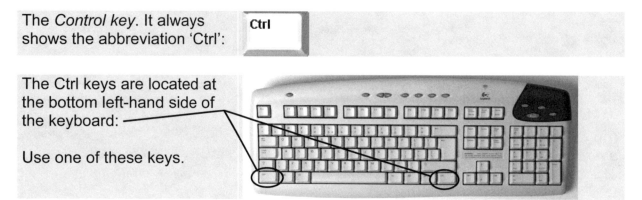

The Ctrl key is used together with the mouse. The first letter file is still selected.

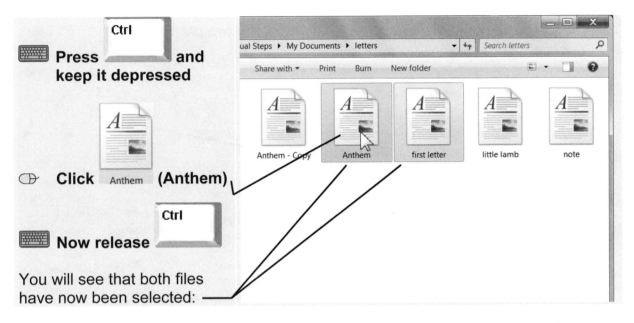

Press Ctrl **and keep it depressed**

Click Anthem **(Anthem)**

Now release Ctrl

You will see that both files have now been selected: ──

You can select even more files by using the Ctrl key. Then you can copy and paste, or cut and paste, or drag the group of selected files to their destination folder. For now, that is not necessary. This is how you clear the selection:

Click on any blank area of the folder window ──

The selection is cleared.

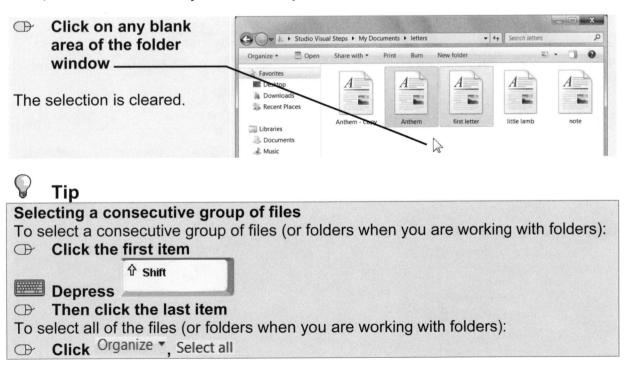

💡 Tip

Selecting a consecutive group of files
To select a consecutive group of files (or folders when you are working with folders):

Click the first item

Depress ⇧ Shift

Then click the last item

To select all of the files (or folders when you are working with folders):

Click Organize ▾, Select all

6.12 Changing the File Name

Sometimes you may want to give a file a different name. Maybe because you have several documents about the same subject, for example, and you want to be able to clearly distinguish one document from another.
You can try changing the name of a file with one of the two practice letters.

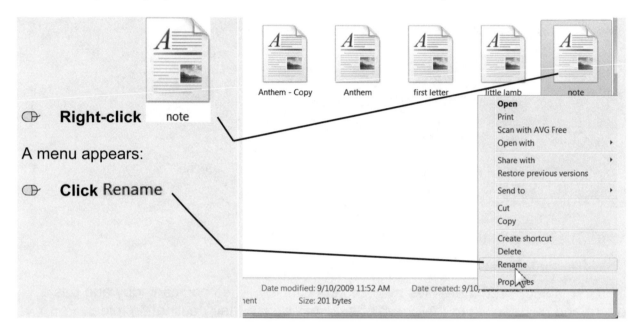

Right-click note

A menu appears:

Click Rename

Date modified: 9/10/2009 11:52 AM   Date created: 9/10/...
Size: 201 bytes

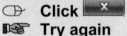 HELP! I see another window

Do you unexpectedly see the window for *WordPad* or *Microsoft Word*?
If so, you have double-clicked the file name, and opened the program. To close the program:

Click

Try again

Now the word *note* is highlighted with a blue background color:

Type the new name:
exercise do not save

Press Enter

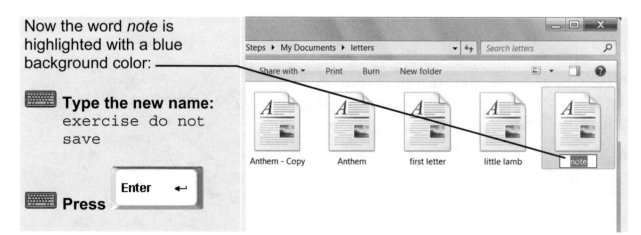

The name has changed:

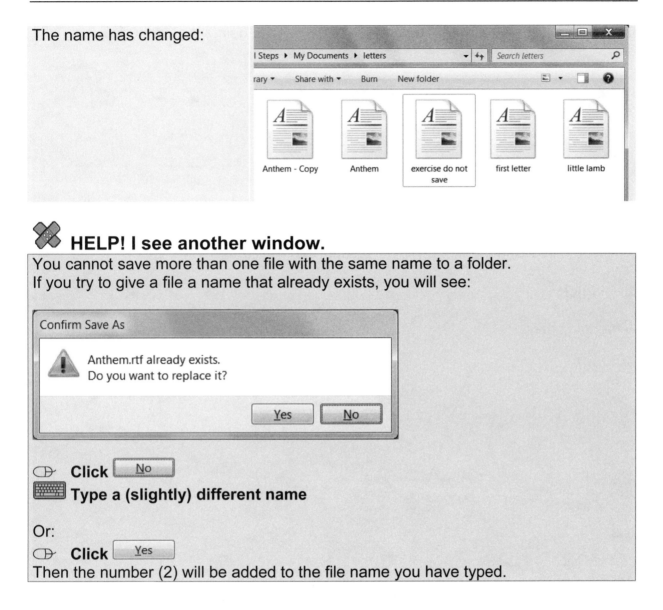

HELP! I see another window.

You cannot save more than one file with the same name to a folder.
If you try to give a file a name that already exists, you will see:

Confirm Save As

Anthem.rtf already exists.
Do you want to replace it?

Yes   No

Click ⬚ No ⬚
Type a (slightly) different name

Or:

Click ⬚ Yes ⬚
Then the number (2) will be added to the file name you have typed.

6.13 Deleting Files

It is wise to plan a regular 'spring cleaning' of your hard disk. To keep your hard disk manageable, you can delete files you no longer need. To practice, you can delete the *Anthem - Copy* file in the *letters* folder, because this is a copy that you do not really need.

Please note:

Select first … then act.

It is important to select the file carefully, so you will not delete the wrong files.

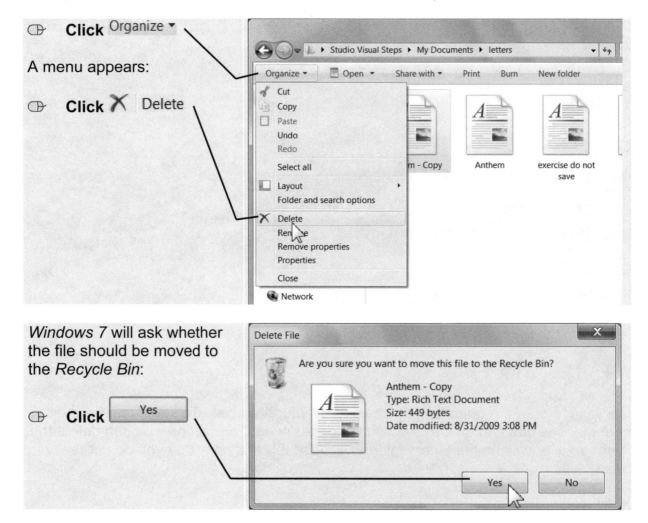

Now you can delete the file. It will be 'tossed' into the *Recycle Bin*.

The file (Anthem-Copy) has now disappeared from the *letters* folder window. Files that have been deleted are not gone forever. As a kind of safety measure, they are moved to the *Recycle Bin* first. They are not really gone forever until you empty the *Recycle Bin*. As long as a file is in the *Recycle Bin*, you can retrieve it later if you need it.

Tip

Selecting multiple files
You can also delete multiple files at the same time. You must select them first by clicking them while pressing the Ctrl key or the Shift key. Then you can delete them.

Tip

Selecting an entire folder

You can also select an entire folder you want to delete. You can select a folder by clicking it; then you can delete it.

Tip

Only your files
Be careful when deleting files. Only delete files that you yourself have made.
If you did not create the file, you might not be able to delete it.
Also, you cannot delete a file (or the folder that contains it) if the file is currently opened in a program. Make sure that the file is not opened in any program, and then try to delete the file or folder again.
Never delete files or folders for programs that you do not use. Program files have to be deleted in a different way.

6.14 The Recycle Bin

All the files that you delete from your hard disk end up in the *Recycle Bin*. You can open the *Recycle Bin* to see its contents. It will contain all the files you have deleted. You can open the *Recycle Bin* with its own icon on the desktop:

☞ **Minimize the *letters* window** ✂¹

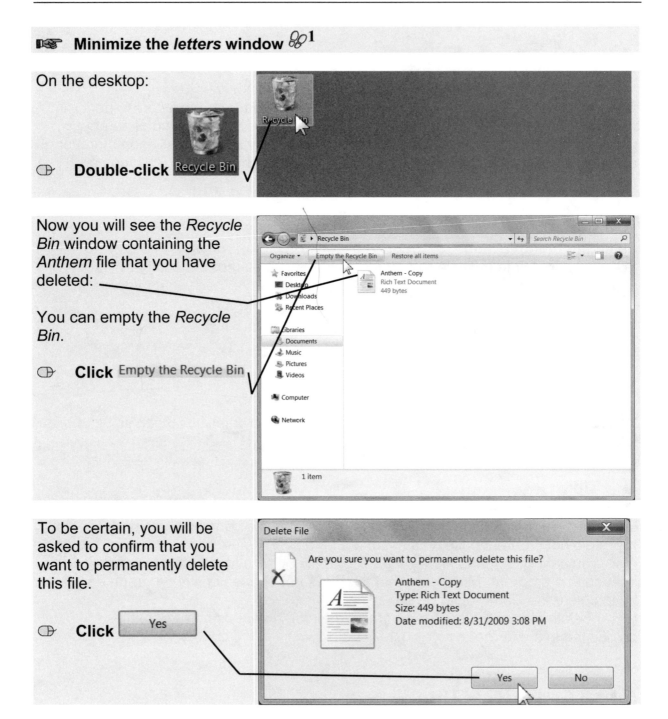

On the desktop:

⊕ **Double-click** Recycle Bin

Now you will see the *Recycle Bin* window containing the *Anthem* file that you have deleted: —

You can empty the *Recycle Bin*.

⊕ **Click** Empty the Recycle Bin

To be certain, you will be asked to confirm that you want to permanently delete this file.

⊕ **Click** Yes

Now the file has been permanently deleted and cannot be retrieved.

☞ **Close the *Recycle Bin* window** ✂⁴

☞ **Open the *letters* window with the button on the taskbar** ✂²⁵

Tip

When should you empty the Recycle Bin?
You do not need to empty the *Recycle Bin* every time you delete a file. You only need to empty it when you want to permanently delete a file. It is better to collect your deleted files in the *Recycle Bin* and to wait until you do your 'spring cleaning'; then you can empty the whole bin.

 Tip

Is there anything in the Recycle Bin?
You can tell by the icon for the *Recycle Bin* on the desktop whether there is anything in it. The icon changes its appearance:

not empty   empty

6.15 Copying to a USB Stick

You may sometimes need to copy something to a USB stick. For example, you might want to transfer a file to another PC or store a backup copy of the file away from the computer. Try this now by copying the *Anthem* file to a USB memory stick.

➥ Please note:

In order to work through this section, you will need a USB stick.
A USB stick is a small, portable device that plugs into a computer's USB port. Like a hard disk drive, a USB flash drive stores information, but with a flash drive you can easily transfer that information from one computer to another.
If you do not have a USB stick, you can skip this section.

First you have to insert the USB stick into the computer.

☞ Locate the USB port on your computer

A USB port can be situated on the front or the back of the computer, or both.
On a laptop, a USB port could also be located on one of its sides.

☞ **Insert the USB stick into the USB port and gently push it in**

Having trouble?

☞ **Then turn the stick over and try again**

The first time you use the USB stick you will see this:

On the right side of the taskbar you see this notification:

Installing device driver software ⚡ ✕
Click here for status.

11:49 AM
9/7/2009

Wait a moment until you see this text balloon appear:

The USB stick is ready to use.

Your device is ready to use ⚡ ✕
Device driver software installed successfully.

Windows 7
Evaluation copy. Build 7100

11:51 AM
9/7/2009

You will also see this window:

⊕ **Click**

Open folder to view files
using Windows Explorer

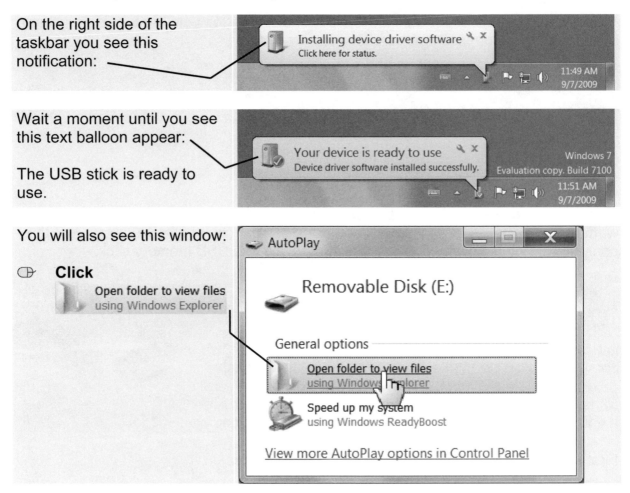

AutoPlay

Removable Disk (E:)

General options

Open folder to view files
using Windows Explorer

Speed up my system
using Windows ReadyBoost

View more AutoPlay options in Control Panel

A second folder window
appears on top of the window:

> ▶ Studio Visual Steps ▶ My Documents ▶ lett

In the address bar you see
this is the folder window of
the USB stick:

▶ Computer ▶ Removable Disk (E:)

In this figure the USB stick is
called *Removable Disk (E:)*.
On your computer a different
letter may be used.

By the icon on the taskbar
you can tell that two windows

have been opened :

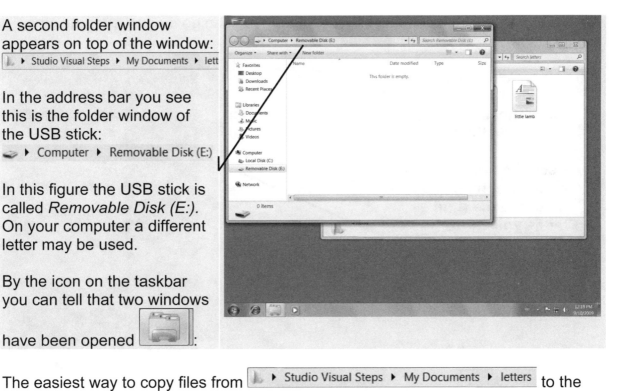

The easiest way to copy files from ▶ Studio Visual Steps ▶ My Documents ▶ letters to the
USB stick folder Removable Disk (E:) is by using both folder windows. First you need to
position both folder windows next to each other. *Windows 7* has a very handy option
for this: drag both windows to the exterior of the window, as far as you can. Now the
windows will appear side by side. This is how you do it:

In the window of the
Removable Disk:

☞ **Place the mouse
pointer on the title bar**

☞ **Keep the mouse
button depressed and
drag it to the left as far
as you can**

☞ **Release the mouse
button**

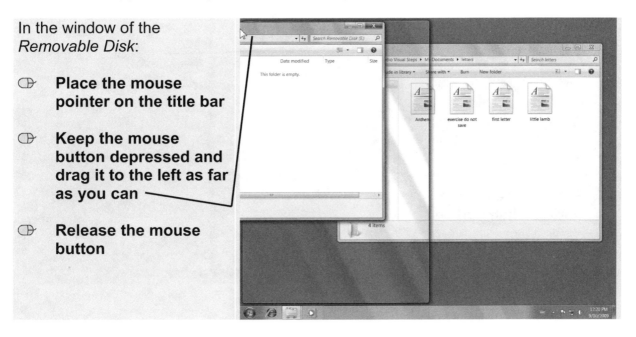

Now the window will take up half of the desktop. You can do the same for the other folder window:

In the *letters* folder window:

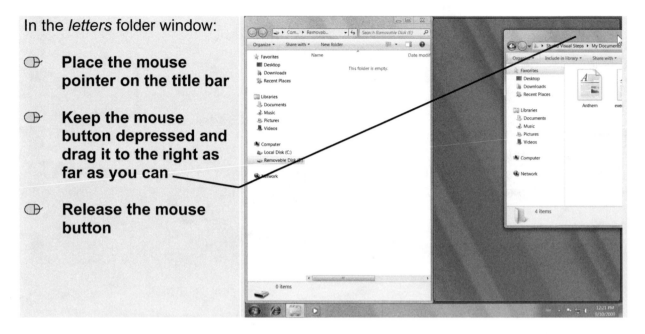

☞ **Place the mouse pointer on the title bar**

☞ **Keep the mouse button depressed and drag it to the right as far as you can**

☞ **Release the mouse button**

You can see the content of both folder windows. Now you can drag and drop a file from the window ▋ ▸ Studio Visual Steps ▸ My Documents ▸ letters to the Removable Disk (E:) folder.

In the right window:

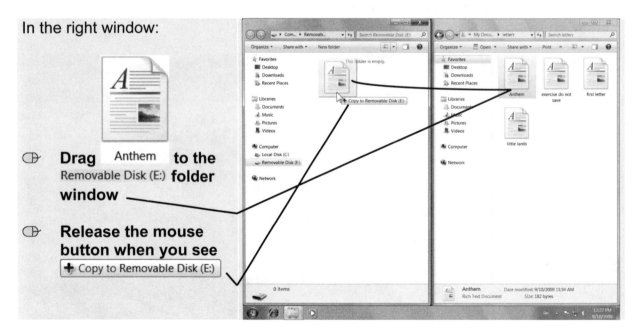

☞ **Drag** Anthem **to the Removable Disk (E:) folder window**

☞ **Release the mouse button when you see** ✚ Copy to Removable Disk (E:)

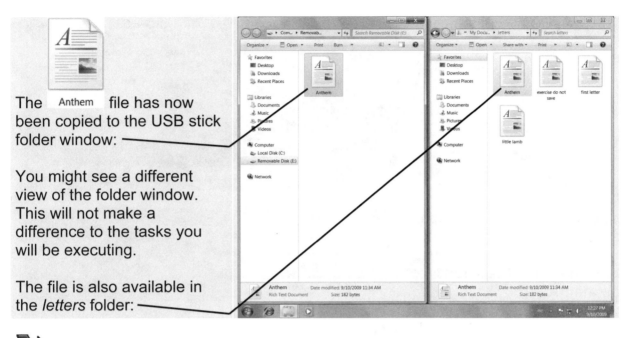

The Anthem file has now been copied to the USB stick folder window: ——

You might see a different view of the folder window. This will not make a difference to the tasks you will be executing.

The file is also available in the *letters* folder: ——

Please note:

- When you drag a file (or folder) into a folder on the same hard disk (your own computer), the file (or folder) will be *moved* to the destination folder.
- When you drag a file (or folder) into a folder on a different hard disk or USB stick, the file will be *copied* to the folder on the destination disk or stick.

Close both folder windows ♺⁴

6.16 Safely Removing a USB Stick

Before removing storage devices, such as USB sticks, you need to make sure that the computer has finished saving any information to the device. If the device has an activity light flashing, wait for a few seconds until the light has finished flashing before removing it.

You can use the *Safely Remove Hardware* icon 🔌 that appears after you have clicked ▲, to ensure that the USB stick will be ready to be removed. You can display the icon like this:

At the lower right-hand side of the taskbar:

⊕ **Click ▲** ——

⊕ **Double-click the icon** 🔌 ——

Click the USB Stick

Eject USB FLASH DRIVE

- Removable Disk (E:)

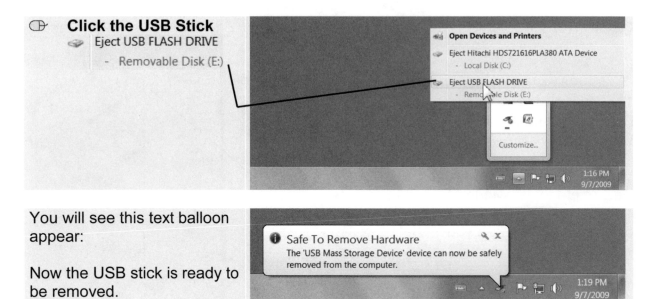

You will see this text balloon appear:

Now the USB stick is ready to be removed.

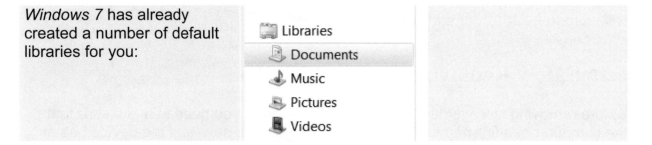

☞ **Remove the USB stick from the computer**

6.17 Libraries

In *Windows 7* you can link folders and files to a *library*.

Windows 7 has already created a number of default libraries for you:

📁 Libraries

   📄 Documents

   🎵 Music

   🖼 Pictures

   🎞 Videos

These libraries allow you to quickly and easily retrieve your own files and folders. For instance, the *Documents library* contains all the files from the *My Documents* folder in your *Personal folder*, as well as the *Public Documents* folder. The *Public Documents* folder is a folder you share with the other users on your computer.

Using folders and files in libraries works exactly the same way as using files and folders in a regular folder. If you want to open and save a file while using a program, such as *WordPad*, the first thing you will see is the library.

First you need to open the libraries. You can use the button on the taskbar to do this:

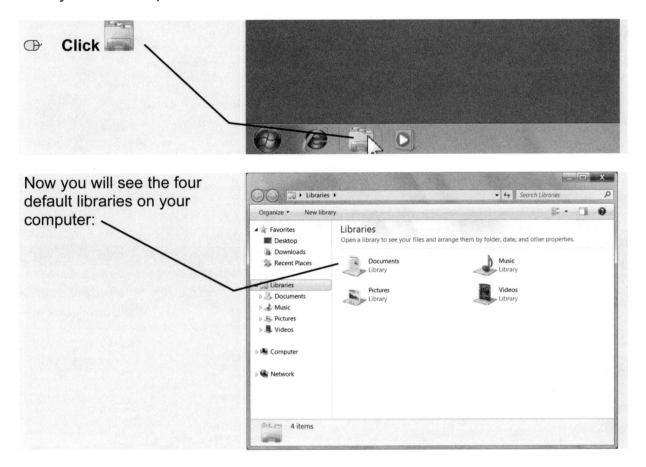

6.18 Creating a Library

In *Windows 7* you can also add a new library yourself, and organize certain folders on your computer within this library. In this example you will create a library containing the following folders:

- the *letters* folder;
- the *Samples Pictures* folder, which is a default folder stored on your computer's hard disk.

By adding these folders to a library you will see how easy it is to collect files from different locations on your computer and organize them in a single library.

Tip

Library with holiday pictures and stories
For example, try to create a library for your collection of holiday pictures and stories.

To create a new library:

⊕ **Click** New library

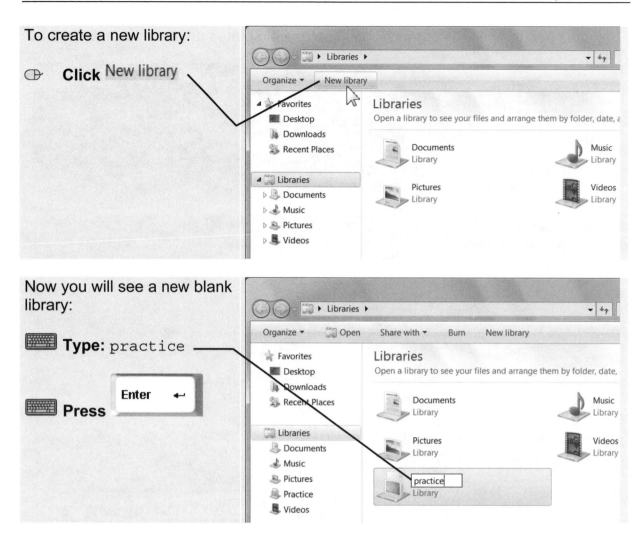

Now you will see a new blank library:

⌨ **Type:** practice

⌨ **Press** Enter ←

Now you have created a new library. You can start adding folders to this library right away:

⊕ **Double-click** Practice Library

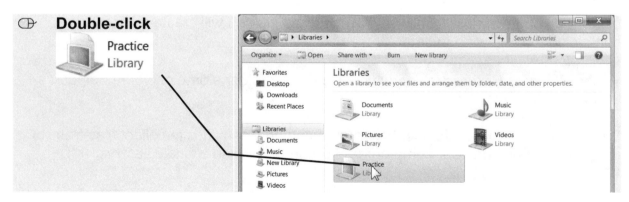

You will see that this library is still empty. Now you are going to add a folder:

⊕ **Click** Include a folder

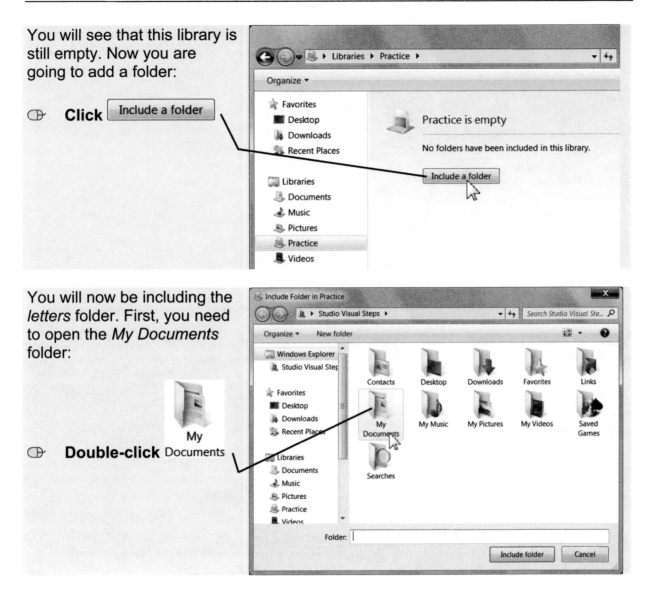

You will now be including the *letters* folder. First, you need to open the *My Documents* folder:

⊕ **Double-click** My Documents

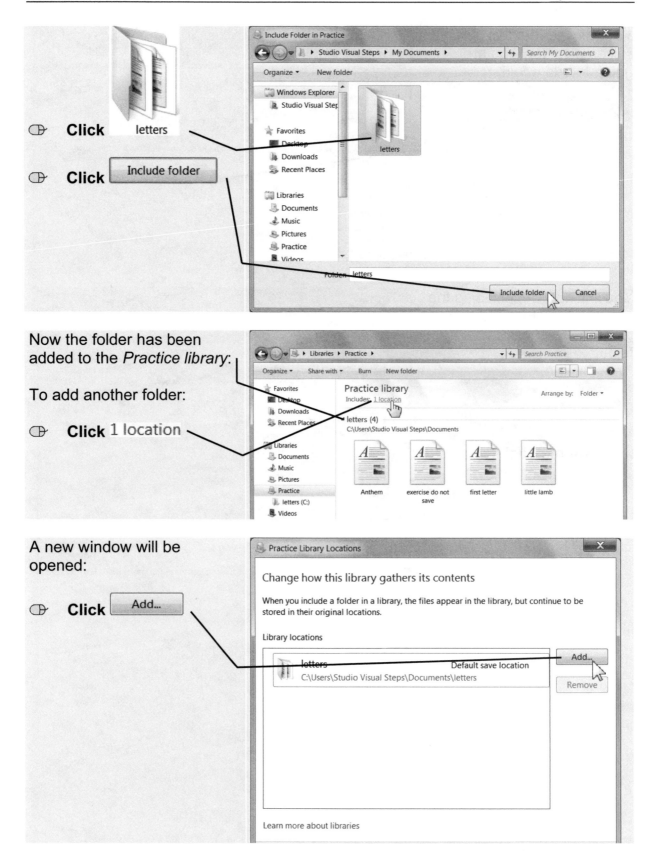

👆 **Click** letters

👆 **Click** Include folder

Now the folder has been added to the *Practice library*:

To add another folder:

👆 **Click** 1 location

A new window will be opened:

👆 **Click** Add...

You will again see the *Include Folder in Practice* window:

⊕ **Click** 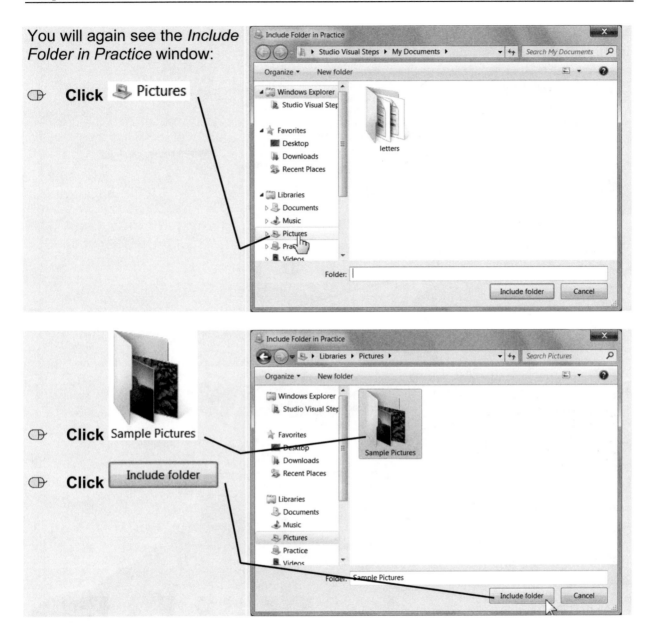 Pictures

⊕ **Click** Sample Pictures

⊕ **Click** Include folder

Now you will see both folders in this window:

Click OK

Here you see the files in the library:

To return to the window with all the libraries:

Click Libraries

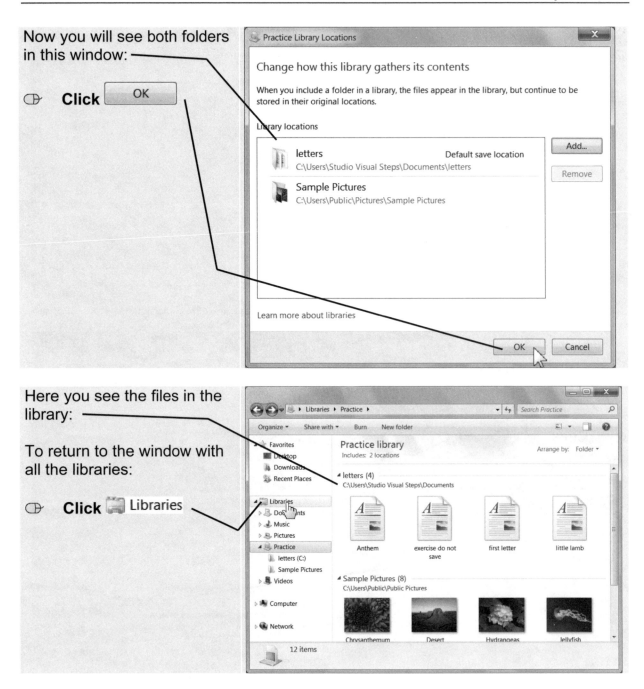

Now you can remove the *Practice library*. This action will only remove the library. The *letters* and *Sample Pictures* folders will remain stored in the same location on your computer's hard disk.

☞ **Right-click** Practice Library

☞ **Click** Delete

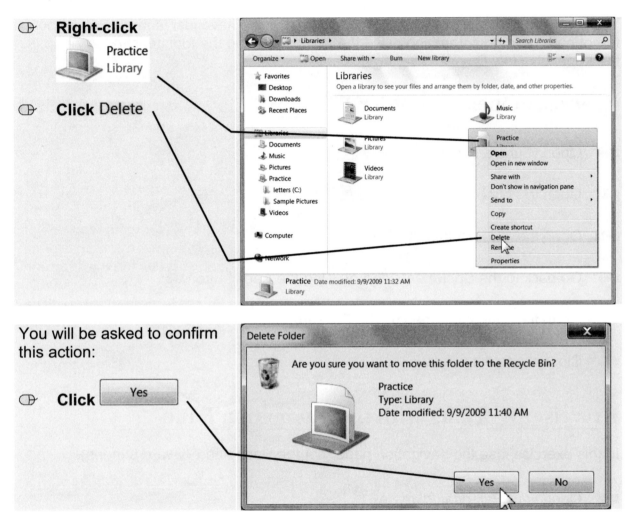

You will be asked to confirm this action:

☞ **Click** Yes

Now the *Practice library* has been removed from your computer.

🖙 **Close the *Libraries* window** ❪❪⁴

In this chapter you have learned how to use the folder windows. You have practiced moving, deleting and copying files, dragging files to a USB stick and creating a library.

You can practice a little more by doing the exercises in this chapter.

6.19 Exercises

☙

The following exercises will help you master what you have just learned. Have you forgotten how to do something? Use the number beside the footsteps to look it up in the appendix *How Do I Do That Again?*

Exercise: Opening Folder Windows

☞ Open your *Personal folder*. ☙^{63}

☞ Open the *My Documents* folder. ☙^{41}

☞ Open the *letters* folder. ☙^{38}

☞ Go back to the *Documents library* using the Back button. ☙^{39}

☞ Go to the *letters* folder using the Forward button. ☙^{39}

☞ Close the folder window. ☙^{4}

Exercise: Working with the Navigation Pane

In this exercise, use the navigation pane (not the Back and Forward buttons).

☞ Open your *Personal folder*. ☙^{63}

☞ Open the *Documents library*. ☙^{41}

☞ Open the *Pictures library*. ☙^{41}

☞ Open the *Documents library*. ☙^{41}

☞ Close the folder window. ☙^{4}

Exercise: Creating a New Folder

☞ Open your *Personal folder*. 🦶🦶63

☞ Open the *My Documents* folder. 🦶🦶41

☞ Create a new folder with the name *practice*. 🦶🦶65

☞ Open the new *practice* folder. 🦶🦶41

☞ Close the folder window. 🦶🦶4

Exercise: Copying Files

Please note: in order to do this exercise, you need to do the exercise above first.

☞ Open your *Personal folder*. 🦶🦶63

☞ Open the *My Documents* folder. 🦶🦶41

☞ Copy the *Anthem* file to the *practice* folder. 🦶🦶42

☞ Close the folder window. 🦶🦶4

Exercise: Renaming a File

Please note: in order to do this exercise, you need to do the exercises above first.

☞ Open your *Personal folder*. 🦶🦶63

☞ Open the *My Documents* folder. 🦶🦶41

☞ Open the *practice* folder. 🦶🦶41

☞ Change the name of the *Anthem* file to *song*. 🦶🦶43

☞ Close the folder window. 🦶🦶4

Exercise: Deleting Files

Please note: in order to do this exercise, you need to do the exercises above first.

☞ Open your *Personal folder*. 𝒮𝒮⁶³

☞ Open the *My Documents* folder. 𝒮𝒮⁴¹

☞ Open the new *practice* folder. 𝒮𝒮⁴¹

☞ Delete the *song* file in this folder. 𝒮𝒮⁴⁴

☞ Close the folder window. 𝒮𝒮⁴

Exercise: Renaming and Deleting a Folder

To rename and delete folders you just need to do the same thing as you do with files. Try it:

☞ Open your *Personal folder*. 𝒮𝒮⁶³

☞ Open the *My Documents* folder. 𝒮𝒮⁴¹

☞ Rename the *practice* folder and call it *my letters*. 𝒮𝒮⁴³

☞ Delete the *my letters* folder. 𝒮𝒮⁴⁴

☞ Close the folder window. 𝒮𝒮⁴

Exercise: Creating a New Library

☞ Open the *Libraries* window. 𝒮𝒮⁶⁴

☞ Create a new library with the name *exercise*. 𝒮𝒮⁶⁶

☞ Add the *letters* folder to the *Exercise library*. 𝒮𝒮⁶⁵

☞ Delete the *Exercise library*. 𝒮𝒮⁴⁴

☞ Close the folder window. 𝒮𝒮⁴

6.20 Background Information

Dictionary

Address bar	The address bar appears at the top of every library or folder window and displays your current location as a series of links separated by arrows. By using the address bar, you can see which folder is opened.
File	The generic name for everything saved on the computer. A file can be a program, a data file with names, text you have written, or a photo. Actually, everything that is on the hard disk of your computer is called a *file*.
File list	This is where the contents of the current library or folder are displayed.
Folder	A folder is a container that helps you organize your files. Every file on your computer is stored in a folder, and folders can also hold other folders. Folders can also be organized into libraries.
Folder list	List of folders in the navigation pane. By using the folder list in the navigation pane, you can navigate directly to the folder or library you are interested in by clicking on this folder.
Folder window	When you open a folder on the desktop, a folder window appears. A folder window has specific areas that are designed to help you navigate around the folders on the hard disk of your computer or work with files, folders and libraries more easily.
Hard disk	The primary storage device located inside a computer. Also called a hard drive or hard disk drive, it is the place where your files and programs are typically stored.
Library	In libraries you can organize and manage documents, music, images, and all other files. You can search for files in exactly the same way you search folders, and you can order files by their properties, such as the date, type, or author. The difference is, that in a library the files that are included will still remain stored in their original location on your computer. The actual files will not be stored in the library.

- Continue reading on the next page -

Navigation pane	Shows a list of folders and libraries that can be opened in the folder window.
Recycle Bin	When you delete a file or folder, it goes to the *Recycle Bin*. You can retrieve a file from the *Recycle Bin*. But if you empty the *Recycle Bin*, all of its contents are permanently gone.
Search box	A box you find in a folder window. If you type something in the search box, the contents of the folder are immediately filtered to show only those files that match what you have typed. However, the search box does not automatically search your entire computer. It only searches the current folder and any of its subfolders.
USB port	A narrow, rectangular connection point on a computer where you can connect a universal serial bus (USB) device such as a USB stick.
USB stick	A small portable device, to store files and folders. Plugs into a computer's USB port. *Windows 7* will show a USB stick as a removable disk.

Source: Windows Help and Support

USB sticks, CDs and DVDs

USB sticks, CDs and DVDs are storage media often used to store files outside the computer. For example, you can use them to transfer files to another computer or to save a *backup* copy. Software manufacturers often provide their products on a CD-ROM or DVD-ROM.

USB stick

A USB stick is a small storage medium with a large storage capacity. You can insert it directly into your PC's USB port. The storage capacity can vary from 16 MB to 32 GB or more. The price depends on the capacity. You can write files directly to a USB stick in *Windows 7*. The memory can be reused.

External hard disk

An external hard disk is also a portable hard disk. Usually, it has a larger storage capacity than a USB stick. An external hard disk can have a storage capacity of up to one terrabite (about 1000 GB).

CD-ROM and DVD-ROM

Many software manufacturers deliver their software on CD-ROMs. These days, software manufacturers deliver very large programs on DVD-ROMs. Large files like movies are also released on DVD-ROM. You can play these CD-ROMs and DVD-ROMs in your CD player or DVD player, but you can not write data to them. ROM means Read Only Memory.

Writable CDs and DVDs

If your computer includes a CD or DVD recorder, you can copy files to a writable disc.

The parts of the Open window

This is the window that you use in *WordPad*, for example, to open a file from your hard disk. It looks like the *Save As* window. Windows such as these are easy to use.

Libraries ▸ Documents ▸

The address bar identifies the library or folder you are in.

The files contained in this library are shown as icons here.

The navigation pane shows the libraries or folders that can be opened.
When you click a folder, the content appears.

This button is used to view the list of files in a different way.

New folder
With this button you can create a new folder within the current library or folder.

Search Documents 🔎

Use this box to search files.

File name: Anthem

This box will automatically show the name of the file you just clicked.

At All Wordpad Documents (*. ▼ , you can see which document types can be opened.

Open ▼ With this button you can open a file or folder.

Cancel With this button you can return to the program. The file will not be opened.

6.21 Tips

Tip

The folder list in the navigation pane

When you use the folder list in the navigation pane in the folder window, you can navigate directly to the library or folder that contains the (sub)folders or files you are interested in.

All you have to do is click a folder or library name and the content will be displayed in the file list.
Here you see the content of the *Personal folder*:

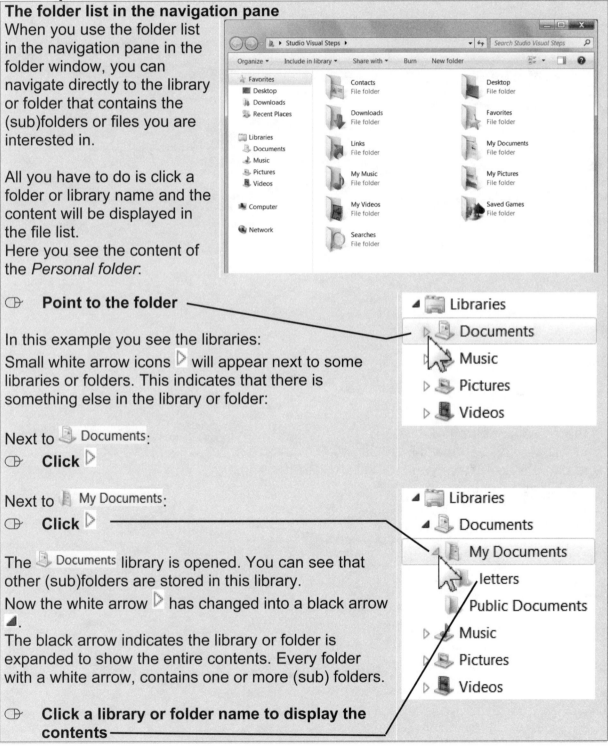

☞ **Point to the folder**

In this example you see the libraries:

Small white arrow icons ▷ will appear next to some libraries or folders. This indicates that there is something else in the library or folder:

Next to 🗎 Documents:
☞ **Click** ▷

Next to 🗎 My Documents:
☞ **Click** ▷

The 🗎 Documents library is opened. You can see that other (sub)folders are stored in this library.
Now the white arrow ▷ has changed into a black arrow ◢.
The black arrow indicates the library or folder is expanded to show the entire contents. Every folder with a white arrow, contains one or more (sub) folders.

☞ **Click a library or folder name to display the contents**

💡 Tip

Searching files in a folder

There are many ways to find your files on your computer. Most of the time, you will start by using the search box that is available within any folder or library window.

👉 **Click in the search box**

⌨️ **Start typing**

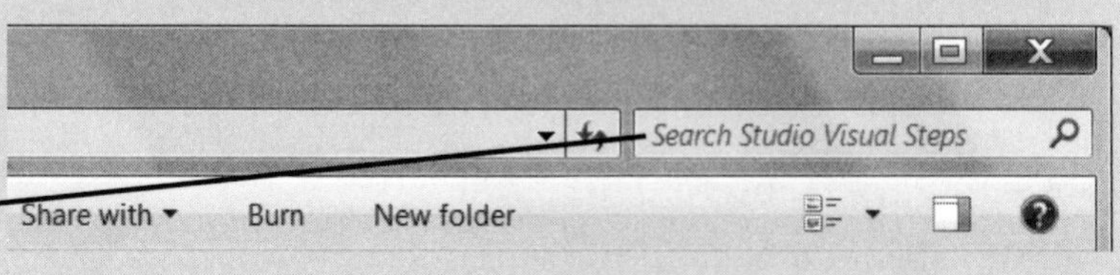

As you type, the search results appear above the file list:

Just click a file name to open it.

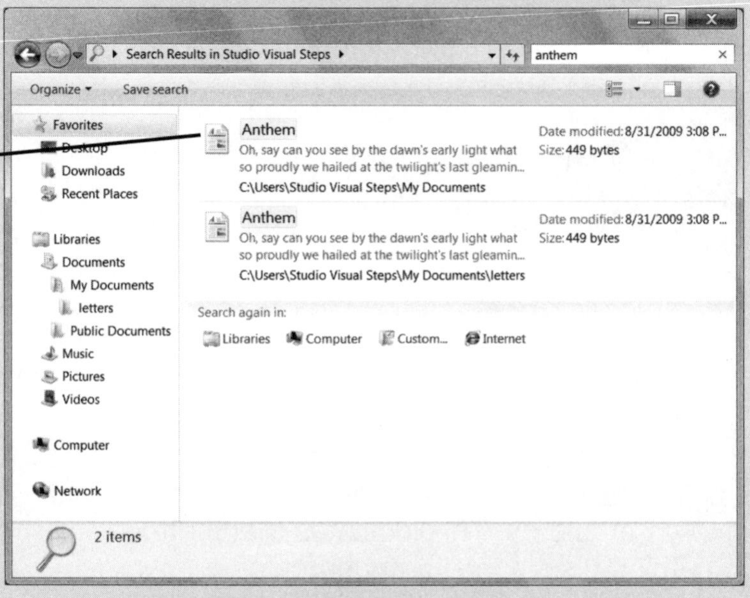

If there are no search results, you will see this window. Now you can choose where you would like to continue searching, for instance your computer's entire hard disk:

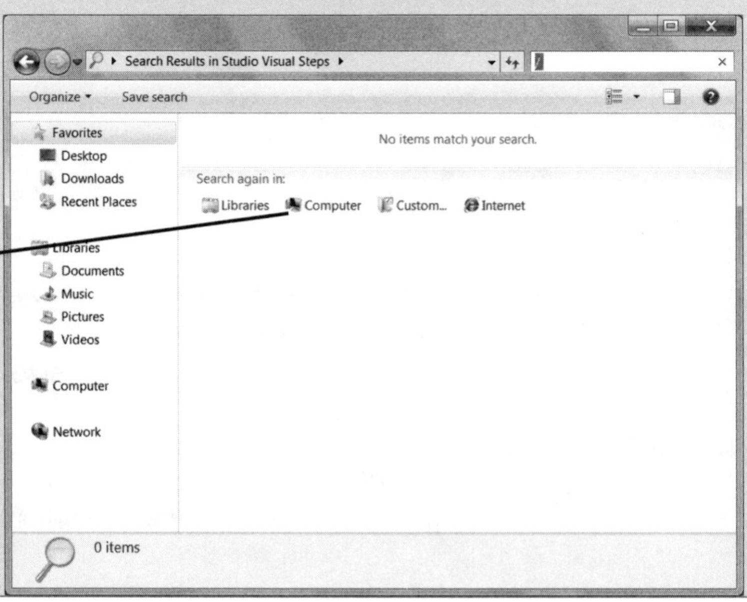

Tip

Finding a file

Have you forgotten where you have saved an important file?
Then you can use the *Windows 7 search box*:

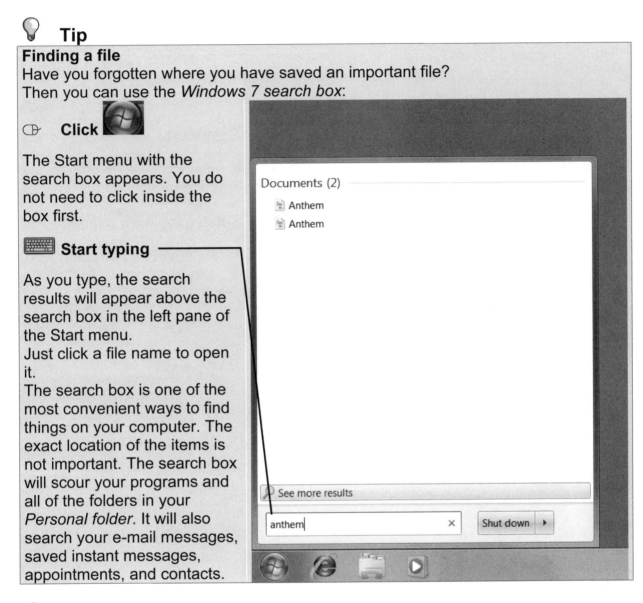

☞ **Click**

The Start menu with the
search box appears. You do
not need to click inside the
box first.

⌨ **Start typing**

As you type, the search
results will appear above the
search box in the left pane of
the Start menu.
Just click a file name to open
it.
The search box is one of the
most convenient ways to find
things on your computer. The
exact location of the items is
not important. The search box
will scour your programs and
all of the folders in your
Personal folder. It will also
search your e-mail messages,
saved instant messages,
appointments, and contacts.

Tip

File names

You cannot use any of the following characters in a file name: \ / ? : * " > < |

🔆 Tip

Finding the My documents folder
There are various ways to find the *My Documents* folder. Here are some examples:

Example 1:

🖰 **Click**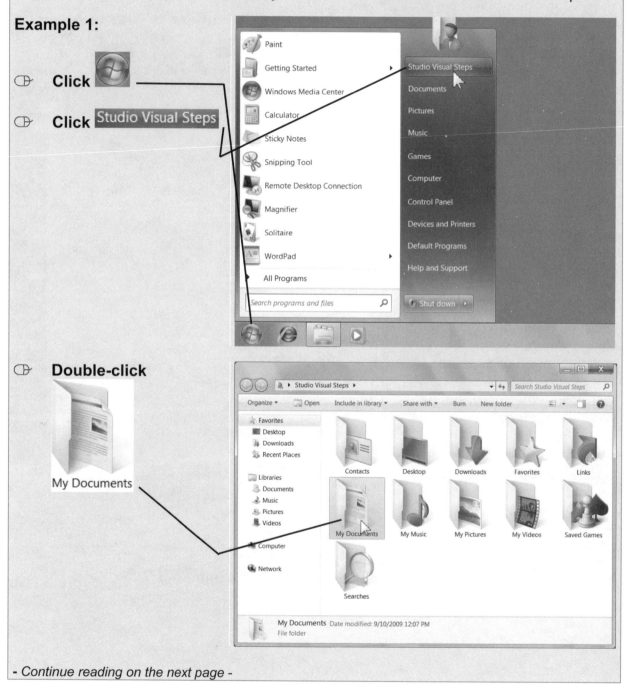

🖰 **Click** Studio Visual Steps

🖰 **Double-click**

My Documents

- Continue reading on the next page -

Now you will see the *My Documents* folder window:

This is the actual *My Documents* folder.

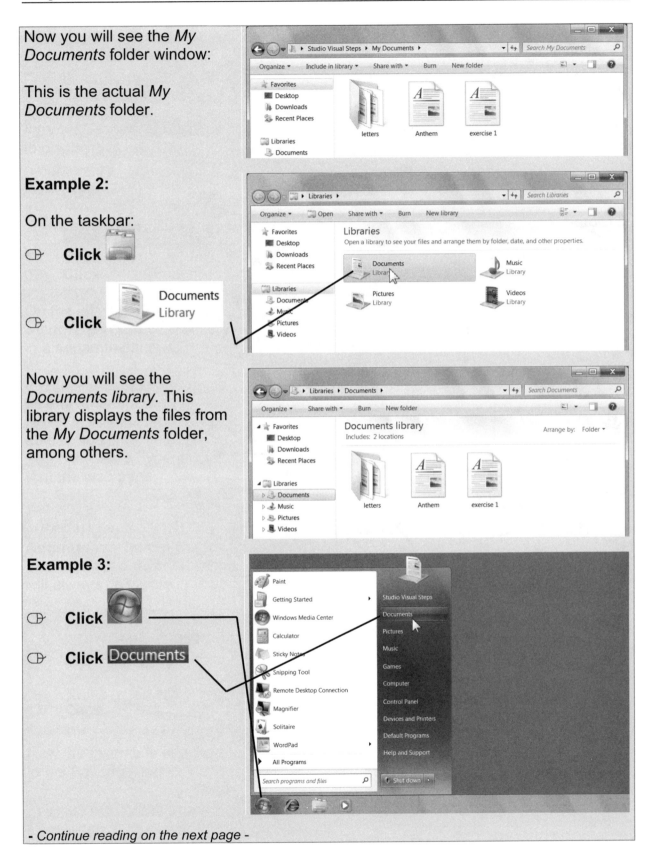

Example 2:

On the taskbar:

⊕ **Click**

⊕ **Click** Documents Library

Now you will see the *Documents library*. This library displays the files from the *My Documents* folder, among others.

Example 3:

⊕ **Click**

⊕ **Click** Documents

Now you will see the *Documents library*. This library displays the files form the *My Documents* folder, among others.

Example 4:

In every open folder window:

⊕ **Click** 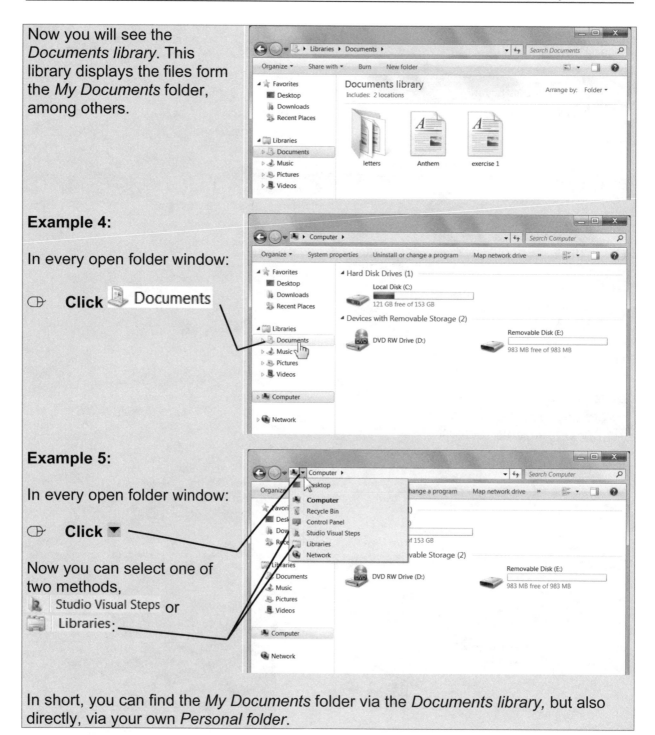 **Documents**

Example 5:

In every open folder window:

⊕ **Click** ▼

Now you can select one of two methods,

🔳 Studio Visual Steps or

📁 Libraries:

In short, you can find the *My Documents* folder via the *Documents library,* but also directly, via your own *Personal folder*.

7. Surfing the Internet

The Internet consists of millions of computers that are all interconnected. The *World Wide Web* is one of the most exciting parts of the Internet. *World Wide Web* means exactly what it says: a web of computers where an infinite amount of information is located regarding every imaginable topic. No matter where you are in the world, you can access that information with your computer.

On the Internet, a source of information is called a *website*. It is a site somewhere on the Web. Within the website, you can browse from one page to another by clicking with your mouse. You can even jump from one website to another. This is called *surfing*. The type of program you need to surf the Internet, is called a *browser.* You might browse through a printed catalog, but these days you can also *browse* just as easily through the company's online catalog.

In order to get on the Internet, you must initiate a connection with a computer that is permanently connected to the Internet. This is done by means of an *Internet Service Provider* (ISP). If you want to use the provider's services, you must subscribe to them or pay for them in another way. The provider then assigns you a *user name* and a *password*. The user name and password will give you access to the Internet.

If you are connected to the Internet, you are *online*. In this chapter, first you will learn to go *online* and then how to *surf.* For this purpose the browser *Internet Explorer* is used, which is provided with *Windows 7*.

In this chapter, you will learn how to:

- open *Internet Explorer*;
- use a web address;
- browse forward and backward;
- save a web address;
- use a *favorite*;
- stop using the Internet.

Please note:

For the exercises in this chapter, you must have an Internet connection that works. If necessary, contact your *Internet Service Provider* or your computer supplier.

7.1 Some Information First: The Modem

The modem
Telephone networks are used to connect computers which may be hundreds or thousands of miles apart from one another. This makes sense, since nearly everyone has a telephone. It is also not uncommon for cable television providers to offer Internet services, using their cable network to connect to the Internet.

In order to connect to the Internet via the telephone line or cable, you need a special piece of equipment: called a *modem*. A modem makes it possible for your computer to communicate with the *Internet Service Provider*. There are two different types of modems: internal and external.

An *external modem* is a separate box that is connected to your computer with a cable.
Another cable leads from the modem to the plug for the telephone line or the cable connection.

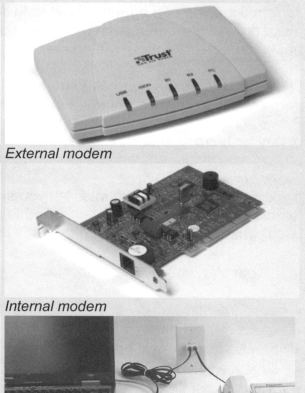

External modem

Nearly all new computers, however, have a modem that is built in. This is called an *internal modem.*
The only thing you see in this type of modem is a contact point for a telephone plug or the cable connection, located at the back of your computer.

Internal modem

Modems that are connected to the telephone line also have a cable that leads to the telephone's plug. Sometimes a double plug is used, so that your telephone can remain plugged into the same contact point.

Laptop computer with external modem and double plug

7.2 Is Your Modem Ready?

Before you continue with this chapter, you need to make sure your modem is ready.

☞ **Check to make sure your modem is connected to the telephone or cable network**

Do you have an external modem?
☞ **If so, turn the modem on**

Do you have an internal modem?
☞ **If so, you do not need to take any action**

7.3 Starting Internet Explorer

The program that is used to connect to the Internet in *Windows 7* is called *Internet Explorer*.
This is how to open the program:

⊕ **Click**

You will see the Start menu:

⊕ **Click ▶ All Programs**

⊕ **Click 🅴 Internet Explorer**

Adobe Reader 9
Default Programs
Desktop Gadget Gallery
Internet Explorer
Windows DVD Maker
Windows Fax and Scan
Windows Media Center
Windows Media Player
Windows Update
XPS Viewer
Accessories
AVG Free 8.5
Games
Maintenance
Microsoft Office
SolidDocuments
Startup
Visual Steps Alarmklok

◀ Back

Search programs and files

Studio Visual Steps

Documents

Pictures

Music

Games

Computer

Control Panel

Devices and Printers

Default Programs

Help and Support

Shut down ▶

The program will open, after which an Internet connection can be established.

💡 Tip

Opening Internet Explorer with the taskbar
If you see the icon on the taskbar, you can open *Internet Explorer* just by clicking this icon:

☞ **Click**

If you are using *Internet Explorer* for the first time and you have a *broadband* connection to the Internet (DSL or cable), you will probably see a window like this floating on top of the *Internet Explorer* window:

☞ **Check** Connect

If you are using *dial-up networking* to connect to the Internet, you will see a *Dial-up Connection* window.

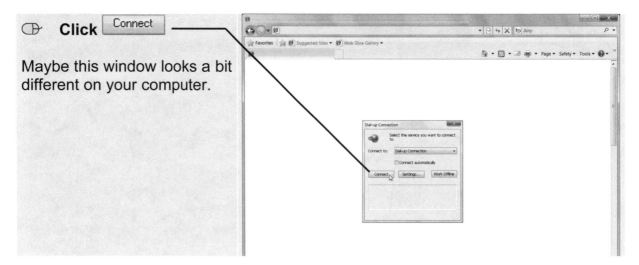

☞ **Click** Connect

Maybe this window looks a bit different on your computer.

If you have an Internet access subscription, your ISP has given you a *user name* and a *password*. If everything is set up properly, both of these will already be displayed in the next window.

If your user name and password are *not* displayed:

⌨ **Type your user name and password in the appropriate boxes**

👆 **Check mark the box** ☐ Save this user name and

👆 **Click** ○ Me only

👆 **Click** [Dial]

Maybe this window looks a bit different on your computer.

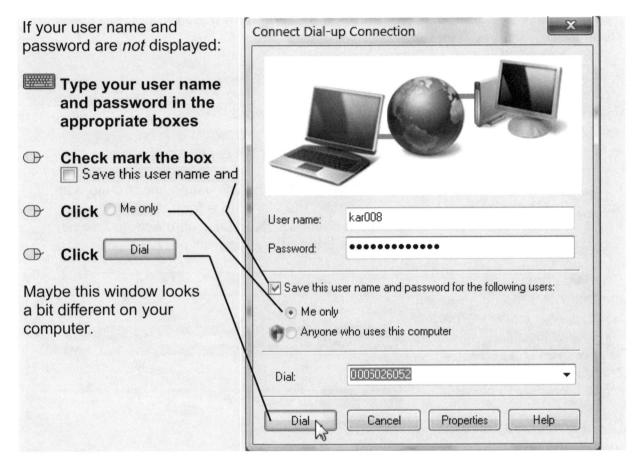

A connection is made to your ISP (*Internet Service Provider*).

HELP! I do not see windows like these.

Are these windows not shown on your screen? If you are connected to the internet by cable or DSL, then this *Dial-Up Connection* window will not appear. You will have a different set up on your computer. *Internet Explorer* automatically connects with the Internet when you open it.

👉 **Just continue reading**

7.4 Contacting Your Internet Service Provider

If you are using dial-up networking to connect to the Internet, your computer will now try to contact your ISP by using the modem. The modem goes through the following steps:

- the modem dials the number of the internet provider;
- then it connects to your ISP's computer;
- your computer sends your user name and password to the ISP's computer;
- the ISP's computer checks your user name and password;
- if they are correct, your connection to the Internet is established.

If your modem is connected to the telephone line, you will usually hear quite a bit of static noise. Your modem is busy converting the signal to a form that allows it to travel over the phone line. If you have a cable, ISDN or DSL connection, *Internet Explorer* automatically connects with the Internet and you will not hear any noise.

Once you are connected to the Internet, a home page will be displayed in the *Internet Explorer* window.
This is usually a page from *Microsoft*, the company that makes *Internet Explorer*.

Down in the right corner of the taskbar, you will see an icon with a computer and a plug indicating that you are *online*:

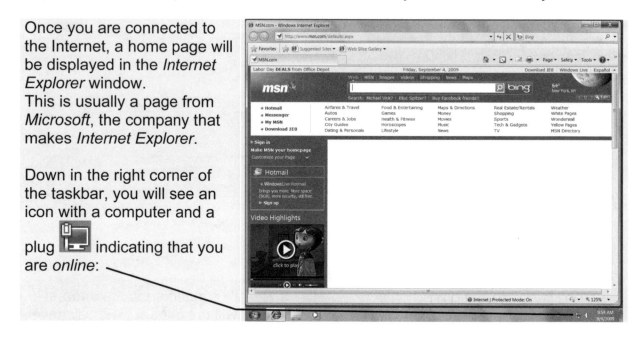

The modem is busy doing something if the computer displays this icon.

Please note:

The initial start page on your computer may not be the same as the one in the illustration. You might, for example, see a web page that someone else has specified in your browser's settings.

HELP! No connection?

Were you unable to connect to the Internet? This could be because your ISP's number is 'busy'. You might see a window like this one:

> Dialing...
> Dialing attempt 1.
> Unable to establish a connection.

When that happens, try again later.

 HELP! Still no connection?

If you have tried to connect to the Internet a number of times and you still unable to do so, it is probable that the settings on your computer are not correct.
Contact your ISP for assistance.

7.5 Typing an Address

Every website has its own web address on the *World Wide Web*. These are the addresses that start with 'www' that you see everywhere.
You can use these addresses to find a website on any computer that is connected to the Internet. The web address of Visual Steps publishing company is:

www.visualsteps.com

⊕ **Click in the Address bar at the top left of the window**

The web address

☑ http://www.msn.com/default

will turn blue as a sign that it is selected.

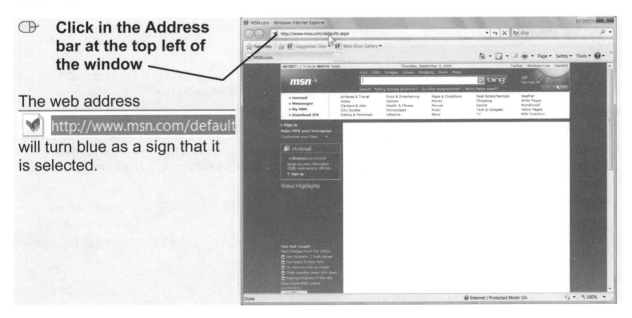

Now you can type the address in this Address bar:

 Type:
www.visualsteps.com

Enter

Press

After a few moments, you see the opening page for this website:

This web page is updated frequently. You may see other pictures in your window.

7.6 Wrong Address

Once in a while a typing error is made when typing an address, or a certain address no longer exists. This is especially true because the Internet is highly dynamic, changing every day. Private individuals may change their web addresses. Sometimes you will see an address that starts with *http://*. That is additional information, indicating that the address is for a website. With *Internet Explorer*, you do not need to type *http://*. The program automatically understands that you want a website and will add it to the address.

When typing a web address, you should take note of the following:

- Make sure that any dots (.) or forward slashes (/) are typed in the correct places. If they are not, you will receive an error message.
- Never type spaces in a web address.

If even one dot is missing, an error message will appear. Try it:

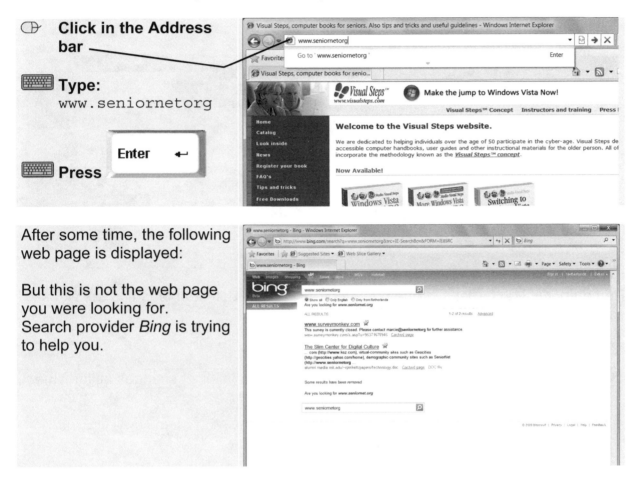

Click in the Address bar

Type:
www.seniornetorg

Press *Enter* ←

After some time, the following web page is displayed:

But this is not the web page you were looking for.
Search provider *Bing* is trying to help you.

Bing asks: Are you looking for **www.seniornet.org** *Bing* has made this assumption because the address you typed - www.seniornetorg - was wrong. The dot before 'org' is missing. The correct address for the *SeniorNet* website is:

www.seniornet.org

Try the correct address:

Click in the Address bar

Type:
www.seniornet.org

Press *Enter* ←

In a little while, the homepage for *SeniorNet* is displayed:

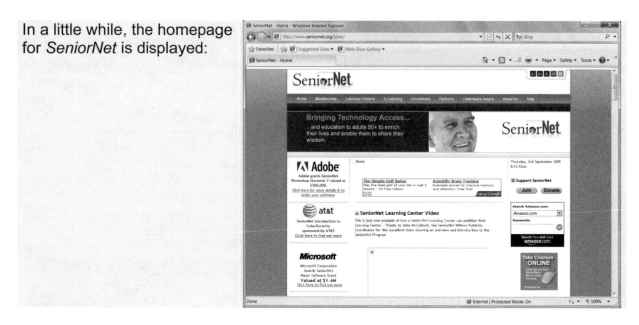

Remember, if you forget just one dot the program may not be able to find the website you want.

➤ **Please note:**
The website shown above may look different now. The Internet changes all the time.

7.7 Refreshing a Page

Sometimes a page is not displayed on your screen as it should be. When that happens, you can tell *Internet Explorer* to reload the page again: to *refresh* it. Just watch what happens:

☞ **Click**

You will see that the window will be refreshed and the information is collected once again.

Everything that is shown on your screen must be sent in through the telephone line or cable. This may take awhile. Sometimes it will seem like nothing is happening. But there is a way to check if *Internet Explorer* is still busy loading a page that you have requested:

At the bottom of the screen, the green bar indicates that information is being received:

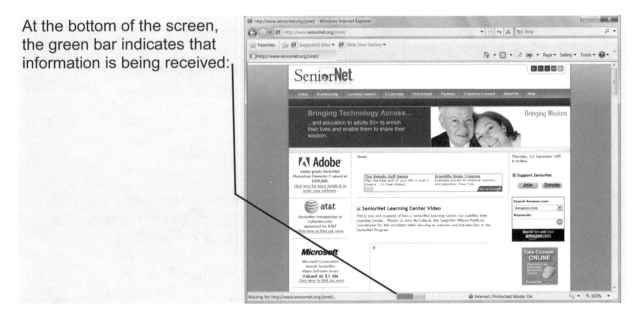

Not all information appears immediately on your screen; it may take time to *draw* (load) the entire page, especially if you are using dial-up networking to connect to the Internet.

7.8 Forward and Backward

You do not need to retype the web address of a website if you want to revisit it. *Internet Explorer* has a number of buttons that help you *navigate* the Internet.

At the top left of the window:

☞ **Click**

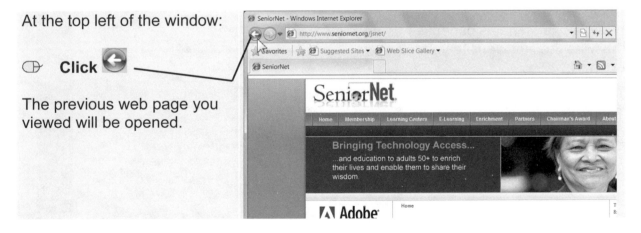

The previous web page you viewed will be opened.

What you see now is the website where search provider *Bing* was helping you:

Perhaps you noticed how quickly this is done. *Internet Explorer* retains the websites you recently visited in its memory so that you can quickly look at them again without needing all of the information sent over the telephone line or cable.

⊕ **Click two more times**

Now the website you first visited will be displayed.

Once again, the start page is displayed:

Now you can no longer browse back. That is because this was the first website you opened.

The button is gray and can no longer be used:

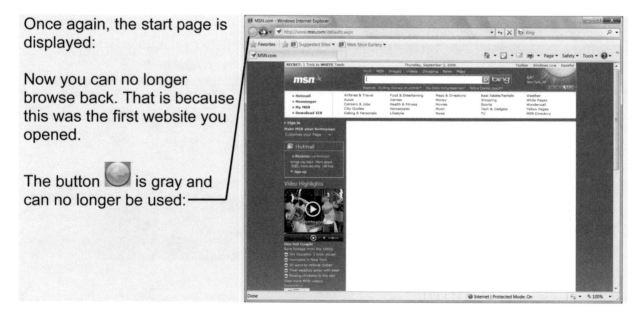

You can, however, browse the other way. There is a special button for this as well.

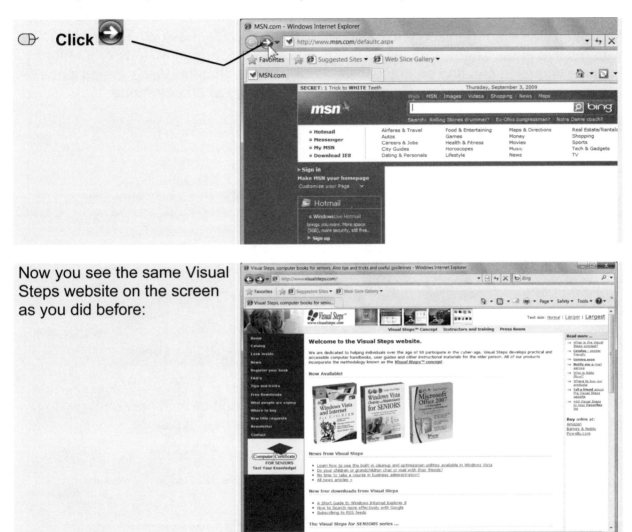

Click ➡️

Now you see the same Visual Steps website on the screen as you did before:

As you have seen, the buttons ⬅️➡️ can easily be used to switch back and forth between the websites you have viewed. This is called *surfing* the Internet.

However, these websites will not remain in memory forever. When you close *Internet Explorer,* the websites will be removed from the browser's memory.

7.9 Clicking to Browse

Most websites are organized and designed to enable you to navigate through the site with relative ease. There is usually a list of topics, in the form of buttons or text that indicate what you can find on the website. You can see that the Visual Steps website has a list of topics on the left. By clicking a topic, you go to another page.

Whenever the mouse arrow changes into a hand, you can click. It may change on a button, but it can also change somewhere in the text or over a picture.

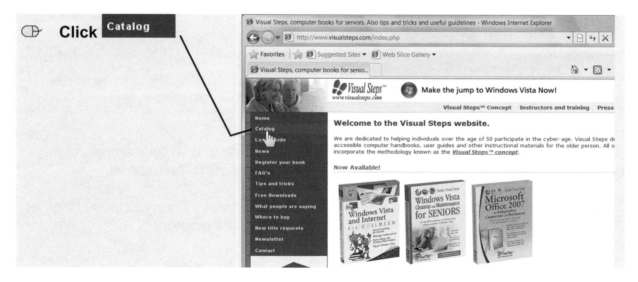

A word, button or picture on which you can click is called a *link*. A link is also called a *hyperlink*.

What you see now is a page with all of the books Visual Steps published:

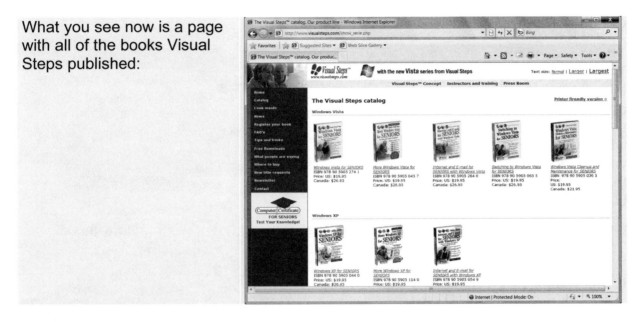

In the example above, you can see that the bottom part of the page is not shown on your screen. You need to use the scroll bar to read that part of the page.

7.10 Using the Scroll Bars

When you view pages on the Internet, you may need to use the scroll bar. Even if you maximize the browser window, it might not be large enough to hold all of the information. In order to see the rest of the page, you must use the vertical scroll bar.

Drag the scroll bar downward

Now you can read the bottom part of the text:

Drag the scroll bar upward

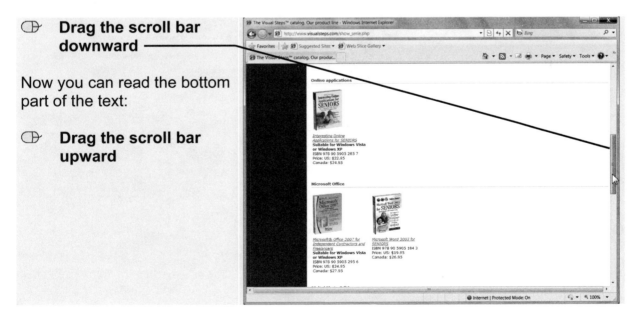

💡 Tip

The mouse wheel
The rapidly growing popularity of the Internet has resulted in various new additions to the mouse, including one called the mouse wheel. By turning the wheel with your finger, the contents of the window will scroll. This is the same thing that happens when you use the scroll bar, but it is much easier and quicker.

Once you have gotten used to a mouse wheel, you will never want to do without!
To scroll down, roll the wheel backward (toward you).
To scroll up, roll the wheel forward (away from you).
If your mouse has a scroll wheel:

☞ **Roll the wheel backward and forward with your index finger**

☞ **End the rolling when the scroll bar is upward**

A good website is made in such a way that you can easily move from one page to the next without getting lost. Most websites, for example, have a button marked *Home* or *Start* that when clicked will return you to the website's home page.

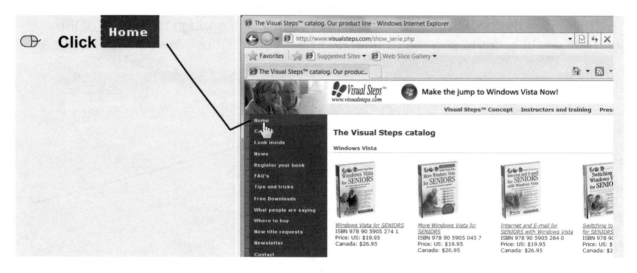

☞ **Click** Home

Once again, the home page is displayed.

7.11 Printing a Web Page

It is not always easy to read a web page on your screen, especially if it contains a lot of text. You can always choose to print the page and read it later.

No printer?
If you do not have a printer, you can skip this section.

This is how to print a page:

☞ **Make sure the printer is turned on**

At the top right of the window:

☞ **Click** 🖶

Shortly thereafter, the page will be printed.

7.12 Saving a Web Address

If you find an interesting website, you can save its address. Then you will always be able to quickly open the site without having to type the address.
Websites for which you have saved the address are called *favorites* in *Internet Explorer*.
You can only save an address of a website while it is being displayed. In this example, this is the Visual Steps website.

At the top left of the window:

☞ **Click** ⭐ Favorites

A menu appears:

☞ **Click** 🌟 Add to Favorites...

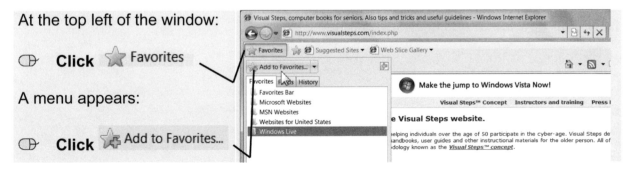

Now you see a small window on top of the web page in which the name has already been inserted:

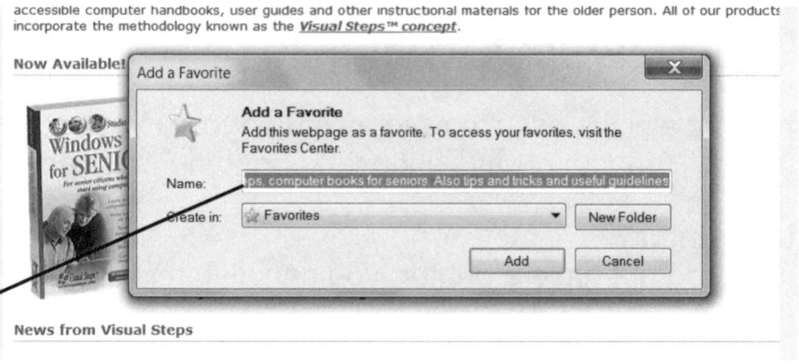

You can put all of your favorite websites in one long list, but you can also save them in separate folders. To practice, you can make a new folder for the websites that go with this book.

⊕ **Click** | New Folder |

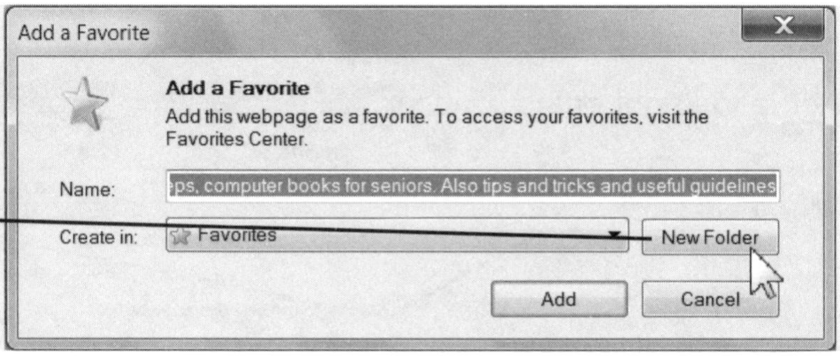

A new window appears on top of the others. Now you can type in the name you want to give the new folder.

⌨ **Type:** Windows for Seniors

⊕ **Click** | Create |

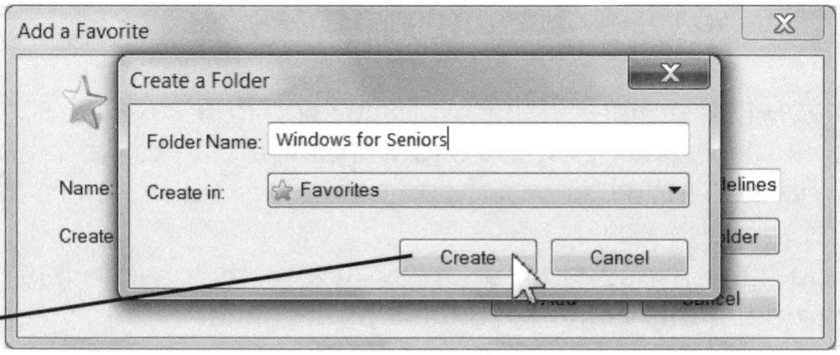

Now your new folder has been given a name.

You see the new folder. It has already been opened for you:

☞ **Click** [Add]

The favorite will be saved in your new folder.

Add a Favorite

Add this webpage as a favorite. To access your favorites, visit the Favorites Center.

Name: ⁞eps, computer books for seniors. Also tips and tricks and useful guidelines

Create in: ⬛ Windows for Seniors ▾   [New Folder]

[Add]   [Cancel]

Now you can check to make sure that you can quickly open this favorite website.

7.13 The Home Button

To see how a favorite works, start by going to a different website. You can go to your homepage, for example. This is the page that automatically opens when you start *Internet Explorer*. There is a special *Home button* for this.

In the top right area of the window:

☞ **Click** 🏠

Your home page is displayed. Now you can open your favorite.

7.14 Opening a Favorite

This is how to quickly open one of your favorite websites:

At the top left of the window:

☞ **Click** ⭐ Favorites

On the left side of the window a white pane is opened:

☞ **Click, in necessary, the** Favorites **tab**

You see the list of favorite folders:

☞ **Click**

🔲 Windows for Seniors

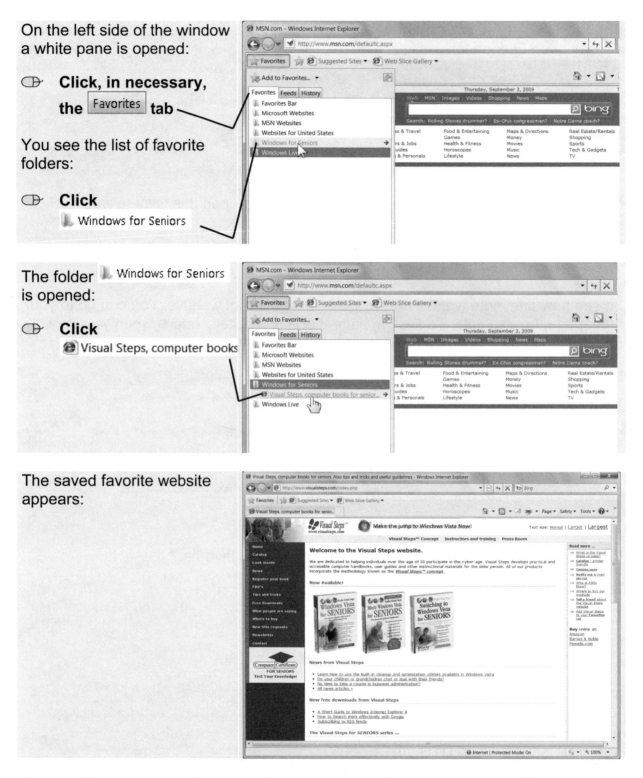

The folder 🔲 Windows for Seniors is opened:

☞ **Click**

🅔 Visual Steps, computer books

The saved favorite website appears:

Internet Explorer remembers your favorites, even after you have closed the program. Without having to remember complicated web addresses, these references to your favorite websites make it possible to quickly return to them at any given time.

7.15 Disconnecting from the Internet

If you have a common analog dial-up connection to the Internet, you have to disconnect each time you stop using the Internet. No other calls can come through to you as long as you are connected to the Internet.
If you have a broadband connection like DSL or cable, you are always connected to the Internet, whether you are using the web or not. You do not have to disconnect.

You can close the *Internet Explorer* window and disconnect in this way:

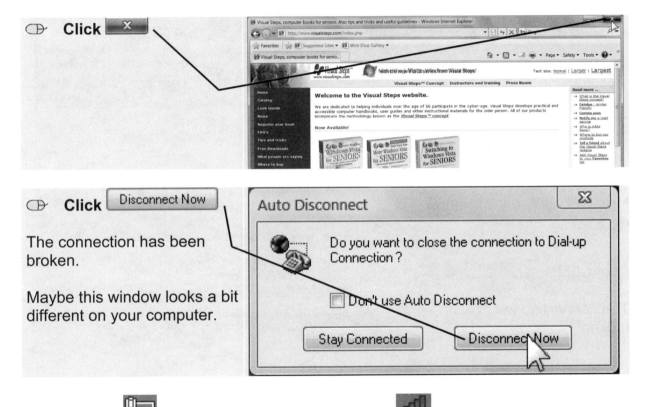

Now the icon from the taskbar will change into . The connection has been broken.

If you have a broadband connection such as DSL or cable you will not see a window

like the one above. You will still see the Internet access icon in the notification area on the far right side of the taskbar because you are continuously online.

✖ HELP! The connection is not broken.

Do you have a dial-up connection to the Internet and you do not see the disconnection window?

Do you still see this icon 🖥 on the taskbar? This means that the connection has not been broken. There is another way to disconnect:

On the taskbar:

👆 **Click** 🖥

👆 **Click**
   Open Network and Sharing Ce

In the window that appears:

👆 **Click** Connect or disconnect

Now you will see this window (or a similar one):

👆 **Click** Disconnect

The connection will now be broken.

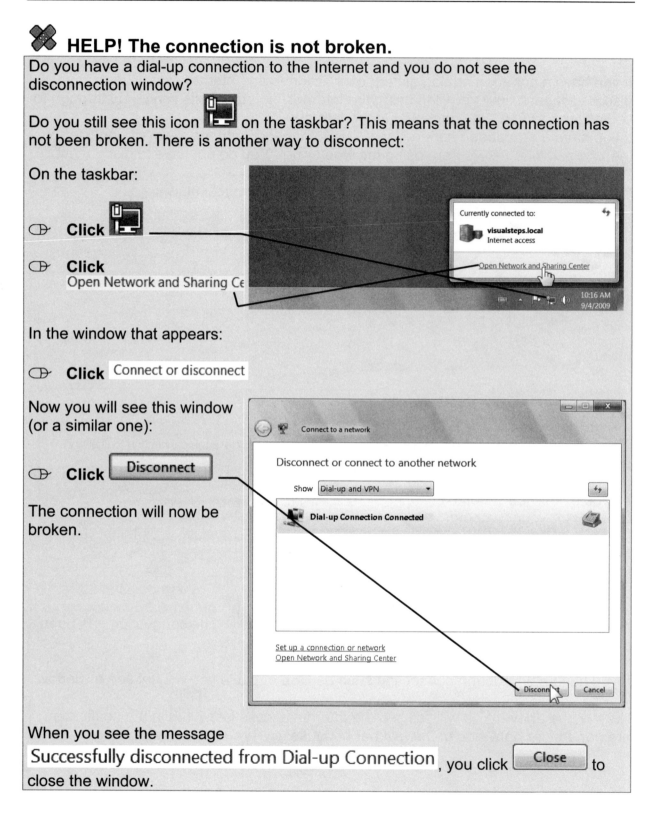

When you see the message
Successfully disconnected from Dial-up Connection , you click Close to close the window.

💡 Tip

Do you want to end the connection but keep viewing the *Internet Explorer* window?

Use this same way to disconnect:

On the taskbar:

👉 **Click** 🖥️

👉 **Click**
Open Network and Sharing Ce

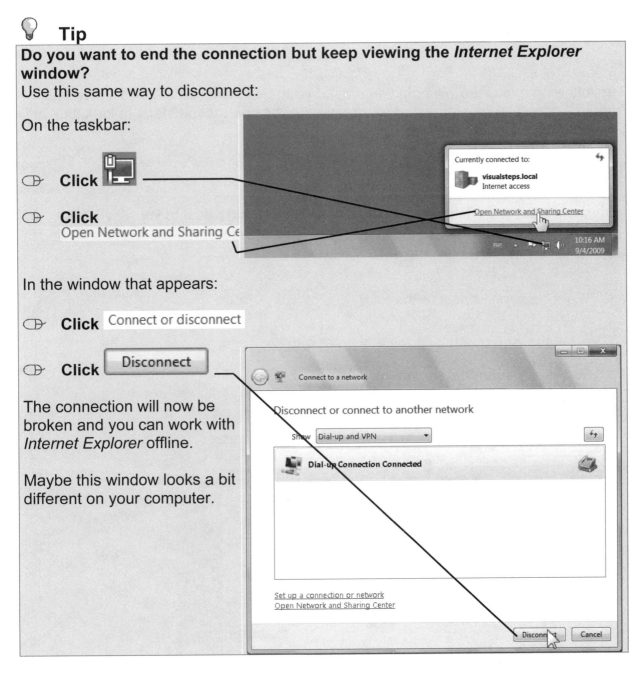

In the window that appears:

👉 **Click** Connect or disconnect

👉 **Click** Disconnect

The connection will now be broken and you can work with *Internet Explorer* offline.

Maybe this window looks a bit different on your computer.

In this chapter you learned how to surf the internet and add websites to your favorites. With the following exercises you can practice what you have learned.

7.16 Exercises

The following exercises will help you master what you have just learned. Have you forgotten how to do something? Use the number beside the footsteps to look it up in the appendix *How Do I Do That Again?*

Exercise: SeniorNet Favorite

In this exercise, you will open the *SeniorNet* website and add it to your favorites.

☞ Open *Internet Explorer.* 🐾45

☞ If necessary: connect to the Internet. 🐾46

☞ Type the web address: www.seniornet.org 🐾47

☞ Browse through the *SeniorNet* website.

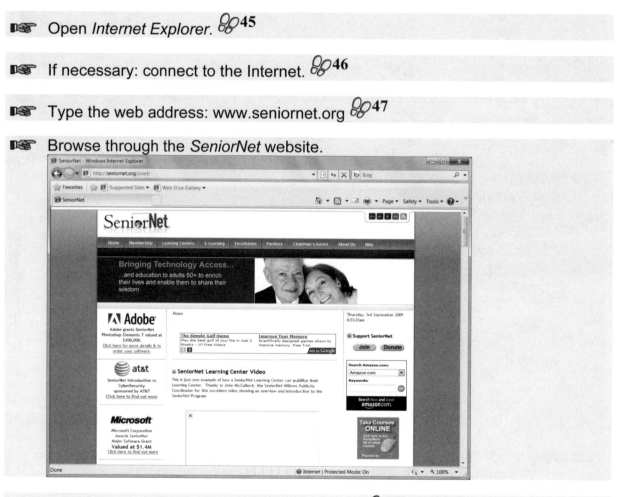

☞ Save the address for *SeniorNet* as a favorite. 🐾48

☞ Close the *Internet Explorer* window. 🐾4

☞ If necessary: disconnect from the Internet. 🐾49

Exercise: Surfing

Going from one website to another is also called surfing. In this exercise you will surf among the sites you visited earlier.

☞ Open *Internet Explorer*. $\mathcal{C\!\!\!\!C}$ ^{45}

☞ If necessary: connect to the Internet. $\mathcal{C\!\!\!\!C}$ ^{46}

☞ Using the *Favorites Center,* open the website www.visualsteps.com $\mathcal{C\!\!\!\!C}$ ^{50}

☞ Using the *Favorites Center,* open the website www.seniornet.org. $\mathcal{C\!\!\!\!C}$ ^{50}

☞ Type the address for the Public Broadcasting Service website: www.pbs.org $\mathcal{C\!\!\!\!C}$ ^{47}

☞ Now go back to www.seniornet.org. $\mathcal{C\!\!\!\!C}$ ^{51}

☞ Go back to the website www.visualsteps.com $\mathcal{C\!\!\!\!C}$ ^{51}

☞ Now go back to www.seniornet.org. $\mathcal{C\!\!\!\!C}$ ^{52}

☞ Go back to the Public Broadcasting Service website. $\mathcal{C\!\!\!\!C}$ ^{52}

☞ Now go back to the home page. $\mathcal{C\!\!\!\!C}$ ^{53}

☞ Close *Internet Explorer*. $\mathcal{C\!\!\!\!C}$ ^{4}

☞ If necessary: disconnect from the Internet. $\mathcal{C\!\!\!\!C}$ ^{49}

7.17 Background Information

Dictionary

ActiveX	Technology for creating interactive web content such as animation sequences or credit card transactions.
Broadband connection	A high-speed Internet connection. Broadband connections are typically 256 kilobytes per second (KBps) or faster. Broadband includes DSL and cable modem service.
Browser	A program used to display web pages and to navigate the Internet. *Internet Explorer* is a web browser.
Cable internet	Cable Internet access is a broadband connection that uses the same wiring as cable TV. To use cable, you need an account with a cable *Internet Service Provider* in your area. The ISP usually provides any necessary equipment, and often sends a technician to set it up for you.
Dial-up connection	Connecting to the Internet by using a modem and a telephone line. Usually a low speed analog connection.
Download	Copying a file from one computer to another using a modem or network. For example, copying software from a website.
DSL	Digital Subscriber Line - a type of high-speed Internet connection using standard telephone wires. This is also referred to as a broadband connection. The ISP is usually a phone company.
Home page	The first or opening page of a website.
Hyperlink, Link	A hyperlink is a navigation element in a webpage that automatically brings the referred information to the user when the user clicks on the hyperlink. A hyperlink can be text or images like buttons, icons or pictures. You can recognize a hyperlink when the mouse pointer turns into a hand.
Internet	A network of computer networks which operates world-wide using a common set of communications protocols. The part of the Internet that most people are familiar with is the World Wide Web (WWW).

- Continue reading on the next page -

ISP	An *Internet Service Provider* (ISP) is a company that provides you with access to the Internet, usually for a fee. The most common ways to connect to an ISP are by using a phone line (dial-up) or broadband connection (cable or DSL). Many ISPs provide additional services such as e-mail accounts, virtual hosting, and space for you to create a website.
Log-in name	User name.
Malware	Malicious software - software designed to deliberately harm your computer. Trojan horses, viruses and worms are examples of malware.
Password	A string of characters that a user must enter to gain access to a resource that is password-protected. Passwords help ensure that unauthorized users do not access your internet connection or your computer.
Security setting	Options that can help protect your computer from potentially harmful or malicious online content.
Spyware	Software that can display advertisements (such as pop-up ads), collect information about you, or change settings on your computer, generally without obtaining your consent.
Web address	The web address of a website uniquely identifies a location on the internet. An example of a web address is: www.visualsteps.com. A web address is also called an URL (Uniform Resource Locator). People use URLs to find websites, but computers use IP addresses to find websites. An IP address usually consists of four groups of numbers separated by periods, such as 192.200.44.69. Special computers on the internet translate URLs into IP addresses (and vice versa).
Web server	A computer that stores information (such as webpages or files) and makes that information available over the Internet.
Web page	A web page or webpage is a resource of information that is suitable for the World Wide Web and can be accessed through a browser.
Website	A website is a collection of interconnected web pages, typically common to a particular domain name on the World Wide Web on the Internet.
WWW	World Wide Web - web of computers, connected to each other - containing an infinite amount of web pages.

Source: Windows Help and Support

Why do I have to wait so long sometimes?
Sometimes it takes quite a long time before a page you want loads into your browser. This depends on a number of things:

- Modems can have various speeds. The faster the speed of the modem, the faster text and pictures are transmitted. The speed of the connection type also plays an important part.
  To date, a modem connected with the normal analog telephone line is the slowest type. Other types of connections, such as ISDN, cable and DSL, are significantly faster.
  New developments will present a range of fast transmission possibilities through the regular analog telephone line.

- Some websites have more pictures and illustrations than others. Some pages have numerous pictures or various graphic effects. All those dancing figures, revolving text, pop-up assistants and other graphic effects require information to be sent to your computer, and it all has to be sent via the telephone line if that is how you are connected.
  Receiving pictures takes a particularly long time. The more efficient the web page is designed, the faster it will appear on your screen.

- Sometimes it is very busy on the Internet. So many people are surfing at the same time that traffic jams occur. When that happens, you will have to wait longer than usual.

What can be done about this?
- You do not always have to wait until all the pictures have been received. Sometimes you immediately see the topic you are looking for.

  ↪ **If this is the case, click** ☒ **next to the Address bar**
  No more information is sent and you can click to go to a different page.

- Sometimes a website's opening page will have a button that says:
  Text only.
  If you click on that button, only the text will be sent, not the illustrations. That takes much less time.

Domain names
A web address is also referred to as a domain name. Every web address has an extension, such as **.com**

For example: *www.visualsteps.**com***

There are various extensions that can be used. In Europe, for example, the extension is usually an abbreviation for the country:

For example: *www.google.**nl***

This site is in the Netherlands. Other country extensions include **.be** for Belgium and **.uk** for the United Kingdom.
In the United States, however, a different system is used. Here, the extension can indicate the type of organization:
.com .... commercial business
.edu .... educational institution
.org .... non-commercial organization

Searching on the Internet
When you want to find information on the Internet, you can use a program called a *search engine*.
This is a program that tries to keep track of the contents of millions of web pages on the Internet. You can ask the search engine to find something for you based on a certain key word or phrase. The engine then uses that word or phrase to find the web addresses of web pages that include this word or phrase.

Well-known search engines are:
www.google.com
www.bing.com
www.altavista.com
www.yahoo.com

You will discover that one search engine will render entirely different results than the other. This is why it is worth the effort to have more than one search engine perform the search.
You can visit the search engines by typing their web addresses in the Address bar of *Internet Explorer.*

Searching with Bing

Internet Explorer has been preprogrammed to use *Bing* as the default search engine.

In the top right corner of the *Internet Explorer* window, you will see this box:
In this box you can type one or more words that you want to base your search on and then click

🔍 .

If you type more than one word, you will get a list of web pages that contain at least one of the words. However, if you put the words between quotation marks, the list will show only those pages that contain that specific combination.

7.18 Tips

💡 **Tip**

Your history
Internet Explorer also keeps track of all the websites that you have visited. It is easy to display this list:

👈 **Click** ⭐ Favorites

👈 **Click the** History **tab**

👈 **Click** 📅 Today

On the left side of the window, you see your history in a separate pane:

If you did not save a website as a favorite but want to revisit it, you will probably be able to find it again in this list. You can click a hyperlink to visit the web page.

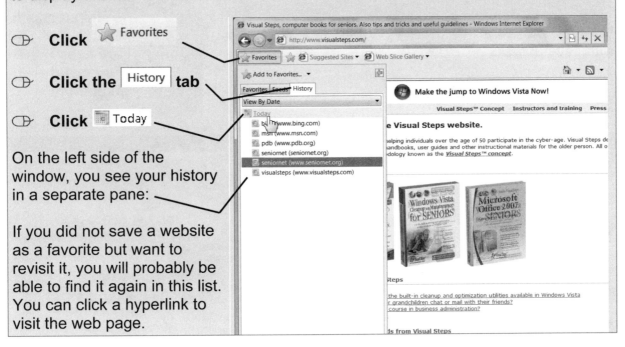

💡 **Tip**

Adding favorites to the toolbar
You can add a favorite website to the Favorites bar as well. In this way, the favorite will always be visible in your window. This is how you do it:

👉 **Surf to www.visualsteps.com**
🔖 45, 47

👈 **Click** ⭐

Now the favorite is attached to the Favorites bar:

To open the favorite, click
🌐 Visual Steps, computer bo... .

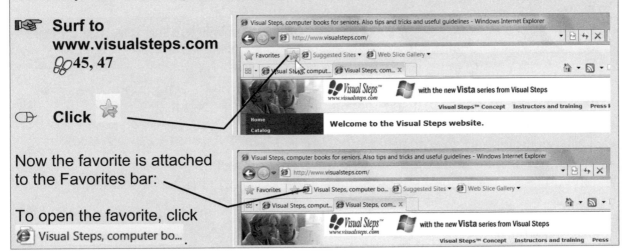

💡 Tip

Opening frequently visited websites directly from the toolbar
It is possible to directly open frequently visited websites from the toolbar. This is how you do it:

👉 **Right-click**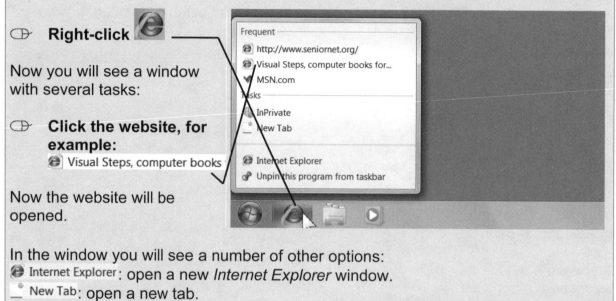

Now you will see a window
with several tasks:

👉 **Click the website, for
example:**
  🔵 Visual Steps, computer books

Now the website will be
opened.

In the window you will see a number of other options:
🔵 Internet Explorer : open a new *Internet Explorer* window.
  New Tab : open a new tab.
🔵 InPrivate : *InPrivate* – browse and visit websites without saving them to your
computer's memory.

💡 Tip

Information bar
Sometimes when you are surfing the Internet, an Information bar in *Internet Explorer*
is shown. The information bar appears below the Address bar and displays
information about downloads, blocked pop-up windows, and other activities.
🛡 To help protect your security, Internet Explorer blocked this site from downloading files to your computer. Click here for options...

If *Internet Explorer* is still using its original settings, you will see the Information bar
in the following circumstances:
• If a website tries to install an *ActiveX control* on your computer or run an *ActiveX*
  control in an unsafe manner. *ActiveX* is technology for creating interactive web
  content such as animation sequences or credit card transactions.
• If a website tries to open a pop-up window.
• If a website tries to download a file to your computer.
• If your security settings are below recommended levels.
When you see a message in the Information bar, click the message to see more
information or to take some action.

- Continue reading on the next page -

Here you see an example of the Information bar:

To get more information:

☞ **Click the information bar**

A small menu appears:

☞ **Click** Information Bar Help

Windows Help and Support window will be opened on your computer and you can read more about the Information bar.

Do you want to know more about the Information bar before surfing the Internet?

☞ **Open *Windows Help and Support*** ⬚6

⌨ **Type in the search box:** Information bar

☞ **Click** 🔍

The information will be displayed.

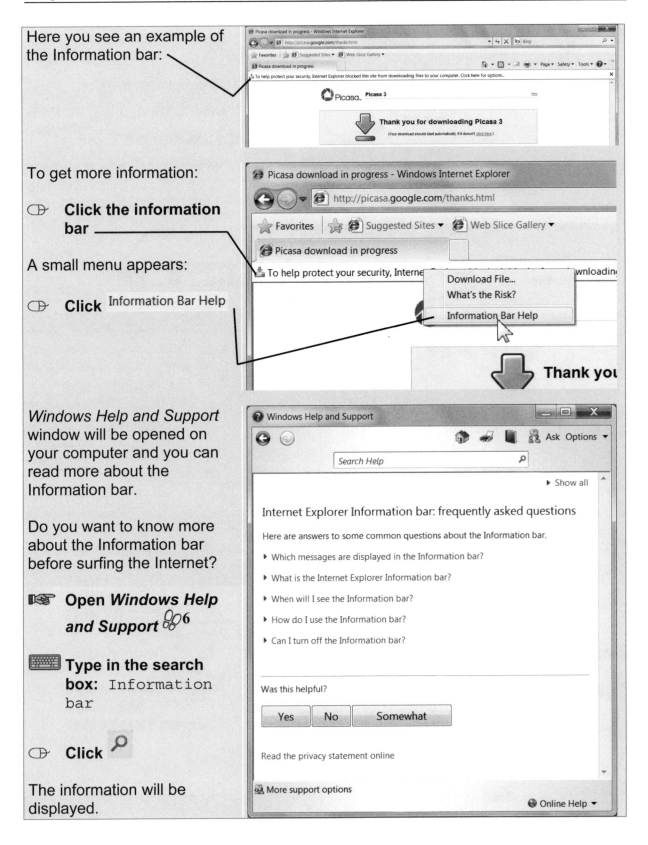

💡 Tip

Tabbed browsing
Tabbed browsing lets you load web pages in separate tabs of a single browser window, so you can switch between them quickly. Here you see the two tabs:

Visual Steps, computer books for seniors. Al... . The right tab in this example is empty.

☞ **Surf to www.visualsteps.com** 👣45, 47

Next to

Visual Steps, computer books for seniors. Al... .

👉 **Point to** [ ]

The tab changes in [ ]:

👉 **Click** [ ]

You will see a webpage with information about tabs:

👉 **Click in the Address bar** ——

⌨ **Type:**
www.seniornet.org

👉 **Click** →

Or:

⌨ **Press** [Enter ↵]

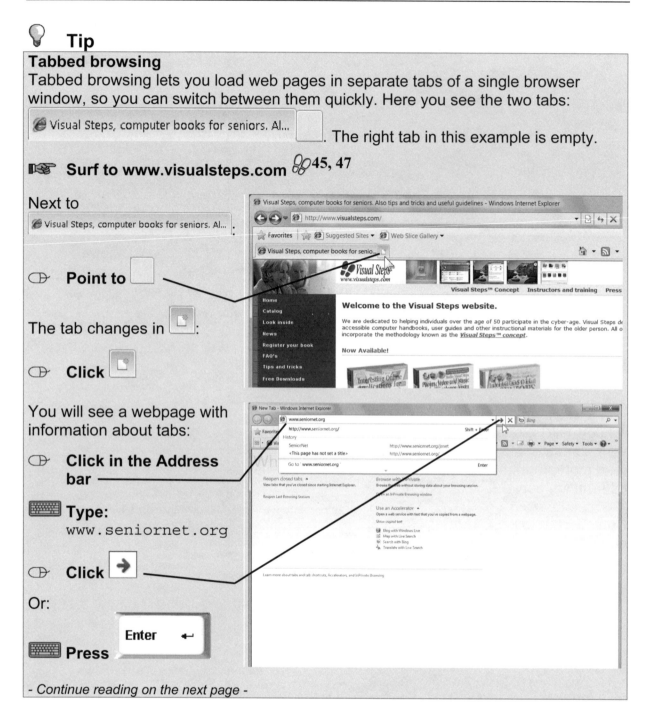

- Continue reading on the next page -

The SeniorNet website appears on this tab:

You can open several tabs if you want.
To go to another webpage, that is listed on a tab, just click that tab.

To close a tab:

☞ **Click** ☒ **on the tab**

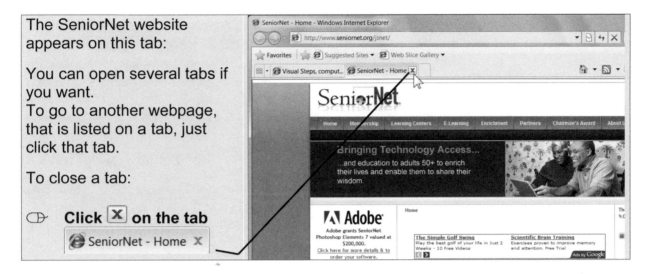

💡 **Tip**

Enlarge the font size and/or zoom in on a web page
Some websites offer the ability to enlarge the font size of the text on the web page. For example the Visual Steps website **www.visualsteps.com**.

There are three text sizes available: Text size: Normal | Larger | Largest.

☞ **Surf to**
   www.visualsteps.com
   🐾45, 47

In the top right corner of the window:

☞ **Click** Largest

The text size is now enlarged. The images and buttons are still the same size.

☞ **Click** Normal

The text size will be normal again.

- Continue reading on the next page -

You can also *zoom in* on a web page. *Zoom* enlarges or reduces everything on the page, including text and images. You can zoom from 10% to 1000%.

In the bottom right corner of the *Internet Explorer* window, there is a zoom button ⚲ 100% ▾:

☞ **Click** ▾ **next to** ⚲ 100%

A menu appears:

☞ **Click** 200%

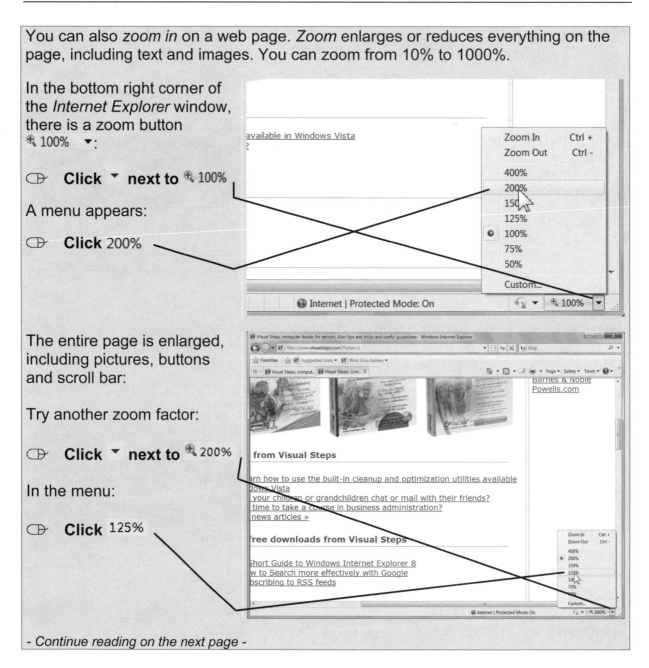

The entire page is enlarged, including pictures, buttons and scroll bar:

Try another zoom factor:

☞ **Click** ▾ **next to** ⚲ 200%

In the menu:

☞ **Click** 125%

- Continue reading on the next page -

This size is better because you can read the information without too much scrolling.

Tip: If you have a mouse with a wheel, hold down the Ctrl key, and then scroll the wheel to zoom in or out.

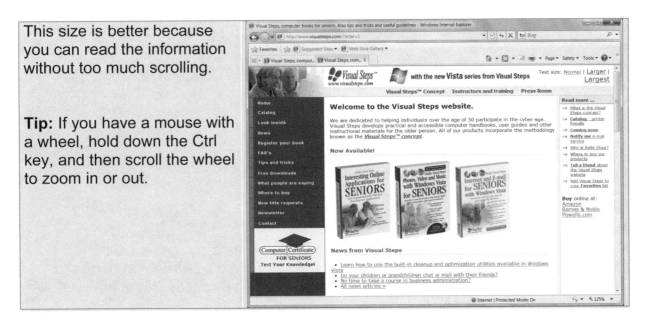

Tip

Register your book

You can register your book. Visual Steps will keep you aware of any important changes that are necessary to you as a user of the book and you will take advantage of our periodic newsletter (e-mail) informing you of our product releases, company news, tips & tricks, special offers, etcetera.

☞ **Surf to www.visualsteps.com/windows7** 🐾**45, 47**

The web page of the book appears. At the left side you see this list:

◑ **Click**
     Register your book

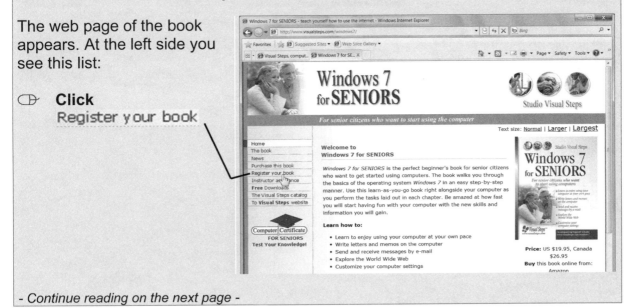

- Continue reading on the next page -

You will see a window like this:

⌨ **Type your e-mail address**

◔ **Click** Submit

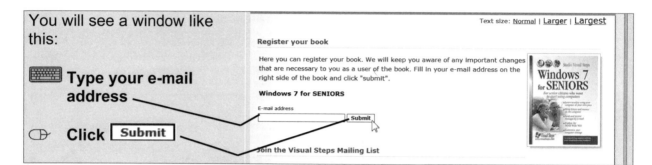

💡 **Tip**

InPrivate Browsing

If you do not want others to know which websites you visit, you can enable the InPrivate Browsing option. This will prevent the system from passing on details to other websites, for instance about the websites you have visited. This is how you enable InPrivate Browsing:

◔ **Click** Safety ▾

◔ **Click** InPrivate Browsing

A new window will be opened.

You will see the InPrivate icon **InPrivate** on the Address bar:

You can type the web address on the Address bar. The InPrivate browsing window works the same way as the regular *Internet Explorer* window.

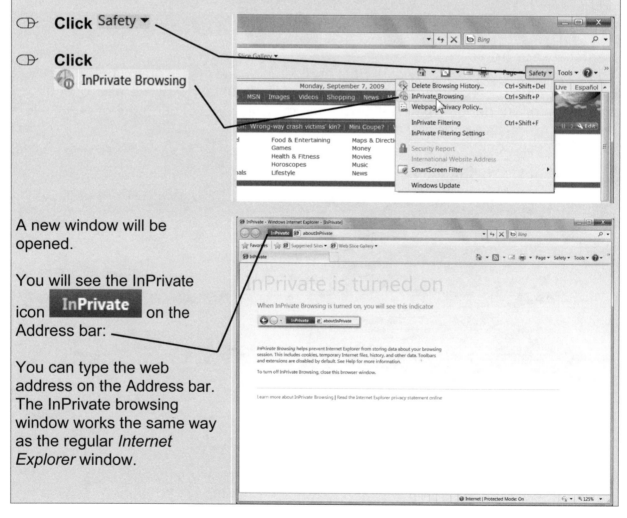

8. E-mail, Your Electronic Mailbox

One of the most widely-used applications on the Internet is electronic mail: e-mail. E-mail uses no pen, paper, envelope or stamp. You type your message into the computer and it is sent via the Internet.

If you have an Internet service subscription, you will automatically be assigned an *e-mail address*. This e-mail address can be used to send and receive mail. Your *Internet Service Provider* (ISP) has a kind of post office, also called a *mail server*. Like with regular mail, this post office handles all of the daily mail traffic.

In order to send an e-mail to someone, the addressee must also have an e-mail address, of course. But it does not matter where that person lives. Sending an e-mail to someone in Germany takes the same amount of time and money as sending an e-mail to your next-door neighbor. Unlike stamps on regular mail, there are no direct costs involved per e-mail, except for your Internet subscription. There is no limit to the number of messages that you can send or receive.

Another significant advantage is that you can send all kinds of things with your e-mail, such as a picture that you have made with a digital camera. E-mail has an extensive effect on communication at work. As the use of e-mail increases, the use of the fax and regular telephone decreases.

With the simple *Windows Live Mail* program you can quickly and easily send and receive electronic 'letters'. You will be using this program in this chapter. Maybe this program has not yet been installed to your computer. If that is the case, you can read how to install this program in *Appendix D Downloading and Installing Windows Live Mail*.

In this chapter you will discover how easy e-mail is: no more stamps to buy and no more trips to the mailbox.

In this chapter, you will learn how to:
- open *Windows Live Mail*;
- create, send, receive and read an e-mail message;
- include an attachment.

Please note:

In order to work through this chapter, you need to have an e-mail address and your e-mail program must be properly installed. If this is not the case, you can read how to do so in *section 8.1 Opening Windows Live Mail*.

8.1 Opening Windows Live Mail

Windows Live Mail is a program that you can use to send and receive electronic mail. In this chapter you will learn how use this program to receive and send e-mail. This is how you open the program *Windows Live Mail:*

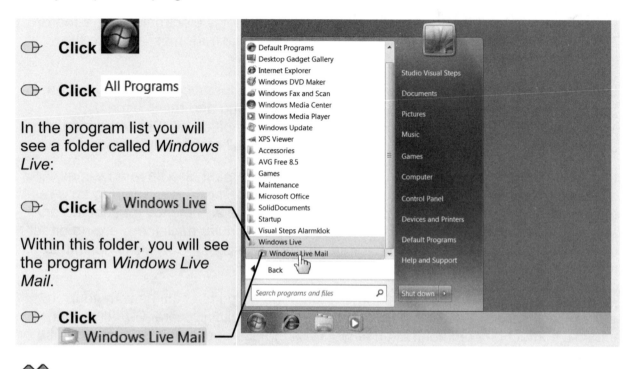

☞ **Click**

☞ **Click** All Programs

In the program list you will see a folder called *Windows Live*:

☞ **Click** Windows Live

Within this folder, you will see the program *Windows Live Mail*.

☞ **Click** Windows Live Mail

HELP! I do not see the Windows Live Mail program.

If you do not see the *Windows Live Mail* program in the start menu, you need to download and install it first. In *Appendix D Downloading and Installing Windows Live Mail* you can read how this is done.

Windows Live Mail will immediately determine whether you are connected to the Internet (online). If you are *offline*, you will see a small window like the one on the next page. You might want to work offline if you want to reduce the amount of time you spend online, either because your Internet Service Provider (ISP) charges you by the hour, or because you have only one phone line and you are not using a broadband connection.

Please note:

If you are using a broadband connection, such as cable or DSL, you will not see the following window. In that case, you can continue with the next step.

If you do not want to connect yet:

☞ **Click** [No]

If you do want to connect, use the [Yes] button.

Possibly your e-mail account in *Windows Live Mail* has not yet been created. This is how you can activate your e-mail account.

HELP! My e-mail account has already been activated.

If you already have an e-mail account you can continue with *section 8.2 The E-mail Address*.

☞ **Click**

Add e-mail account

Now a wizard will be opened. In this wizard you will need to fill in the data you have received from your Internet Service Provider. Such as your e-mail address, your password, and the name of the POP3-server and SMTP-server.

HELP! I want to use a webmail address.

Do you already have a webmail address from Hotmail or Gmail, for example? Then you need to define the settings for your e-mail account in a different way. Check the website that goes with this book (**www.visualsteps.com/windows7**) and you will find the information in *Appendix Setting up a Webmail account in Windows Live Mail*.

Type your e-mail address

Type your password

Type the display name

Click `Next`

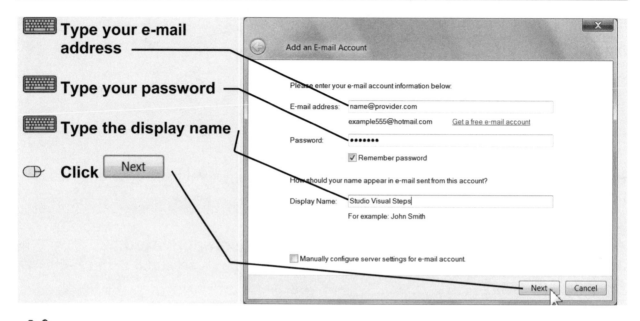

HELP! I do not have this information.

Your Internet Service Provider should have given you these details. If you have not received this information, you should contact your ISP (Internet Service Provider).

Type the name of the POP3 server

Type the name of the SMTP server

Click `Next`

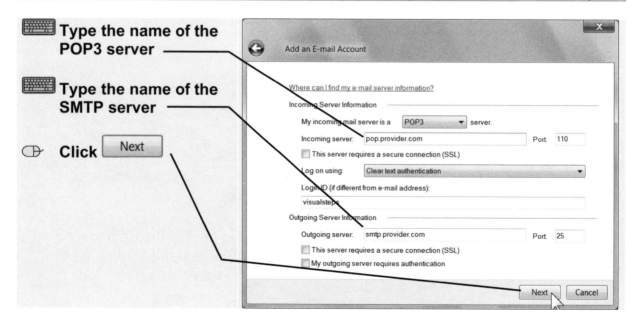

Now you have finished:

Click Finish

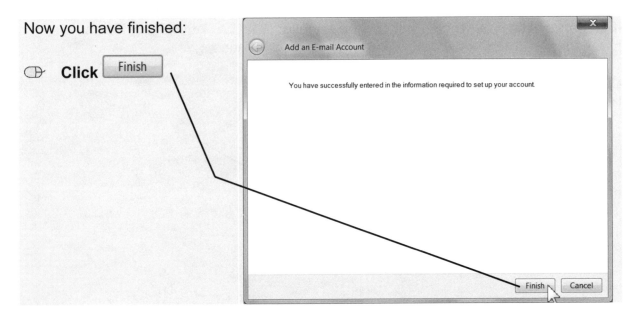

When you are offline, you will see the following window with no messages. You will be asked again if you want to go online. This will not be necessary when you are going to execute the following steps.

Click No

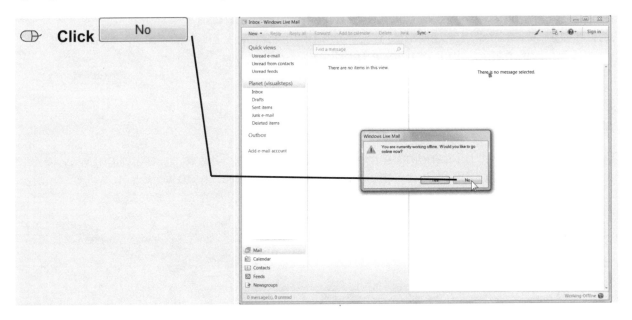

Please note:

From now on you will see the same windows you see when you are online. If you have an Internet connection via a phone line, you can remain offline. Whenever you need to connect to the Internet, the program will ask you to do so.

If you are online, your e-mail will now be retrieved. Maybe you will receive some messages. In the window below you will not see any messages yet.

On the left there is a folder list:

In the middle you will see a message list with headers:
In this example, no messages are yet received.

This is the preview pane:

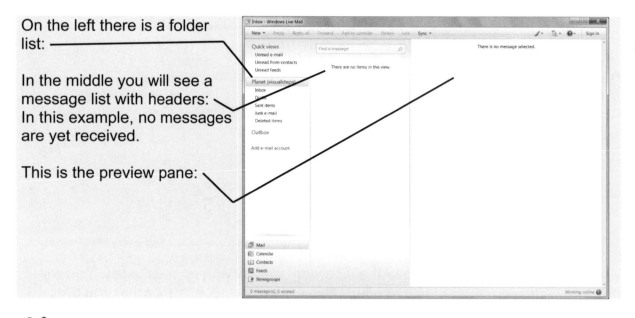

HELP! My window looks entirely different.

When someone else has already used the program, the window may look different. This does not matter. Just continue reading.

8.2 The E-mail Address

To practice, you will be sending a message to yourself. This is an excellent way to learn how to send e-mail. Since the message is sent straight to you, you will also learn how to receive e-mail. This is how to create a new e-mail message:

At the top left of the window:

☞ **Click** New

Now you see the *New message* window on top of the program window:

In this window you can create a new e-mail message:

The first thing to do is to address your message using an e-mail address. Every e-mail address consists of a number of words, with the familiar symbol @ somewhere in the middle. For example:

name@provider.com

The name of the addressee is located in front of the @. Behind it, the address usually contains the name of the Internet Service Provider from which you received the e-mail address.

➥ Please note:

E-mail addresses may not contain spaces.
This is why names or words are sometimes separated by a dot (.). These dots are extremely important. If you forget one in the address, your message will never arrive. Your mailman may understand what the sender means if the address is not completely correct. But a computer does not.

8.3 Sending an E-mail

The best way to test that your electronic mailbox works as it should is to send an e-mail message to yourself.

In the line marked
To: **type your own e-mail address**

Every e-mail message is also given a subject.

Click in the box next to Subject:

Type: test

Now you can start typing the actual text of the message.

Click in the main message window

You can type the message here.

Type: This is a first e-mail as a test.

To change font type, size, style, and effects such as color, use the formatting bar Calibri ▾ 12 ▾ **B** *I* U ̲ A̲ ▾ just like in the *WordPad* program.

When you have finished the e-mail, you can send it.

At the top left of the window:

Click Send

When you work *offline*, the program reminds you that the message is placed in the *Outbox* first:

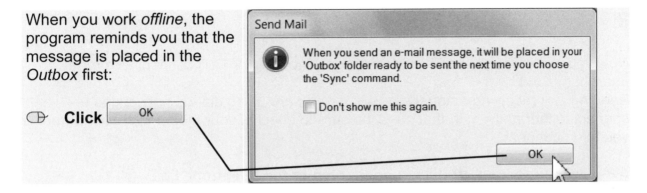

 **Click** OK

HELP! No reminder.

Is the reminder about the *Outbox* not shown on your screen? Then you are probably using a broadband connection, for example a DSL line. This means that *Windows Live Mail* has a different setting, and your e-mail is immediately mailed. If this is the case, skip the following section and continue at *section 8.6 Reading a Message*.

8.4 The Outbox

When you work offline, all of the e-mails you make are collected in the *Outbox* first. Your message will not be sent until you connect to the Internet. This means that you can write all of the e-mails you want, and then send them all at once.

Now you see the *Windows Live Mail* window again. There is one message in the *Outbox*:

8.5 Sending and Receiving

Now you can manually send your message. The program will connect with the Internet to send it.
Sending and receiving manually is useful if you are using dial-up networking to connect to the Internet. In that case, be sure to check if your modem is ready before you try to connect.

☞ **Make sure your modem is connected to the telephone line**

Do you have an external modem?
☞ **If so, turn the modem on**

Do you have an internal modem?
☞ **Then you do not need to do anything**

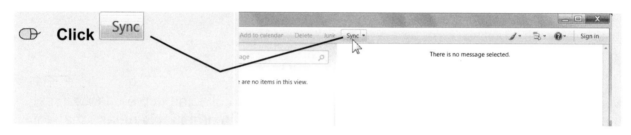

When you work *offline*, *Windows Live Mail* will tell you that you are still offline and ask whether you want to go online.

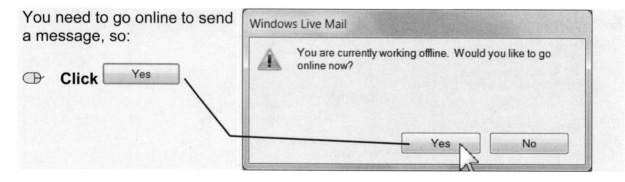

If you are using dial-up networking to connect to the Internet, you will see a *Dial-up Connection* window. It probably looks like this one:

Click `Connect`

Dial-up Connection

Select the service you want to connect to.

Connect to: Dial-up Connection

☐ Connect automatically

Connect   Settings...   Work Offline

If your user name and password are *not* displayed:

Type your user name and password in the appropriate boxes

If you want to save your user name and password:

Check mark the box
☐ Save this user name and pass

Click ○ Me only

Click `Dial`

Connect Dial-up Connection

User name: kar008

Password: ●●●●●●●●●●●●●●

☑ Save this user name and password for the following users:

○ Me only
○ Anyone who uses this computer

Dial: 0005026052

Dial   Cancel   Properties   Help

A connection is made to your ISP (Internet Service Provider). Next your e-mail message is sent. The program also automatically checks to see if you have any new e-mail messages.

HELP! There are no windows like these.

Are these windows not shown on your screen?
This means that *Windows Live Mail* has different settings on your computer. Your

program automatically connects when you click the button Sync.

☞ **Just continue to read**

You can follow this process as it proceeds in the lower right corner of the window:

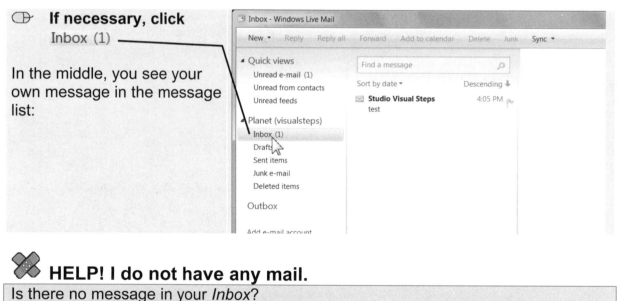

If everything went as it should, your text message was immediately sent to you. Then it is put in the *Inbox*.

8.6 Reading a Message

All e-mail messages you receive are placed in a separate folder that is called the *Inbox*.

⟳ **If necessary, click**
    Inbox (1) ─────

In the middle, you see your own message in the message list:

HELP! I do not have any mail.

Is there no message in your *Inbox*?
Perhaps it has not yet been received. Try again later to receive the message:

⟳ **Click** Sync

You can open the message in a larger window so that you can read it:

In the message list you see the header of your message:

⊕ **Double-click your message**

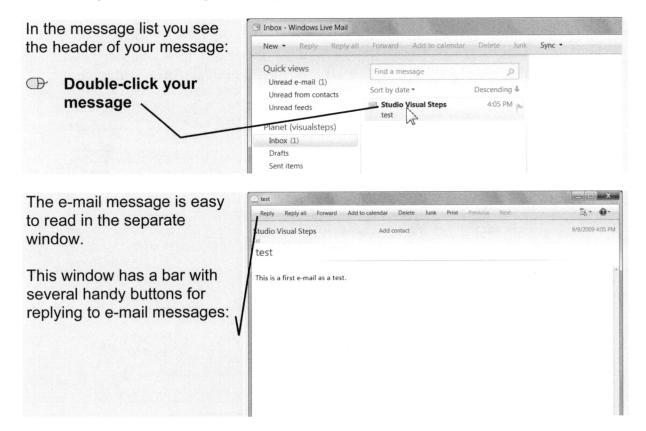

The e-mail message is easy to read in the separate window.

This window has a bar with several handy buttons for replying to e-mail messages:

These buttons have the following functions:

Reply	**Reply** Reply to sender, the 'to' portion already contains the correct e-mail address. The original e-mail message is included.
Reply all	**Reply All** An e-mail message can be sent to more than one person. This button is used to send a reply to everyone to whom the original e-mail was addressed. The original e-mail message is included.
Forward	**Forward** A new e-mail is made from the original message that can be sent to someone else. The original e-mail message is included.

☞ **Close the e-mail message window** ✇⁴

8.7 Including an Attachment

The nice thing about e-mail messages is that you can send all kinds of things with them. You can add a photo, a drawing, or another document, for example. Something that you want to send with an e-mail message is called an *attachment*. This is how to add an attachment to a message:

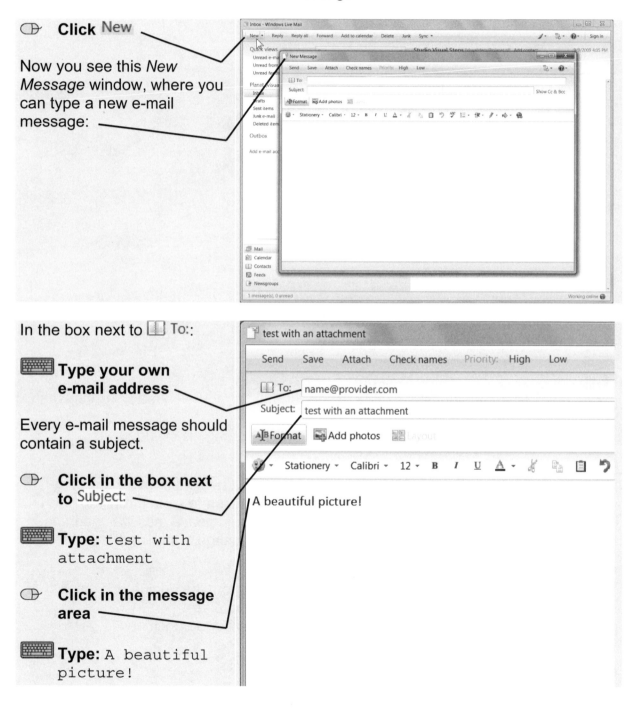

⊕ **Click** New

Now you see this *New Message* window, where you can type a new e-mail message:

In the box next to 📖 To::

⌨ **Type your own e-mail address**

Every e-mail message should contain a subject.

⊕ **Click in the box next to** Subject:

⌨ **Type:** test with attachment

⊕ **Click in the message area**

⌨ **Type:** A beautiful picture!

To attach a picture to your message, you click the 'paper clip' button:

☞ **Click** Attach

```
📄 test with an attachment

    Send    Save    Attach    Check names    Priority:  High    Low

    📧 To:    name@provider.com

    Subject:  test with an attachment

    A|B Format    📷 Add photos    ⊞ Layout

    😊 ▾   Stationery ▾   Calibri ▾   12 ▾   B  I  U  A ▾  ✂  🗐  📄  ↺

    A beautiful picture!|
```

Now you will see this folder window. By default, the *Documents library* will be opened. You are now going to open the *Pictures library*:

You will use one of the sample pictures from *Windows 7*.
First open the folder:

☞ **Click** 🖼 Pictures

☞ **Double-click**

Sample Pictures

```
📄 Open                                                          _ □ ✕

◄ ► ▾ 🗁 ▸ Libraries ▸ Pictures ▸        ▾ ✦  Search Pictures    🔍

Organize ▾    New folder                              ▦ ▾  □  ❓

4 ⭐ Favorites          Pictures library              Arrange by:  Folder ▾
   ■ Desktop           Includes: 2 locations
   📥 Downloads
   📋 Recent Places
                        📁
4 📚 Libraries          Sample Pictures
   ▷ 📄 Documents
   ▷ 🎵 Music
   ▷ 🖼 Pictures
   ▷ 🎬 Videos

4 💻 Computer
   ▷ 💾 Local Disk (C:)

              File name:                    ▾   All Files (*.*)     ▾

                                                Open        Cancel
```

The sample pictures appear in the file list:

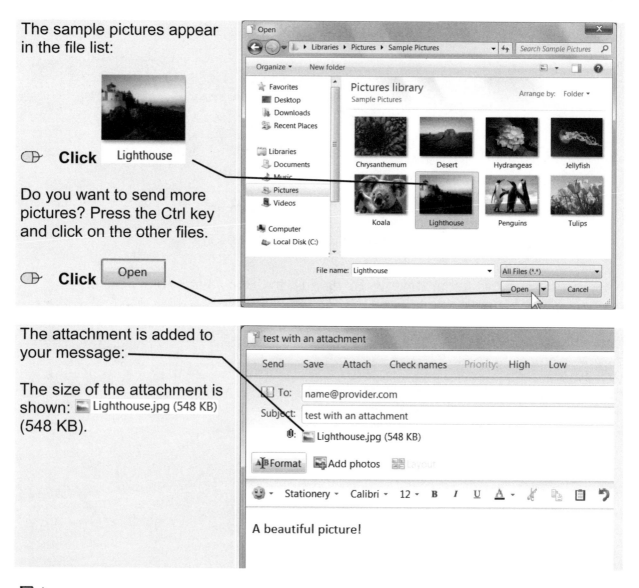

☞ **Click** Lighthouse

Do you want to send more pictures? Press the Ctrl key and click on the other files.

☞ **Click** Open

The attachment is added to your message: ——

The size of the attachment is shown: 🖼 Lighthouse.jpg (548 KB) (548 KB).

🢂 Please note:

Sending and receiving an e-mail with an attachment takes more time than sending and receiving a 'bare' e-mail message, especially if you or the addressee are using dial-up networking to connect to the Internet. Sending pictures takes a particularly long time. You may decide for yourself whether or not you really want to send this message.

If you do not want to send:
☞ **Close the message window**

The program will ask whether you want to save the changes.
☞ **Click** No

If you really want to send the e-mail message, do the following:

At the top left of the window:

☞ **Click** `Send`

> ⬜ test with an attachment
>
> Send Save Attach Check names Priority: High Low
>
> 📖 To: name@provider.com
>
> Subject: test with an attachment
>
> 📎: 🖼 Lighthouse.jpg (548 KB)
>
> AIB Format 🖼 Add photos Layout
>
> ☺ ▾ Stationery ▾ Calibri ▾ 12 ▾ **B** *I* U A ▾ ✂ 📋 📄 ↩
>
> A beautiful picture!

When you work *offline*, the program reminds you that the message is placed in the *Outbox* first:

☞ **Click** `OK`

> Send Mail
>
> ℹ When you send an e-mail message, it will be placed in your 'Outbox' folder ready to be sent the next time you choose the 'Sync' command.
>
> ☐ Don't show me this again.
>
> `OK`

If your message is placed in the *Outbox*, you can send it now manually. If your mail is sent immediately, you do not have to send it manually.

☞ **Send your e-mail** 👣⁵⁵

☞ **If necessary: connect to the Internet** 👣⁴⁶

➥ **Please note:**

Sending this e-mail will take some time if you are using dial-up networking.

8.8 Opening an Attachment

Once your e-mail is sent, it should arrive very quickly. You can see this in the *Inbox:*

⏣   **Click the message**

Here you see the preview of
your own message:

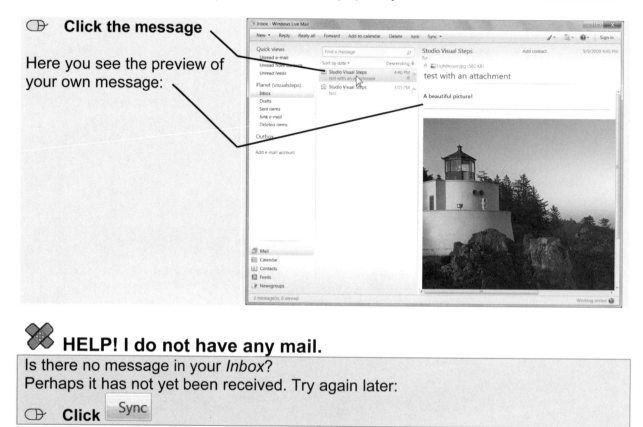

HELP! I do not have any mail.

Is there no message in your *Inbox?*
Perhaps it has not yet been received. Try again later:

⏣   **Click** `Sync`

Next to the header of this
message list, a small paper
clip 📎 indicates that an
attachment has been
included:

⏣   **Double-click your new
        message**

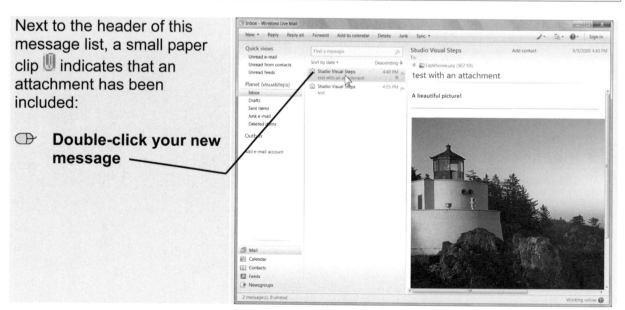

You see your message in a separate window:

The window is too small to show the whole picture. Using the scroll bar you can see the picture:

Double-click
Lighthouse.jpg (562 KB)

The default program to view the picture is called *Windows Photo Viewer*. *Windows Photo Viewer* is a tool included with *Windows 7* that you can use to view, share and print your digital pictures (and videos too). On your computer the picture may be shown in another program.

After you have seen the picture, you can close the program window:

Click X

You see the test message again.

8.9 Saving an Attachment

You can save an attachment from an e-mail on your computer. This is how:

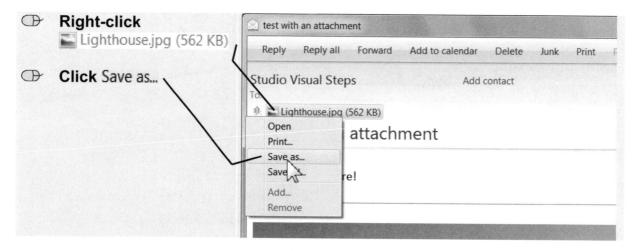

Right-click
🖼️ Lighthouse.jpg (562 KB)

Click Save as...

Windows will suggest storing the picture in the *Sample Pictures* folder on your computer's hard disk drive:

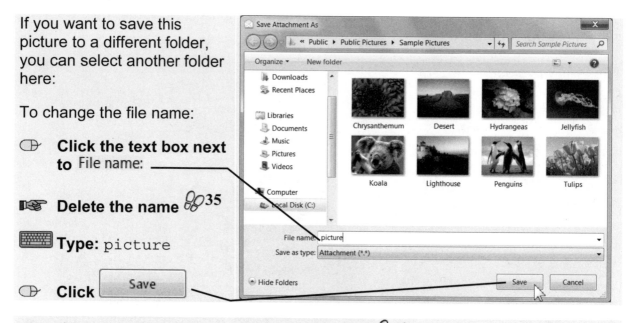

If you want to save this picture to a different folder, you can select another folder here:

To change the file name:

Click the text box next to File name:

☞ **Delete the name** 👣35

⌨️ **Type:** picture

Click Save

☞ **Close the *test with an attachment* window** 👣4

☞ **Close *Windows Live Mail*** 👣4

Now you have learned how to send and receive e-mail messages. You can practice what you have learned by doing the exercises in this chapter.

8.10 Exercises

The following exercises will help you master what you have just learned. Have you forgotten how to do something? Use the number beside the footsteps to look it up in the appendix *How Do I Do That Again?*

Exercise: Creating an E-mail

With this exercise, you can practice writing, sending and receiving a new e-mail message.

☞ Open *Windows Live Mail*. $\wp$54

☞ Create a new e-mail message addressed to yourself. $\wp$56

☞ Send the e-mail message to yourself. $\wp$57

☞ Send and receive your e-mail. $\wp$55 If necessary, connect to the Internet. $\wp$46

☞ Check whether you have new e-mail in your *Inbox*. $\wp$58

☞ Read your e-mail message. $\wp$59

☞ Close *Windows Live Mail*. $\wp$4

Exercise: Receiving E-mail

This exercise is used to practice determining whether or not you have received e-mail messages.

☞ Open *Windows Live Mail*. $\wp$54

☞ Send and receive your e-mail. $\wp$55 If necessary, connect to the Internet. $\wp$46

☞ Check whether you have any new e-mail in your *Inbox*. $\wp$58

☞ Close *Windows Live Mail*. $\wp$4

Exercise: Sending an E-mail with Attachment

With this exercise, you can send another e-mail, this time including the *Anthem* text file as an attachment.

➥ Please note:

You typed and saved the *Anthem* text in *Chapter 5 Word Processing*. If you did not, simply attach a different text.

☞ Start *Windows Live Mail*. 🐾⁵⁴

☞ Create a new e-mail message addressed to yourself. 🐾⁵⁶

☞ Add the *Anthem* text file in the *My Documents* folder as an attachment. 🐾⁶⁰

☞ Send the e-mail message to yourself. 🐾⁵⁷

☞ Send and receive your e-mail. 🐾⁵⁵ If necessary, connect to the Internet. 🐾⁴⁶

☞ Check whether you have e-mail in your *Inbox*. 🐾⁵⁸

☞ Read your e-mail message. 🐾⁵⁹

☞ Open the attachment (*WordPad* or *MS Word* will be opened to show the text). 🐾⁶¹

☞ Close *WordPad / MS Word*. 🐾⁴

☞ Close *Windows Live Mail*. 🐾⁴

8.11 Background Information

Dictionary

Attachment	Documents, images, and other files sent as attachments to an e-mail message. Messages that contain attachments are indicated by a paper clip icon in the attachment column of the message list. For security reasons many e-mail programs (including *Windows Live Mail*) prevent recipients from opening executable file attachments, such as those with .exe, .bat and .inf file name extensions.
Deleted items	Deleted e-mails are moved to the *Deleted items* folder. To permanently remove deleted items from your computer: delete the message in the *Deleted items* folder.
DSL	A type of high-speed Internet connection using existing copper telephone wires. Also referred to as a broadband connection.
E-mail	Short for electronic mail. Messages sent via the Internet.
E-mail account	The server name, user name, password, and e-mail address used by *Windows Live Mail* to connect to an e-mail service. You create the e-mail account in *Windows 7* by using information provided by your Internet Service Provider (ISP).
E-mail header	Information included at the top of an e-mail message: name of the sender and recipient, subject, date, and other information.
Inbox	The *Inbox* is where all of the e-mail messages that you receive are placed.
ISP	Internet Service Provider - A company that provides Internet access. An ISP provides a telephone number, a user name, a password, and other connection information so that users can access the Internet through the ISP's computers.
Message list	List of messages in various folders in *Windows Live Mail*.
Outbox	When you manually send e-mail and you finish writing a message and click on the `Sync` button, the message will be placed in your *Outbox* folder. Messages in the *Outbox* folder will be sent when you click the Sync button.

- Continue reading on the next page -

Preview pane	Here you can view the message's contents without opening the message in a separate window. To view an e-mail message in the preview pane, click the message in the message list.
Sent items	A copy of every message you send is saved in the *Sent items* folder, just in case you need it later.
Virus	A piece of code or program designed to cause damage to a computer system (by erasing or corrupting data) or annoying users (by printing messages or altering what is displayed on the screen).

Source: Windows Help and Support

The smaller, the faster

On the Internet, there is one golden rule: the smaller the message, the faster it is sent. The same applies to attachments. If you send a small attachment, such as a small photograph, the transmission will only take a few seconds. If you send a larger drawing, it will take more time and the telephone line will be used longer.

Along with the name of an attachment, such as a text or a picture, its size is always shown, expressed in MB or KB: Lighthouse.jpg (548 KB).

The size of a file is always indicated in KB or MB. These are measurements for sizes, just like inches and ounces.

A *Kilobyte* is (about) one thousand bytes.
This means that: 20 Kilobytes is 20,000 bytes. The abbreviation of kilobyte is *KB*.

A *Megabyte* is (about) one thousand kilobytes.
This means that one Megabyte is (about) one million (one thousand times one thousand) bytes. The abbreviation of megabyte is *MB*.

How long does it take to send or receive something?

The speed at which something can be sent or received depends on a number of things, including the speed of your modem, the type of connection and how busy it is on the Internet.
If for example, you are using dial-up networking to connect to the Internet, you can receive 6 KB per second with a regular modem. This translates into 360 KB or 0.36 MB per minute.

- Continue reading on the next page

A message that consists of 16 KB therefore takes about three seconds.

The size of the picture attachment you used in this chapter, is 269 KB. It takes about 45 seconds to send or receive. The directions text as shown in our illustrations measures 1.73 MB and will take about three minutes. As you see, this is quite a long time.

You can send different types of files with an e-mail message. You can even send sounds or video clips! But be careful: sound and video files are usually quite large. It may take a long time to send or receive files of this type. However, when you are using a broadband connection, for example a DSL line, this will not be a problem. This type of service offers high speed connection to the Internet.

How much fits?

Now you know what a kilobyte and a megabyte are. You can read here how much data fits on various types of data storage devices:

A diskette (floppy): 1.44 MB.
A CD-ROM (CD-R) / CD-Rewritable (CD-RW): 640 MB.

A larger size is used these days for different kinds of data storage: the Gigabyte.
A Gigabyte is (about) one thousand Megabytes, or one billion bytes.
The abbreviation of Gigabyte is *GB*.

A USB stick: 16 MB to 32 GB or even more.
A DVD-ROM (DVD-R) / DVD-Rewritable (DVD-RW): 4,7 GB or more (double layer).
Hard disks on today's computers have a capacity of at least 320 GB.
More powerful computers may have hard disks with 750 GB or even more!

Busy?

Do you connect to the Internet via the telephone line (dial-up networking)? If you are connected to the Internet and someone tries to call you, the caller will get a busy signal. So if you are expecting a call, do not connect to the Internet.
Do you connect by using an ISDN or DSL line? Then you can receive calls while you are connected to the Internet.
Do you have a cable connection? In that case, you can continue regular telephone service because your Internet connection does not interfere with your telephone.

Attachment blocked

Windows Live Mail blocks certain types of file attachments that are commonly used to spread e-mail viruses. A *virus* is a piece of code or program designed to cause damage to a computer system (by erasing or corrupting data) or annoying users (by printing messages or altering what is displayed on the screen).

When an e-mail message contains a blocked picture or other content, a red 'X' will appear in place of the blocked content.

If *Windows Live Mail* blocks an e-mail or an attachment, the Information bar will display a message letting you know that it has done so.

Although it is not recommended, you can enable access to blocked attachments. This should only be done by advanced users, and only with an up-to-date virus checker running.

Blocked e-mail message

8.12 Tips

💡 **Tip**

Wrong address?
If you make a mistake in the address to which the message is to be sent, it will be returned to you by the Internet post office. This post office will return your message as an attachment to a message explaining why it is being returned.
This message will be sent to your *Inbox*:

✉ System Administrator   Yesterday 🚩
　　Undeliverable: test   📎

Open the Sent items folder to see whether you made a typing error in the address. You can create a new message with the correct address.

💡 **Tip**

Keeping a list of addresses
Generally, you will have to keep track of the e-mail addresses you want to use yourself. There is no book of reference that lists everyone's e-mail address (like a telephone directory for telephone numbers). You can find lists of e-mail addresses on the Internet, but it is unlikely that you will find all the addresses you want.

Windows Live Mail can help you to keep track of e-mail addresses that you have used, which can be saved in the *Contacts* folder
📖 Contacts :

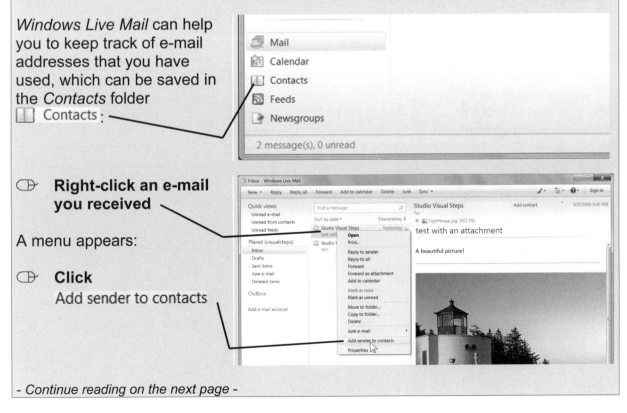

☞ **Right-click an e-mail you received**

A menu appears:

☞ **Click**
Add sender to contacts

- Continue reading on the next page -

If you wish, you can add more information here, or click one of the categories:

When you have finished:

⊕ **Click** Add contact

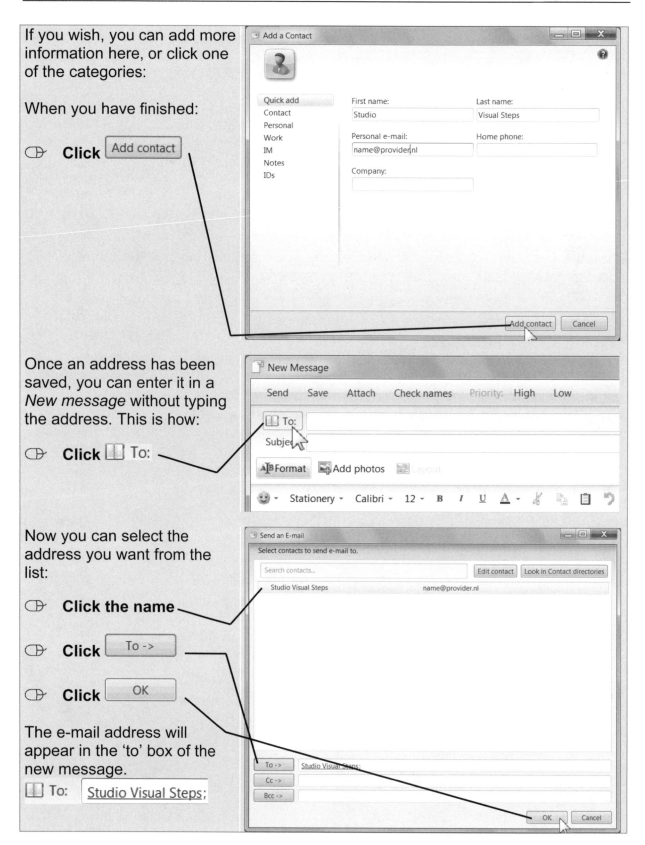

Once an address has been saved, you can enter it in a *New message* without typing the address. This is how:

⊕ **Click** 📖 To:

Now you can select the address you want from the list:

⊕ **Click the name**

⊕ **Click** To ->

⊕ **Click** OK

The e-mail address will appear in the 'to' box of the new message.

📖 To: Studio Visual Steps;

Tip

Printing an e-mail
Use this button Print on the toolbar if you want to print an e-mail message.

 Tip

Deleting an e-mail
Use the delete button Delete on the toolbar if you want to delete an e-mail message.
First click the message you want to delete in the message list. Then click this button
Delete.

The message will be stored in the Deleted items folder. Open the Deleted items folder
and delete the message once more.
Now it is permanently removed from your computer.

 Tip

E-mails to more addresses
If you want to send your e-mail to more than one address, you must type a semi-
colon (;) or comma between the addresses.
If you select more than one address from your list of addresses, *Windows Live Mail*
will automatically enter these for you.

💡 Tip

Security settings in Windows Live Mail
Take a look at security settings in *Windows Live Mail:*

👉 **Click**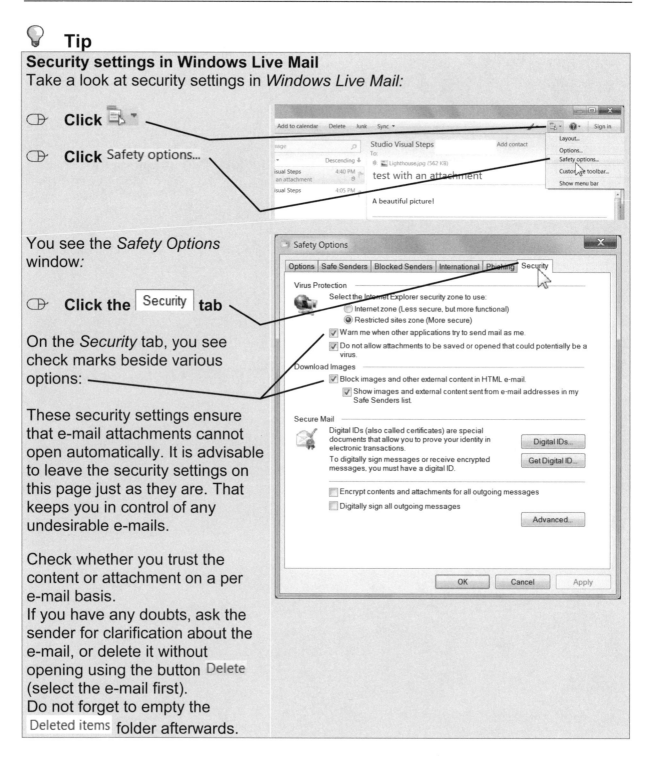

👉 **Click** Safety options...

You see the *Safety Options* window:

👉 **Click the** Security **tab**

On the *Security* tab, you see check marks beside various options:

These security settings ensure that e-mail attachments cannot open automatically. It is advisable to leave the security settings on this page just as they are. That keeps you in control of any undesirable e-mails.

Check whether you trust the content or attachment on a per e-mail basis.
If you have any doubts, ask the sender for clarification about the e-mail, or delete it without opening using the button Delete (select the e-mail first).
Do not forget to empty the Deleted items folder afterwards.

9. Bonus Online Chapters and Extra Information

Now you have come to the last chapter of this book. However, on the website that goes with this book you can find a number of bonus chapters and appendices. In this chapter you will learn how to open these additional chapters and appendices.

Furthermore, you will take a look at the Visual Steps website. You will see that this website contains lots of useful, extra information.

In this chapter:

- you will learn how to open the Bonus Online Chapters;
- you will visit the Visual Steps website.

9.1 Opening the Bonus Online Chapters

The website that accompanies this book contains a number of bonus chapters, namely:

- *Chapter 10 Text Layout*
- *Chapter 11 How to Make Working with Your Computer More Pleasant*
- *Chapter 12 Photo Editing with Paint*

You will also find an extra appendix:

- *Extra Appendix Setting Up a Webmail Account in Windows Live Mail*

These chapters and the appendix are provided as PDF files. These files can be opened with the free *Adobe Reader* software program. This is how you open these files on this book's website:

☞ **Open** *Internet Explorer* ✀⁴⁵

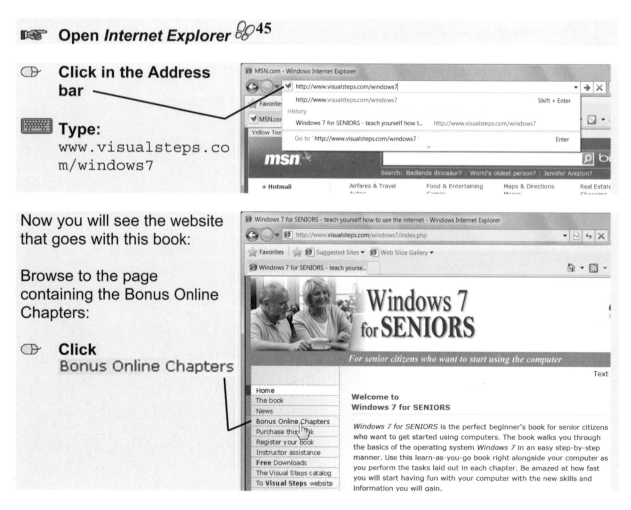

☞ **Click in the Address bar**

⌨ **Type:**
www.visualsteps.com/windows7

Now you will see the website that goes with this book:

Browse to the page containing the Bonus Online Chapters:

☞ **Click**
Bonus Online Chapters

Now you will see this web page:

To open a chapter:

☞ **Click**
Start downloading »»

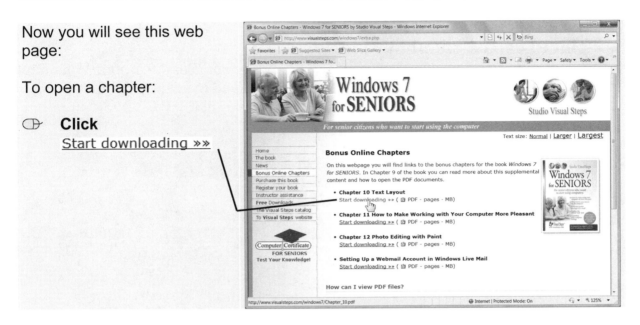

You can use the free *Adobe Reader* program to open these PDF files. This program allows you to view the files and even print them, if you wish.
The PDF files are secured by a password. To open the PDF files, you need to enter the password:

Type: 76957

☞ **Click** OK

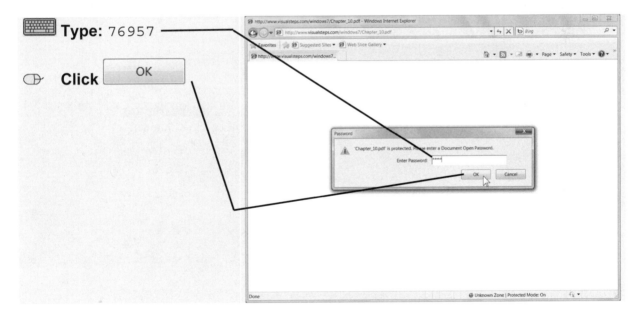

HELP! I see a different window.

If the window below is displayed on your screen, the *Adobe Reader* program has not yet been installed to your computer. In that case you need to follow a number of steps to install the program:

Click Cancel

Drag the scroll bar down

Click
Click here for more informa

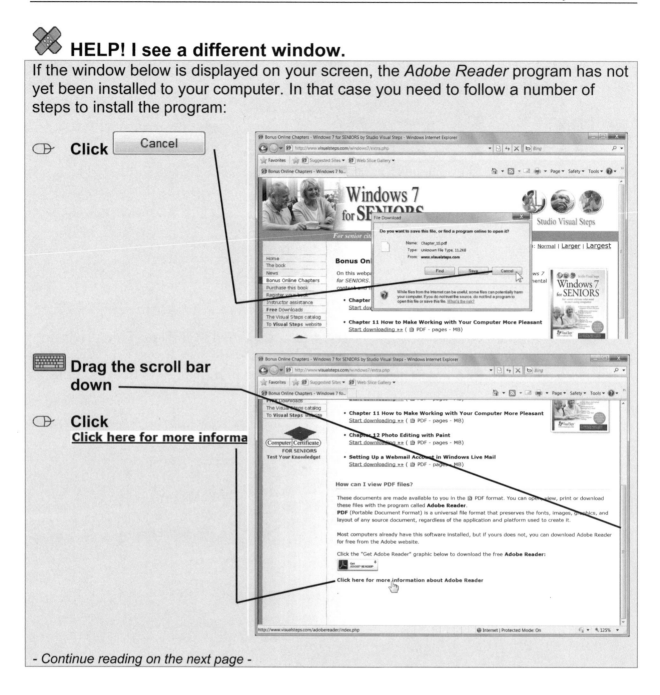

- Continue reading on the next page -

Now you will see a web page with information on downloading *Adobe* Reader in an easy way:

☞ **Follow the steps in this window**

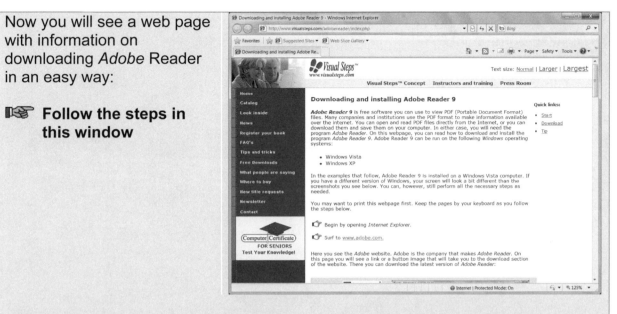

Now you will be guided through the installation procedure, step-by-step. After the installation has been completed:

☞ **Close the *Internet Explorer* window about installing *Adobe Reader*** 🐾⁴
☞ **Open the Bonus Online Chapter as described in this section**

HELP! I see a different window.

When you open the program *Adobe Reader* for the first time, you see a window like the following:

👆 **Click** [Allow]

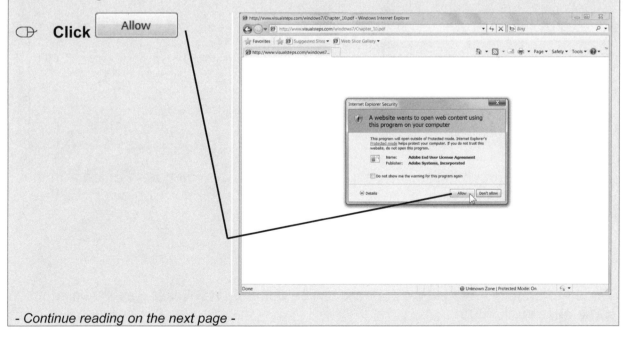

- Continue reading on the next page -

You will be asked to accept the license agreement:

⊕ **Click** [Accept]

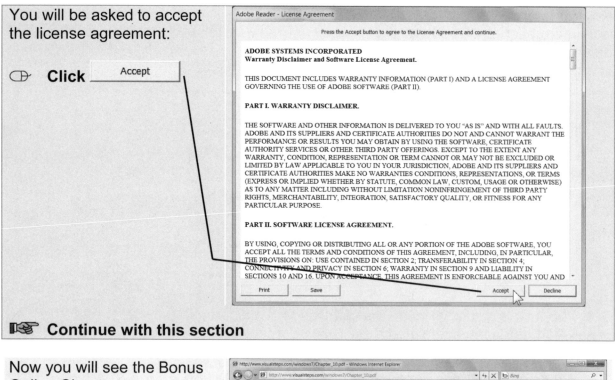

☞ **Continue with this section**

Now you will see the Bonus Online Chapter:

You can view this document by using the scroll bars:

You can print the document as well. Click the 🖶 button to print the document:

You can work through this online chapter in the same way you have worked with the chapters in the book. After you have read or printed the chapter, you can close the window.

☞ **Close all windows** ⚹⁴

The other chapters and extra appendix can be opened in a similar way, by using the same password: 76957.

♀ Tip

More about Adobe Reader
On the www.visualsteps.com/info_downloads web page you will find a free PDF file
with information on the use of *Adobe Reader*. This is how you open this file:

☞ **Open *Internet Explorer* ∂∂45**

☞ **Open the www.visualsteps.com/info_downloads web page ∂∂47**

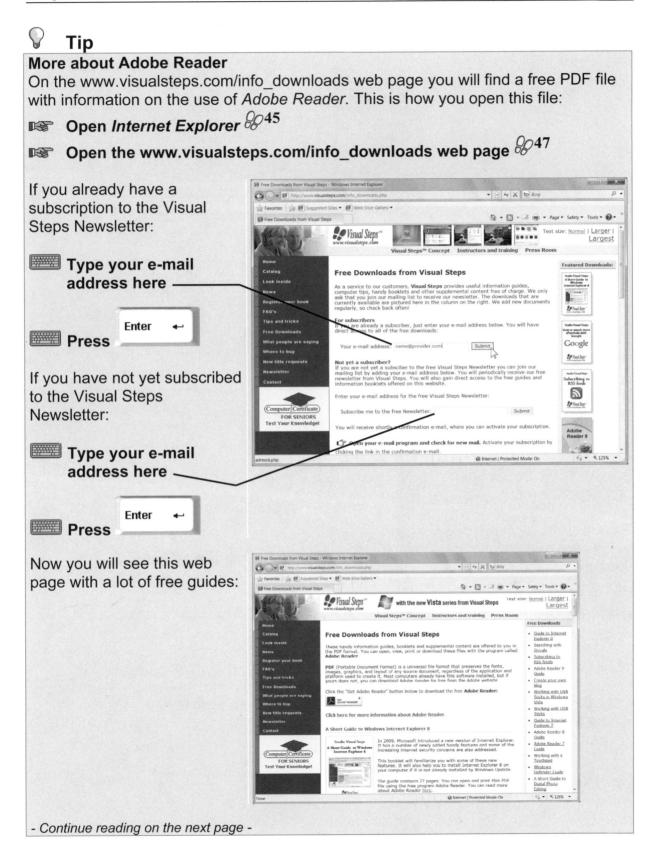

If you already have a
subscription to the Visual
Steps Newsletter:

⌨ **Type your e-mail
address here**

⌨ **Press** Enter ←

If you have not yet subscribed
to the Visual Steps
Newsletter:

⌨ **Type your e-mail
address here**

⌨ **Press** Enter ←

Now you will see this web
page with a lot of free guides:

- *Continue reading on the next page* -

Click

Start downloading »»

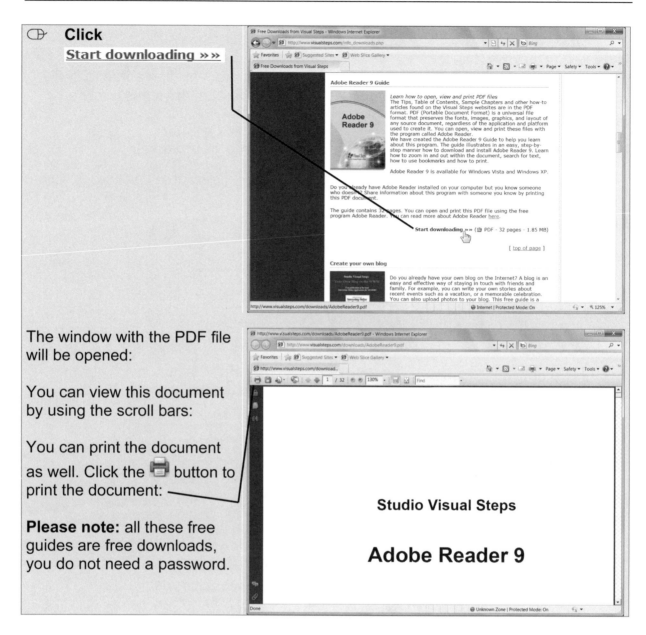

The window with the PDF file will be opened:

You can view this document by using the scroll bars:

You can print the document as well. Click the 🖶 button to print the document:

Please note: all these free guides are free downloads, you do not need a password.

9.2 Visual Steps Website and Newsletter

So you have noticed that the Visual Steps method is a great method to gather knowledge quickly and efficiently. All the books published by Visual Steps have been written according to this method. There are quite a lot of books available, on different subjects. For instance about *Windows*, photo editing, and about free programs, such as *Google Earth* and *Skype*.

Book + software
One of the Visual Steps books includes a CD with the program that is discussed. The full version of this high quality, easy-to-use software is included. You can recognize this Visual Steps book with enclosed CD by this logo on the book cover:

Website
Use the blue *Catalog* button on the **www.visualsteps.com** website to read an extensive description of all available Visual Steps titles, including the full table of contents and part of a chapter (as a PDF file). In this way you can find out if the book is what you expected.

This instructive website also contains:
- free computer booklets and informative guides (PDF files) on a range of subjects;
- free computer tips, described according to the Visual Steps method;
- a large number of frequently asked questions and their answers;
- information on the free Computer certificate you can obtain on the online test website **www.ccforseniors.com**;
- free 'Notify me' e-mail service: receive an e-mail when the book of interest is published.

Visual Steps Newsletter
Do you want to keep yourself informed of all Visual Steps publications? Then subscribe (no strings attached) to the free Visual Steps Newsletter, which is sent by e-mail.

This Newsletter is issued once a month and provides you with information on:
- the latest titles, as well as older books;
- special offers and discounts;
- new, free computer booklets and guides.

As a subscriber to the Visual Steps Newsletter you have direct access to the free booklets and guides, at **www.visualsteps.com/info_downloads**

9.3 More Visual Steps Books

The **Windows 7 for SENIORS** book has taken you through the basics of computing and *Windows 7*. Now you can write a letter, surf the internet, send an e-mail and personalize *Windows 7*. Interested in gaining more skills? Try the following Visual Steps books in the *Windows 7 for SENIORS series*:

Internet and E-mail for SENIORS with Windows 7
ISBN 978 90 5905 116 4

In this book you will learn how to:
- search the Internet effectively to find information;
- download free software from the Internet;
- prevent virus attacks, spyware, pop-ups, phishing websites and spam;
- personalize your e-mail;
- send, receive, open and save attachments;
- save e-mail addresses in the *Contacts* folder.

Interesting Online Applications for SENIORS
ISBN 978 90 5905 285 7

In this book you will learn how to:
- explore the world with *Google Earth* and *Google Maps*;
- make free long distance phone calls with *Skype*;
- buy and sell your goods with *eBay*;
- create your own blog on the Internet with *Blogger*;
- make new friends with *Facebook*;
- use e-mail worldwide with *Windows Live Hotmail*;
- chat with *Windows Live Messenger*;
- put your videos online with *YouTube* and many more.

In preparation:

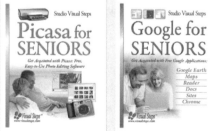

If you would like to know more about these books, please visit our website,
www.visualsteps.com

Appendices

A. Clicking, Dragging and Double-Clicking in Solitaire

The card game *Solitaire* is not only very popular among computer users, but also an extremely pleasant way to practice working with the mouse. The game requires a lot of clicking and dragging. This section describes how to play the game.

Starting Solitaire

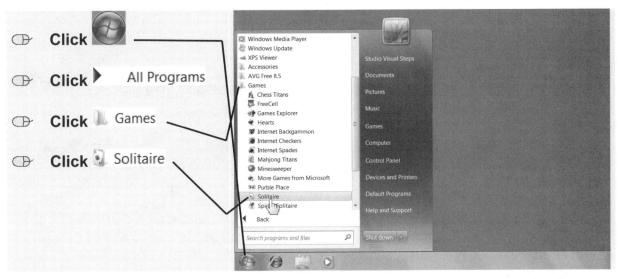

☞ **Click**

☞ **Click** ▶ All Programs

☞ **Click** Games

☞ **Click** Solitaire

You now see this window with seven piles of cards:

This is how to play the game: At the top left there is a pile of cards that are face down, called the *deck*. You can turn over the cards in this pile by clicking the deck.

☞ **Click the deck**

The top three cards are turned over:

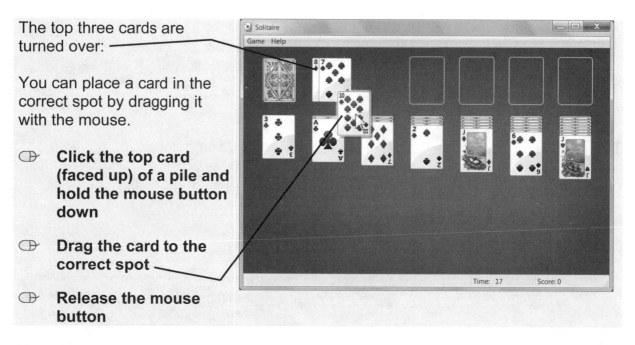

You can place a card in the correct spot by dragging it with the mouse.

◉ **Click the top card (faced up) of a pile and hold the mouse button down**

◉ **Drag the card to the correct spot**

◉ **Release the mouse button**

You can move the card to one of the seven lower piles, called 'row stacks'. There you release the mouse button.

- If the card can be played here, it will remain there.
- If the card cannot be played here, it will remain face up and returns automatically to the pile.

Do you already know how to play this version of the card game *Solitaire*?
Then you really already know how to play: try to play all of the cards and get them all up to the suit stacks.

Do you not know how to play this version of the card game *Solitaire*?
Then you can read the objective of the game and the rules below.

The Rules for Solitaire

The Objective

- The objective of this game is to play all of the cards in proper order (from aces to kings) on the suit stacks at the top right. Next to the deck, you see the empty spaces for the four suit stacks:

- The first card that you can play on these piles is the ace; then you must play the two, three, four, and so on, up to the king.
- Spades, clubs, diamonds and hearts each have their own pile.

Some of the cards are divided over seven stacks:

The rest of the cards are in the deck at the top left.

The Beginning

You must try first to play cards on the seven playing stacks.

You can take a card from these stacks by *dragging* it with your mouse:

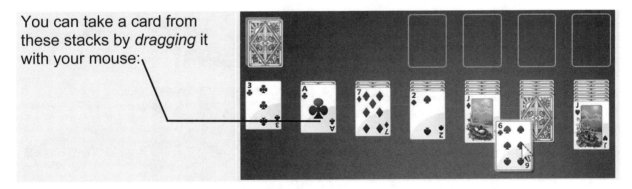

👉 Please note:

A card can only be played on these seven stacks if it is the next descending card of the opposite color: red eight on black nine, black jack on red queen, and so on.
In *Solitaire*, the *king* is the *highest* card and the *ace* is the *lowest*.

The Seven Stacks

You can play a card from one of the playing stacks to a different playing stack:
This can only be done if the card fits.

In this way you must try to turn over all of the cards and play them on one of the row or suit stacks.
But there are a few more things you need to know:

If there is a stack of cards that fits onto a different stack, you can move the entire stack by dragging the first card in the stack:

In this case the stack with the 7 of diamonds underneath is being dragged:

If one of the seven playing stacks at the bottom is emptied, you can only start it again by placing a *king* there:

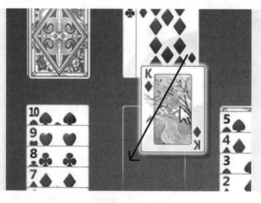

Once your entire deck has been turned over, you will see a circle in the empty space. You can turn back the pile of cards from the deck that could not yet be played by clicking the circle:

Playing Suits

You can also play cards by suit. There is a space for each of the four suits at the top right of the screen.

If an *ace* has turned up, you should start the suit stacks by moving it to one of the four spaces, as illustrated here with the ace of spades. You can move cards to a suit stack not only by dragging them, but also by double-clicking with the left mouse button:

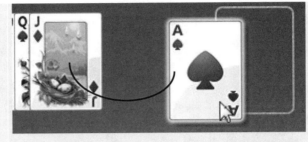

If a two of spades turns up later, you can play it on top of the ace of spades:

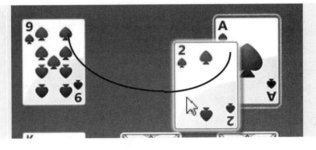

End of the Game

You have *won the game* if you succeed in completing all of the four suit stacks, one for clubs, one for diamonds, one for hearts and one for spades.

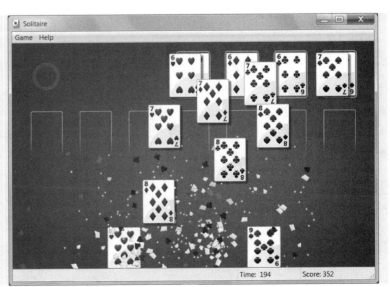

A New Game

You are 'stuck' if you can no longer turn over cards from the deck or move any of the cards in the stacks. The best thing to do when this happens is to start a *new game*. This is how to start a new game:

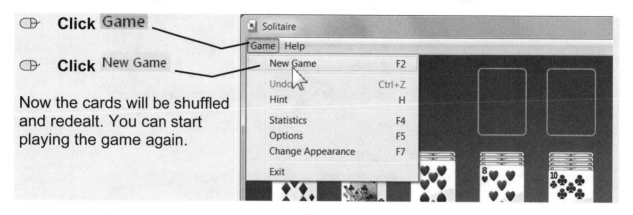

☞ **Click** Game

☞ **Click** New Game

Now the cards will be shuffled and redealt. You can start playing the game again.

Tips

 Tip

Paying attention and a bit of luck!
Solitaire is a game in which you must pay attention. You have to continually look carefully to see if a card can be played somewhere. But you also need a bit of luck. Even the very best players can not win every game.

 Tip

Always pay attention to the following:
- Look to see if a card can be played on one of the seven row stacks.
- Check to see if you can play a card on one of the four suit stacks.
- Do not turn cards over from the deck until you have played all of the cards that you can.

Tip

Do you want a different deck of cards?
You can change the deck as follows:

- **Click** Game

- **Click**
Change Appearance

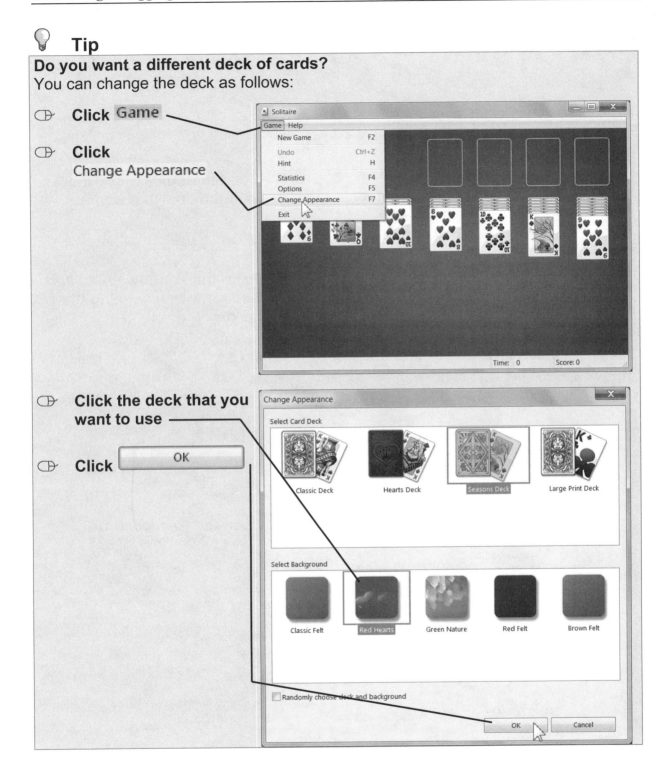

- **Click the deck that you want to use**

- **Click** OK

B. How Do I Do That Again?

In this book you will find many exercises that are marked with footsteps. x
Find the corresponding number in the appendix below to see how to do something.

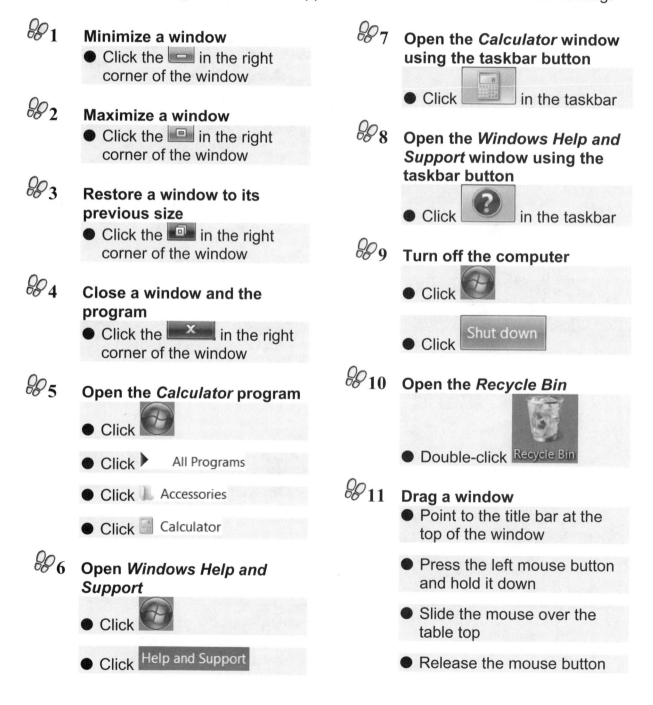

1   Minimize a window
- Click the ▬ in the right corner of the window

2   Maximize a window
- Click the ▢ in the right corner of the window

3   Restore a window to its previous size
- Click the ◱ in the right corner of the window

4   Close a window and the program
- Click the X in the right corner of the window

5   Open the *Calculator* program
- Click
- Click ▶ All Programs
- Click Accessories
- Click Calculator

6   Open *Windows Help and Support*
- Click
- Click Help and Support

7   Open the *Calculator* window using the taskbar button
- Click in the taskbar

8   Open the *Windows Help and Support* window using the taskbar button
- Click in the taskbar

9   Turn off the computer
- Click
- Click Shut down

10   Open the *Recycle Bin*
- Double-click Recycle Bin

11   Drag a window
- Point to the title bar at the top of the window
- Press the left mouse button and hold it down
- Slide the mouse over the table top
- Release the mouse button

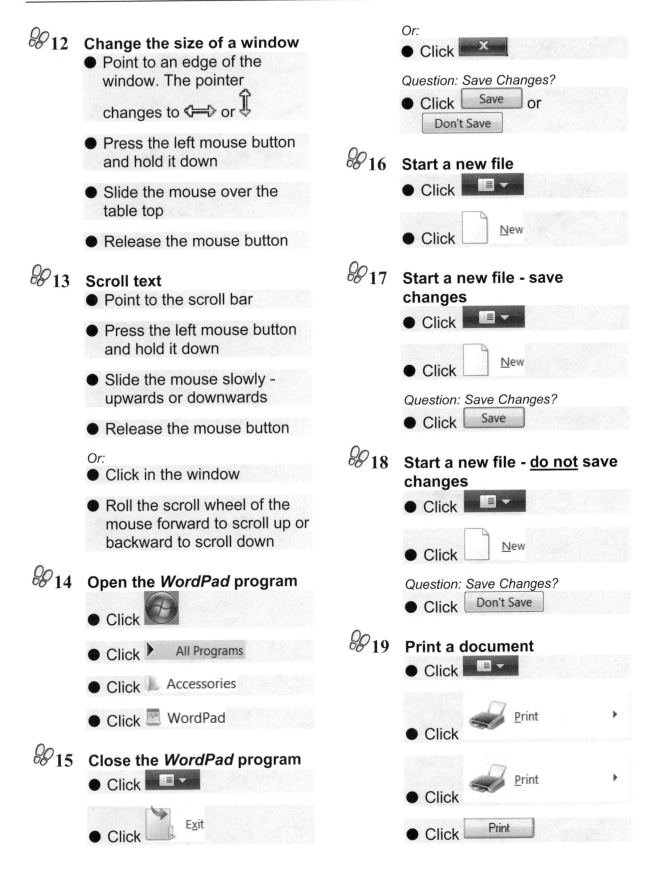

12 Change the size of a window
- Point to an edge of the window. The pointer changes to ⟷ or ↕
- Press the left mouse button and hold it down
- Slide the mouse over the table top
- Release the mouse button

13 Scroll text
- Point to the scroll bar
- Press the left mouse button and hold it down
- Slide the mouse slowly - upwards or downwards
- Release the mouse button

Or:
- Click in the window
- Roll the scroll wheel of the mouse forward to scroll up or backward to scroll down

14 Open the *WordPad* program
- Click
- Click ▶ All Programs
- Click Accessories
- Click WordPad

15 Close the *WordPad* program
- Click
- Click Exit

Or:
- Click x

Question: Save Changes?
- Click Save or Don't Save

16 Start a new file
- Click
- Click New

17 Start a new file - save changes
- Click
- Click New

Question: Save Changes?
- Click Save

18 Start a new file - do not save changes
- Click
- Click New

Question: Save Changes?
- Click Don't Save

19 Print a document
- Click
- Click Print ▶
- Click Print ▶
- Click Print

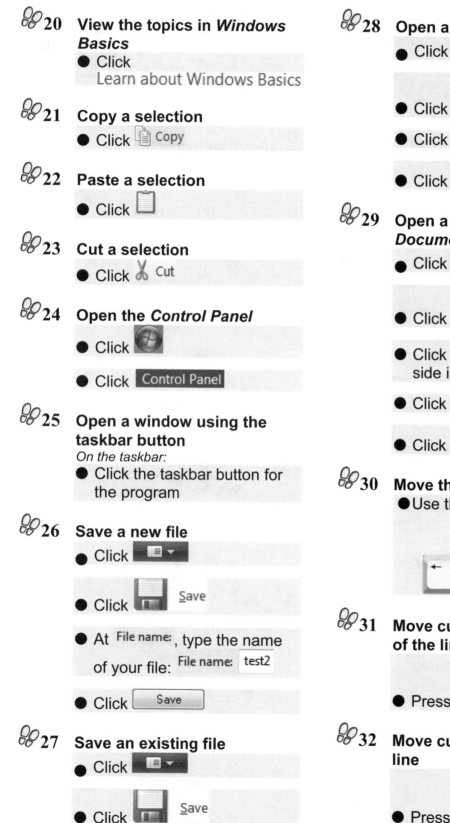

20 View the topics in *Windows Basics*
- Click
  Learn about Windows Basics

21 Copy a selection
- Click 🗐 Copy

22 Paste a selection
- Click 📋

23 Cut a selection
- Click ✂ Cut

24 Open the *Control Panel*
- Click 🪟
- Click Control Panel

25 Open a window using the taskbar button
On the taskbar:
- Click the taskbar button for the program

26 Save a new file
- Click
- Click 💾 Save
- At File name: , type the name of your file: File name: test2
- Click Save

27 Save an existing file
- Click
- Click 💾 Save

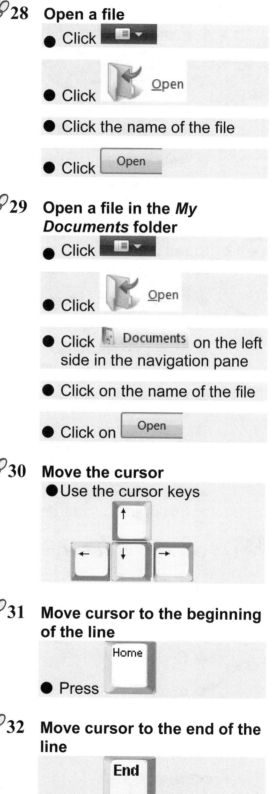

28 Open a file
- Click
- Click 📁 Open
- Click the name of the file
- Click Open

29 Open a file in the *My Documents* folder
- Click
- Click 📁 Open
- Click Documents on the left side in the navigation pane
- Click on the name of the file
- Click on Open

30 Move the cursor
- Use the cursor keys
  ↑ ← ↓ →

31 Move cursor to the beginning of the line
- Press Home

32 Move cursor to the end of the line
- Press End

33 Start a new paragraph / line
- Press Enter ↵

34 Erase letters or a selection (word, sentence or paragraph / line)
- Press ← Backspace

35 Erase letters or a selection
- Press Delete

36 Selecting a word
- Double-click on the word

To select several words:
- Click in front of the first word
- Drag the mouse pointer over the words

37 Paste two paragraphs / lines together
- Move the cursor to the beginning of the last paragraph / line
- Press ← Backspace

38 Open the *letters* folder
- Double-click letters

39 Return to a previously visited folder or return to a folder visited after the current one
- Click ← or →

40 Make a new folder
- Click New folder
- Type the name of the folder
- Press Enter ↵

41 Open a folder
In the file list:
- Double-click the folder

Or:
- Click the relevant folder name on the left side in the navigation pane

42 Copy a file to a folder
- Select a file by clicking it
- Click Organize ▾
- Click 📄 Copy
- Open the correct folder
- Click Organize ▾
- Click ☐ Paste

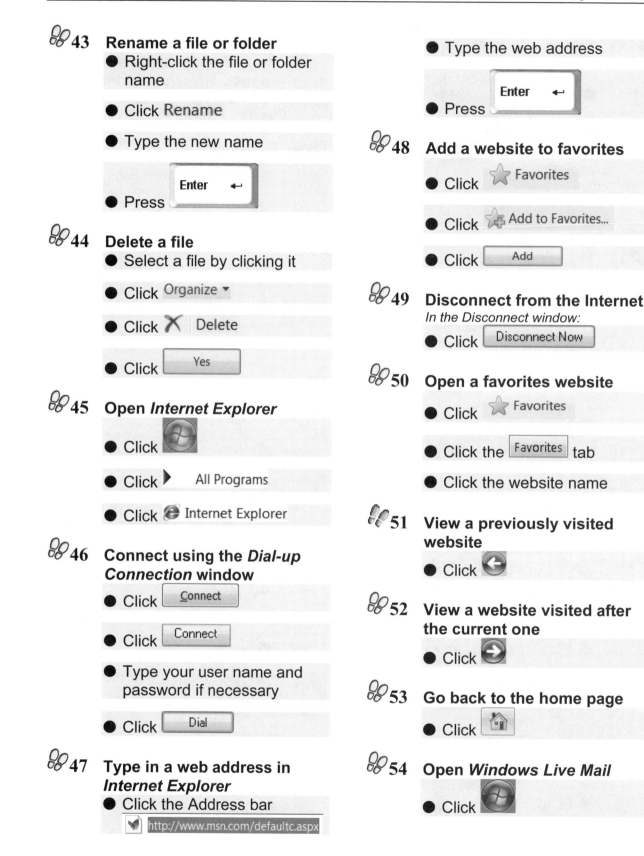

43   Rename a file or folder
- Right-click the file or folder name
- Click Rename
- Type the new name
- Press [Enter ↵]

44   Delete a file
- Select a file by clicking it
- Click Organize ▾
- Click ✗ Delete
- Click [Yes]

45   Open *Internet Explorer*
- Click [start]
- Click ▶ All Programs
- Click ⌬ Internet Explorer

46   Connect using the *Dial-up Connection* window
- Click [Connect]
- Click [Connect]
- Type your user name and password if necessary
- Click [Dial]

47   Type in a web address in *Internet Explorer*
- Click the Address bar
  http://www.msn.com/defaultc.aspx

- Type the web address
- Press [Enter ↵]

48   Add a website to favorites
- Click ☆ Favorites
- Click ⊕ Add to Favorites...
- Click [Add]

49   Disconnect from the Internet
In the Disconnect window:
- Click [Disconnect Now]

50   Open a favorites website
- Click ☆ Favorites
- Click the [Favorites] tab
- Click the website name

51   View a previously visited website
- Click ⬅

52   View a website visited after the current one
- Click ➡

53   Go back to the home page
- Click 🏠

54   Open *Windows Live Mail*
- Click [start]

● Click All Programs

● Click Windows Live

● Click Windows Live Mail

55 Send and receive e-mail
In the Windows Live Mail window:

● Click on Sync

If necessary:

● Click Yes

● Connect to the Internet

56 Create an e-mail message
In the Windows Live Mail window:
● Click New

57 Send an e-mail message
In the New Message window:

● Click Send

58 View the message list in the Inbox
In the Windows Live Mail window:
● Click Inbox (1)

59 Open an e-mail
In the Inbox message list:
● Double-click the message

60 Add an attachment
In the New Message window:
● Click Attach

61 Open an attachment
In the opened message window:
● Double-click the name of the attachment
Lighthouse.jpg (562 KB)

62 Undo last change
In the WordPad window:
● Click

63 Open your *Personal folder*
● Click

● Click your name on the top right of the Start menu, for instance Studio Visual Steps

64 Open the *Libraries* window
● Click

65 Add a folder to a library
● Double-click the library

The first folder:
● Click Include a folder

● Click the folder

● Click Include folder

The second folder (or third etcetera):
● Click 1 location

● Click Add...

● Click the folder

● Click Include folder

66 Create a new library
● Click New library

● Type the name

● Press Enter ↵

C. Changing Your Keyboard Settings

In order to type foreign language characters and symbols such as ñ, á, ö, and ç, you may need to change your keyboard settings. You can do this with the *Control Panel*.

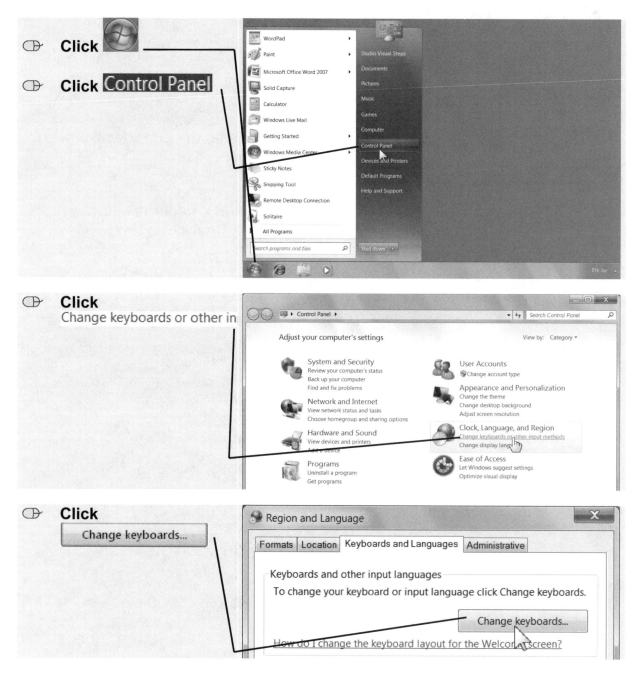

You will see a window with several language settings. The setting
English (United States) - United States-International is the one you need to type foreign letters
on a QWERTY keyboard. If this setting does not appear in your list, you can choose
an international keyboard setting. Here is how to do that:

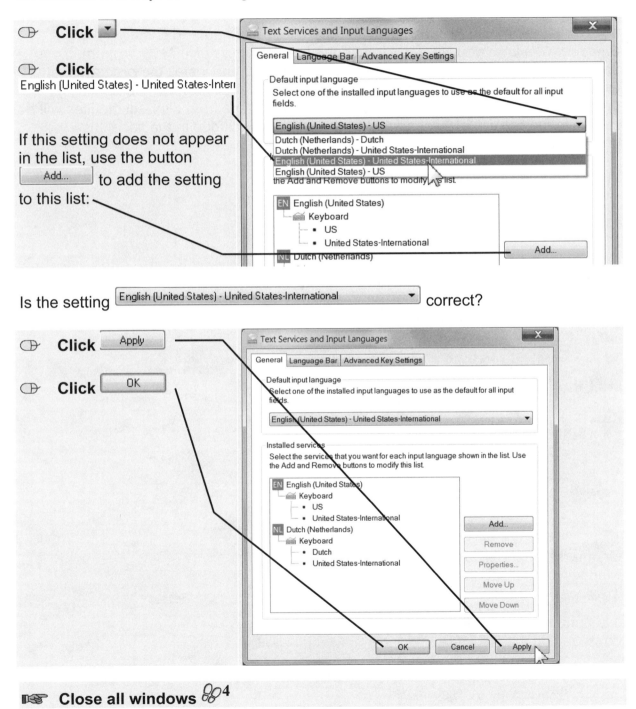

☞ **Click** ▼

☞ **Click**
English (United States) - United States-Interi

If this setting does not appear
in the list, use the button
Add... to add the setting
to this list:

Is the setting English (United States) - United States-International correct?

☞ **Click** Apply

☞ **Click** OK

☞ **Close all windows** ℰℰ4

Now you can type accents and umlauts just as we have described in this book.

D. Downloading and Installing Windows Live Mail

If you want to be able to execute all the operations in *Chapter 8 E-mail, Your Electronic Mailbox*, you will need to use the free *Windows Live Mail* program. If you are not yet using this program, you need to download and install the program first. Downloading means copying the files from the Internet to your own computer. Installing means putting the program on your computer's hard disk. All the files will be copied to the correct folder, and the program will be included in the list of installed programs.

This is how you do it:

☞ **Open *Internet Explorer*** &98;&98;45

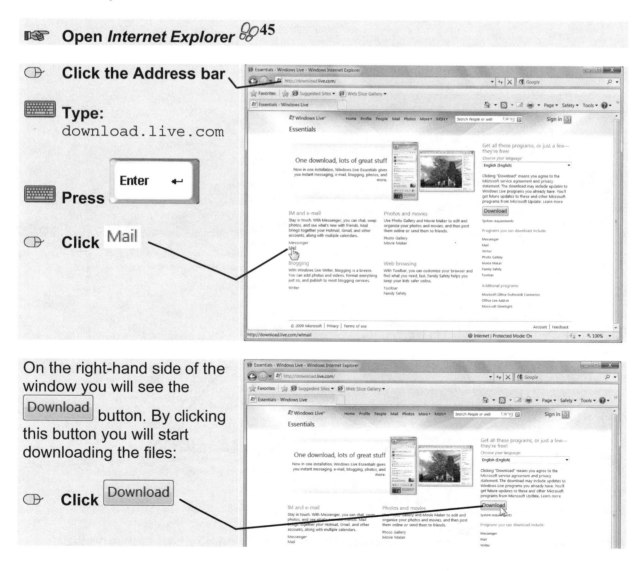

⊕ **Click the Address bar**

⌨ **Type:**
download.live.com

⌨ **Press** | Enter ↵ |

⊕ **Click** | Mail |

On the right-hand side of the window you will see the | Download | button. By clicking this button you will start downloading the files:

⊕ **Click** | Download |

Here you need to choose whether you want to run or save the file:

⊕ **Click** [Run]

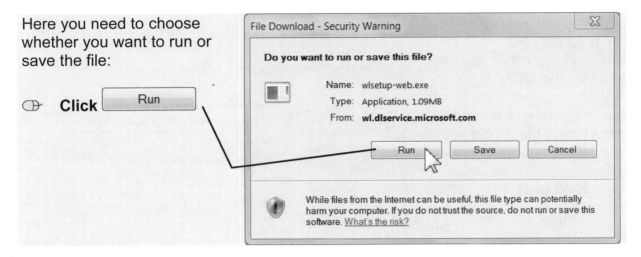

Now your screen will turn dark and you will be asked for permission to continue:

⊕ **Click** [Yes]

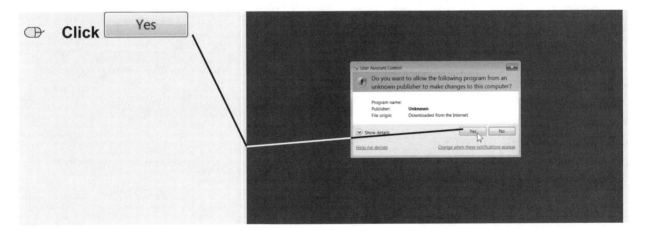

Now you will need to select the programs you want to install. In this case, you need to install the *Mail* program. So, you need to uncheck all the boxes next to the other programs. This is how you do it:

☞ **Next to** 👥 Messenger, **click** ☑

☑ will change into ☐:

Now, you need to uncheck all the other boxes as well, except for the 🗐 Mail box:

☞ **Uncheck all the other boxes** ☑, **except** 🗐 Mail

☞ **Click** [Install]

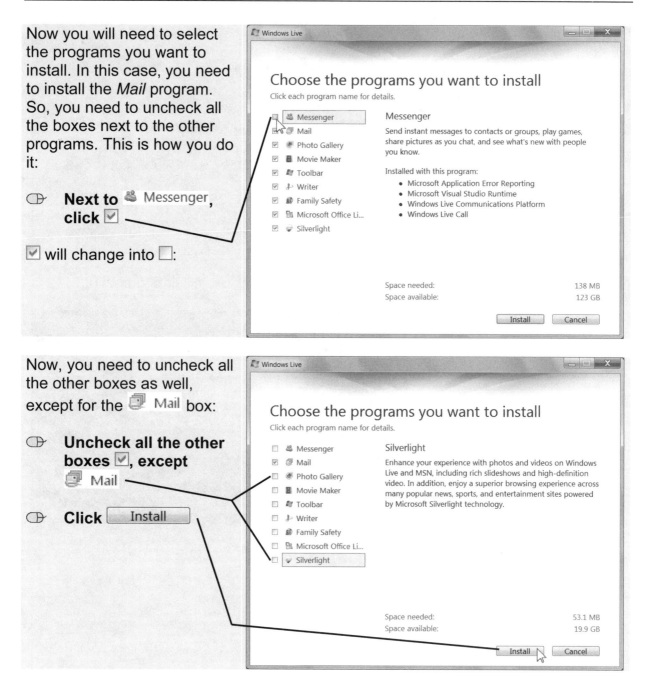

Now you will be asked to close all open programs:

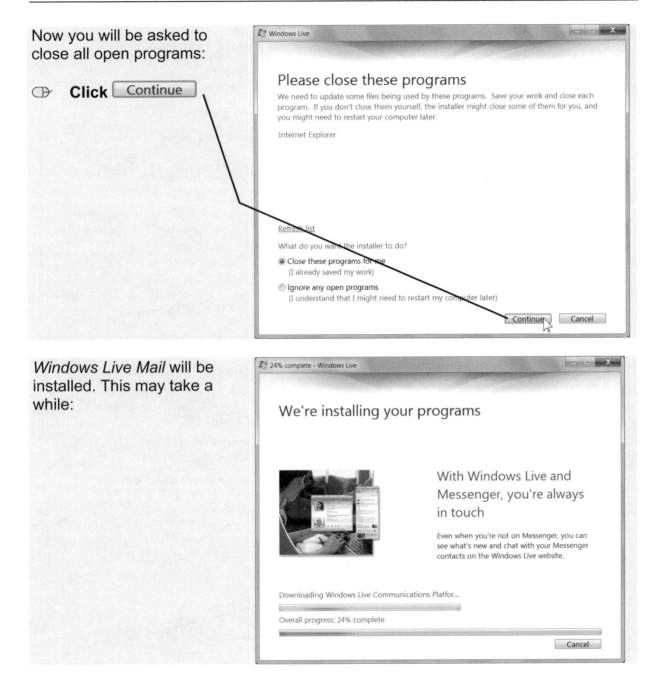

Click **Continue**

Please close these programs

We need to update some files being used by these programs. Save your work and close each program. If you don't close them yourself, the installer might close some of them for you, and you might need to restart your computer later.

Internet Explorer

Refresh list

What do you want the installer to do?

⦿ Close these programs for me
   (I already saved my work)

◯ Ignore any open programs
   (I understand that I might need to restart my computer later)

Continue   Cancel

Windows Live Mail will be installed. This may take a while:

24% complete - Windows Live

We're installing your programs

With Windows Live and Messenger, you're always in touch

Even when you're not on Messenger, you can see what's new and chat with your Messenger contacts on the Windows Live website.

Downloading Windows Live Communications Platfor...

Overall progress: 24% complete

Cancel

The installation procedure is almost completed:

☞ **Uncheck all the** ☑
   boxes

☞ **Click** [Continue]

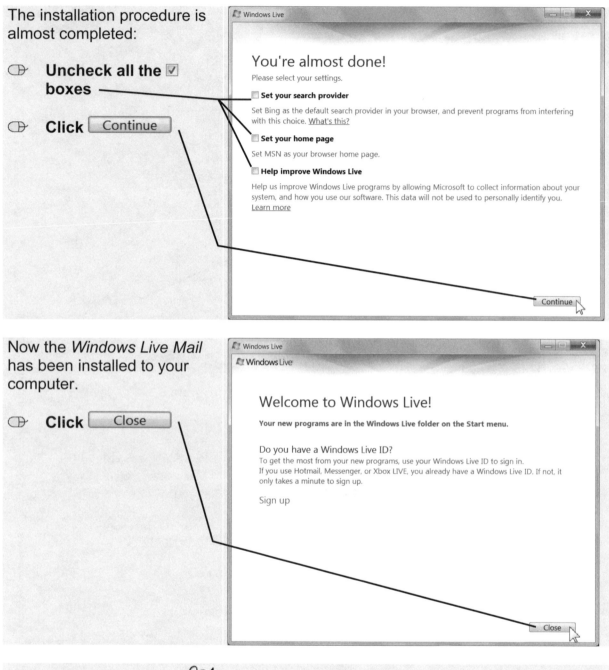

Now the *Windows Live Mail* has been installed to your computer.

☞ **Click** [Close]

☞ **Close all windows** ✂️4

E. Index

Interesting Online Applications for SENIORS

Interesting Online Applications for SENIORS
Get acquainted with thirteen free internet applications

Author: Studio Visual Steps
ISBN 978 90 5905 285 7
Book type: Paperback
Nr of pages: 392 pages
Accompanying website:
www.visualsteps.com/online

The World Wide Web (WWW) has rapidly become a treasure trove of free online tools and applications that allow better communication with friends and family and give the opportunity to enjoy many other fun and useful activities. Today you can view almost every spot on the globe with the amazingly sharp satellite imagery of *Google Earth*. Or create your own blog or journal about any subject that interests you with *Blogger*. Other very popular applications include *eBay* where you can buy and sell just about anything you want and *Facebook* – the website where you can create your own personal webpage. Invite all your friends to view your latest vacation pictures or family event in your online photo album created with *MyPhotoAlbum*. This book introduces you to thirteen of the most popular online applications.
Use this learn as-you-go book right alongside your computer as you perform the tasks laid out in each chapter.

You will learn how to:
- explore the world with *Google Earth*;
- plan a trip with *Google Maps*;
- make free long distance phone calls with *Skype*;
- get the news you want quickly and easily with RSS Feeds;
- buy and sell your goods with *eBay*;
- create your own blog on the Internet with *Blogger*;
- make new friends with *Facebook*;
- use e-mail worldwide with *Windows Live Hotmail*;
- chat with *Windows Live Messenger*;
- put your digital photos into a web album with *MyPhotoAlbum*;
- put your videos online with *YouTube*;
- *Windows Live Spaces*: your own personal space on the Internet;
- useful online reference sites such as Wikipedia, Dictionary.com, the Library of Congress, the Smithsonian, the Mayo Clinic and more.